WOMEN AND THE LIFE CYCLE

Women and the Life Cycle

Transitions and Turning-Points

Edited by
Patricia Allatt, Teresa Keil, Alan Bryman
and Bill Bytheway

St. Martin's Press   New York

First published in the United States of America in 1987

Printed in Great Britain

ISBN 0–312–01343–4

Library of Congress Cataloging-in-Publication Data
Women and the life cycle: transitions and turning-points/edited by
Patricia Allatt ... [et al.].
p. cm.
Selected papers originally presented at the British Sociological
Conference, "The Sociology of the Life Cycle," held at Loughborough
University of Technology in April 1986.
Bibliography: p.
Includes indexes.
ISBN 0–312–01343–4: $30.00 (est.)
1. Women—Psychology—Congresses.   2. Life cycle, Human—
—Congresses.   3. Life change events—Congresses.   4. Sex role—
Congresses.   I. Allatt, Patricia.   II. British Sociological
Conference (1986: Loughborough University of Technology)
HQ1206.W8743 1987
305.4'2—dc19
                                                    87–20281
                                                        CIP

Contents

List of Tables and Figures

Tables

Figure

Acknowledgements

The papers which appear in their final version in this book were originally presented at the British Sociological Association Conference, 'The Sociology of the Life Cycle', held at Loughborough University of Technology in April, 1986. Volumes of this kind are necessarily organised around a theme and in consequence several excellent conference papers had to be excluded from this and the sister volume *Rethinking the Life Cycle*. We should like to thank all those who gave papers, the participants and those who helped with the organisation, all of whom contributed to the success of the conference. We should also like to thank Anne Dix and Mike Milotte of the British Sociological Association, Gwen Moon of the Department of Social Sciences, Loughborough University of Technology, and the Computer Unit of Teesside Polytechnic for their contribution to the completion of this volume.

P. A.
T. K.
A. B.
B. B.

Notes on the Contributors

Sheila Abrams was a Research Officer with the Rowntree Research Unit at Durham University, where she worked on communes and various forms of neighbourhood and community life. Formerly with Age Concern, she has also done research on skilled workers in engineering. She is joint author of various works concerning community care.

Patricia Allatt is Principal Lecturer in Social Administration at Teesside Polytechnic. She has previously held posts at the Universities of Keele and Durham and at Newcastle upon Tyne Polytechnic. She has published on the Youth Service, crime prevention, the family and youth unemployment. Her current researches are on children's perception of other cultures, tenant populations and youth unemployment.

Kristine Beuret is a Lecturer in Social Policy at Leicester Polytechnic and Director of 'Social Research Associates'. She specialises in work on the social aspects of transport and is interested in the re-interpretation of social policy from a feminist perspective.

Elizabeth Bird is Staff Tutor in Sociology in the Department of Extramural Studies at the University of Bristol, where amongst other duties she is responsible for organising a variety of training and educational programmes for women. As well as researching and writing on women, she has published in the area of adult education and cultural and media studies.

Julia Brannen, sociologist, is a research officer at the Thomas Coram Research Unit, University of London Institute of Education, where she is engaged on a longitudinal programme of research including a project concerned with dual-earner households after the birth of the first child.

Alan Bryman is Senior Lecturer in the Department of Social Sciences at Loughborough University. He has previously held research posts in the Industrial Administration Research Unit at Aston University and in the Department of Theology at Birmingham University. His main research interests lie in the fields of organisation studies, research methodology, and labour market studies. He is co-author of *Clergy, Ministers and Priests* (1977), author of *Leadership and Organizations* (1986), and editor of *Doing Research in Organizations* (1988).

Bill Bytheway is Senior Research Fellow in the Institute of Health Care Studies in the University College of Swansea. He has recently completed a research project funded by the Joseph Rowntree Memorial Trust concerning the organisation of care within the families of older redundant steelworkers. He is also involved in a number of studies of health services for elderly people in south-west Wales. He has been active in the study of ageing for a number of years, being a founder member of the British Society of Gerontology. Before taking his present post, he was engaged in research in the Centre for Social Science Research, University of Keele, and before that in the MRC Medical Sociology Unit at Aberdeen.

Sheila Cunnison has carried out participant and observational research in industrial, service and professional work situations, and into women's participation in trade unions, and is currently involved in research work about housing and care of the elderly. She is an Honorary Fellow of Humberside College.

Rosemary Deem is Lecturer in Education at the Open University and has published several books on gender and education. She has been researching women and leisure since 1980 and published *All Work and No Play* in 1986. She was British Sociological Association Treasurer in 1985–6, and Chairperson of the Association from 1986 to 1987.

Christine Griffin lectures in Social Psychology at Birmingham University. During the early 1980s, she worked at Birmingham's Centre for Contemporary Cultural Studies on a study which became *Typical Girls? Young Women from School to the Job Market* (1985). She has recently completed a survey of racism and youth unemployment in Leicester, and is currently writing a critical review of research on youth and adolescence. She has been involved in youth work with young women in Birmingham since 1979.

Vivienne Griffiths is Lecturer in Education at the University of Sussex, and has a particular interest in gender and education.

Formerly a teacher, she has also worked in drama-in-education groups, and is interested in using drama to explore gender issues. Her current research is on adolescent girls and their friends.

Teresa Keil is Senior Lecturer in Sociology in the Department of Social Sciences at Loughborough University of Technology. She has previously held posts at the Universities of Liverpool, Leicester and Aston in Birmingham. She has published on the process of entry into work and, with members of the Work and Employment Group at Loughborough, on labour markets. Her current research interests are in labour market studies and in the social organisation of food preferences.

Lynn Makings is Lecturer in Sociology at Leicester Polytechnic, where she specialises in teaching the sociology of law. Her previous research has focused on women factory workers.

Dennis Marsden is Reader in Sociology at the University of Essex. Formerly at the Institute of Community Studies in Bethnal Green, he later moved to Essex to work on the national poverty survey. He has published on education, mothers alone, unemployment, and family violence. He is currently engaged on a five-year study of the Youth Training Scheme.

Jennifer Mason is Research Officer at Lancaster University on an ESRC-funded project investigating family obligations and social policy. Previously she studied at the Universities of Southampton and Kent, and has carried out research into the married lives of older couples.

Ann Oakley is Deputy Director of the Thomas Coram Research Unit, University of London Institute of Education. She has been researching and writing in the area of the family, gender and health for many years, and is currently working on a project designed to improve the health and well-being of mothers and children by providing them with social support.

Helen Roberts is Visiting Senior Research Fellow in the Social Statistics Research Unit, City University, and Senior Researcher at Bradford and Ilkley Community College. She is the author of *Women and Social Classification*.

Jackie West lectures in Sociology at the University of Bristol. She is the editor of *Women, Work and the Labour Market* (1982) and has written extensively on gender, class and work. She and her co-author have worked together on a number of projects including the collective editorship of *Half the Sky* (1979).

Erica Wimbush is Senior Researcher at the Centre for Leisure Research in Edinburgh. Recent research projects have included a study of the role of leisure in women's health and well-being and an evaluation of the development of community schooling in an Edinburgh secondary school. She is currently involved in research on playing amusement machines as an aspect of popular cultural lifestyles.

Susan Yeandle is Senior Research Officer with the Manpower Services Commission, Sheffield. Previously she worked as a sociologist at Durham University and more recently at University College, Swansea, where she conducted the research for her article in this volume. Her publications include *Women's Working Lives: Patterns and Strategies* (1985) and a book (with Patricia Allatt) concerned with youth unemployment and the family.

1 Introduction

Patricia Allatt and Teresa Keil

The theme of the 1986 BSA conference, the Sociology of the Life Cycle, attracted many contributions which, in addressing the problem of how to conceptualise and analyse the individual's progression through life, raised the issue of the relative utility of a life-cycle approach as compared with a life-course perspective. The former is distinguished by its emphasis on 'ages and stages' in life, the latter emphasises the individual's transitions into those stages in changing historical conditions. The implicit contrast in the two frameworks of analysis is one of a biological and social inevitability, irrespective of individual differerences, set against an approach which allows for the interaction of the individual with social structures which are subject to historical change. While a case could be made for the abandonment of the life-cycle approach because of its apparent simplicity – that is, its lack of fit with the complexities of people's lives and its overtones of determinism – the chapters in the present volume, taken collectively, illustrate the analytical power of both conceptualisations for understanding the ideological mechanisms of control which sustain social structures as well as in unravelling the complex strands which make up an individual's personal history.

Drawing upon recent original research, all the chapters explore transitions and turning-points in women's lives. Of course, these intellectual frameworks could be used to explore the lives of any members of society, male or female. However, a focus on women, whether the life-cycle or life-course approach is adopted, helps to unshackle our conceptualisations of women's life experience from the family cycle, a conceptual problem which has not arisen in analysing the life experience of men. These studies also have a general applicability for sociology in that they highlight the negotiation and renegotiation of the social order which regulates the allocation of responsibilities between men and women in the public and private domains.

The foundations of this approach were laid more than ten years ago at the 1974 British Sociological Association Conference with its theme of sexual divisions in society (Barker and Allen, 1976a and 1976b). The publications arising from this conference opened up many debates within the discipline. Their special contribution was to accord to the private sphere of family, caring, and what was subsequently described as 'people work' (Stacey, 1981) the same weight and prominence traditionally only assigned to the public sphere of economic and political life. They argued, moreover, for a theoretical recognition of the systematic relationship between the two spheres.

This systematic nature of the interrelationship is reflected in the chapters in the present volume. First, although the focus is upon transitions and turning-points in women's lives, the chapters reveal the crucial relevance of gender relationships at these junctures and highlight the interdependence of men's and women's lives in the unfolding of their life histories and trajectories. Second, in showing how the public and private spheres are rendered gender-specific, they illustrate how this is neither random nor 'natural' but critically controlled and influenced by cultural dictates and structural constraints. In looking at these constraints and dictates it is useful to consider the contrasting insights offered by the two conceptual frameworks – the life-cycle perspective and the life-course approach. It should be emphasised that each is essentially a way of categorising and ordering experience rather than explaining or theorising about it. Their power is empirical and ideological; it lies in the fact that they are not only analytical tools for the identification of different features of people's lives but are also ideological instruments for the interpretation and manipulation of people's experience.

The life cycle is a well-established mode of analysis which has been used to frame the stages and to draw attention to the apparent inevitability of certain experiences. In this sense the ideological dimension provides insight into the processes of social control which operate; for while each stage has to be negotiated by each individual, the context of that negotiation is the currently obtaining structure of power between men and women. This structure is discussed more or less explicitly in the chapters, with women's participation in the labour market presenting a particularly useful illustration of the processes involved. Thus the acceptance, by both men and women, of women's responsibility for household organisation and the care of dependants ensures that, for women, entry or re-entry into employment can never be a straightforward commitment to a particular career trajectory. For example, the employment taken may depend on the geographical location of the husband's work and the condition of the local labour market, and may involve the acceptance of the constraints of culturally prescribed roles. Furthermore, because of the discreteness of the stages which constitute the life-cycle model, the life cycle lends itself to ideologial manipulation as a means of controlling all women by reference to one particular stage regardless of whether individual women fall into that category.

It is the life-course approach with its emphasis on the interrelationships of individual, family and historical time which opens up the possibility of a more detailed analysis of the constituent elements of individual lives – for example, the financial and organisational costs and where they fall at each transition and turning-point as trajectories merge and compete for the individual's time and other resources. Although we lack similar documentation of men's lives, the overwhelming impression of the empirical material on the life course of women is of a complexity that contrasts with that of men. From the evidence here, this complexity is, moreover, structurally and culturally created and maintained in order to simplify men's lives. Paradoxically, although life-course analysis emphasises the availability of options and individual choice, the life-course analysts' distinction between family and individual time helps us to recognise the systematic conflation of the two in the lives of most women. Closely linked to such ideological conflation is the empirical overburdening of women's lives today.

The chapters have been grouped under three broad headings. Part I, which explores the conventional social categories, comprises chapters by Oakley and Roberts. Oakley takes as her theme gender and generation and brings together a wide range of empirical material which documents gender trajectories through life from cradle to grave. She analyses these status transitions with particular reference to their inevitability, the amount of control which can be had over them and the extent to which transition from one status to another is legitimised by various authorised agencies. In recognising the key importance of gender and generation, Oakley contrasts the experiences of men and women in Western society and shows how the determinism of biology and its cultural management is more pronounced for women than for men. The role of ascription is addressed in a rather different way by Roberts in her discussion of the social classification of women. She confronts the problems which arise from conventional analyses of stratification and considers the gender bias in the 'scaffolding behind occupational classifications'. The City classification, which is in the process of development, is based on women's work, both waged and unwaged, and includes an evaluation of household work. However, rather than being viewed as a step towards the incorporation of the complexities of the private domain into the public accounting, it should be seen as a move towards integrating the elements of the two domains and a more complete measurement of patterns of social stratification and mobility in modern British society.

The second group of chapters addresses the theme of historical time and private lives. Here some of the attributes of the status passages identified by Oakley are considered in greater detail and placed in specific contexts. In contrast to the conventional wisdom about the experiences of adolescent girls, Griffiths, for example, gives an account of the strategies used by working-class girls to resist pressures to drop their girlfriends and to acquire boyfriends. This detailed ethnographic account describes the struggle to resist 'compulsory heterosexuality' and to maintain friendships with girls at the conventional 'changeover time' from girlfriends to boyfriends. There is an emphasis on the initiatives taken by girls to obtain and manage their relationship with boyfriends in ways which will allow them to continue to maintain their friendships with girls.

The strong emphasis on the value of such friendships raises questions about the extent to which they might be continued through later transitions. The theme of the management of heterosexual relations at a transitional stage also runs through the contribution of Beuret and Makings who raise the question of the effect of recession and the possibility of change in traditional roles. Evidence from earlier studies, both recent and of the depression of the 1930s, suggests that the traditional power hierarchy in marriage may not only remain undisturbed by the unemployment of the husband but may be actively sustained by the wife (Sinfield, 1981, p. 87; Komarovsky, 1971, p. 50). Thus, irrespective of the inhibiting effects of social insurance legislation which make it financially unrealistic for the majority of wives of unemployed men to seek or even to retain a job, some wives purposely forgo paid employment so as to sustain in their husbands that sense of masculinity which is intimately linked to the provider role. In contrast to these studies of older, established marital relationships, Beuret and Makings explore the issue of the effect of mass unemployment on the power relations between men and women at a specific transitional stage in the life course: the 'coupledom' which precedes marriage. It is a stage at which two major life-course careers for women, employment career and wifehood, begin to jostle for dominance, and a period when, for any particular couple, patterns of behaviour are not yet established. Thus traditional and conventional expectations regarding marital roles are perhaps open to both negotiation and redefinition.

It is important to note that the particular group of women studied, young hairdressers with unemployed boyfriends, is atypical; they are, or were, apprenticed to a skill which offers the possibility of long-term opportunities of entrepreneurship and financial independence after marriage (albeit in the form of cottage industry). It is also clear that the young women were well aware of the traditional expectations as to their behaviour *vis-à-vis* the male, whether boyfriend or husband. These young women, however, enjoyed their independence and, unlike the older women in established relationships, they consciously manipulated 'their' men to create the impression that the men were taking the initiative. In doing so they developed strategies for handling their superior financial position, strategies which, it should be emphasised, gave them what they wanted while preserving their boyfriends' masculine image as providers. The authors suggest that these young women's attitudes and the way they appeared to control and manage the relationship may herald a weakening of the 'dependent woman model' of marriage, especially when this is taken in conjunction with contemporary changes in family structure.

Irrespective of the possibilities of renegotiation there are none the less conventional assumptions which surround transitions. These have been particularly strong in the interpretation of the transition from adolescence to adulthood. Griffin argues explicitly that the external structure – in this case high rates of youth unemployment – forces a reappraisal of conventional explanations of young people's transition to adulthood. The continuities and discontinuities in youth research are revealed in the treatment of gender, with her own research on women producing a different and more complex picture than that for men. For example, it is important to recognise that young women are making transitions through the sexual and marriage markets as well as through labour markets, and that they have to balance social and financial pressures in the hope of getting a good job and a boyfriend or husband. Each transition in the changed structure of the 1980s has the potential to change gender relationships, but whether the position of working-class women will be strengthened or whether hardship will lead to entrenched traditional values depends on both the conditions and responses to them.

The continuities and discontinuities of domestic life are considered by Mason, Deem and Yeandle. Mason documents the vocabulary as well as the outcomes of attempts at renegotiation of family relationships amongst older married couples. She demonstrates that by 'analysing the ways in which couples make sense of structured change through their domestic organisation' something can be said about the ways in which gender inequalities were being created, interpreted, maintained or changed. The pattern of 'gendered domestic responsibility' with its emphasis on the wife's responsibility for servicing the family and the husband's role as 'helper' is a major continuity in the lives of the couples studied. Such a pattern prevents challenge to the inequality of husband and wife, and any renegotiations reinforce the tradition and extend the control of husbands over wives' time (for example the freedom to visit friends, to use the car, and to shop). The empirical material illustrates the loss of privacy and the assumptions made about 'togetherness' in later years. The differing interpretations of and responses to nagging made by husbands and wives reflect the continued dominance of the husband and the circumscribed autonomy of the wife. In its emphasis on the difficulties of any renegotiation the research provides an interesting contrast with that of Griffin and Beuret and Makings.

Deem draws attention to the use of the life cycle as an analytical framework for the examination of women's leisure. She argues that, whilst the socio-economic and historical context should not be overlooked, a life-cycle approach does not (as earlier studies might imply) necessarily conceal the influences of class, region, ethnicity or gender; it can, rather, sharpen awareness of their effects. A focus upon life stages, moreover, broadens the perception of women's participation in leisure pursuits beyond the stereotypical representation of women with young children as the norm. This phenomenon is redolent of the ideological use of one stage in the life cycle made by male trade unionists as revealed by Cunnison's analysis. The approach also demonstrates the discontinuities and continuities in the form and extent of women's leisure over their lifespan, illustrating the constraints upon their activity which flow from cultural definitions of appropriate female leisure and the continuities of male power over women in private and public life, control which passes amongst fathers, boyfriends and husbands.

In contrast Yeandle emphasises the use of the framework of the life course to explore the determinants and consequences of economic activity. The empirical material provides comparisons between three cohorts and elaborates the ways in which the characteristics of the cohorts link up with the contextual events of historical time. Of special interest is the interrelationshp between age categories and stage. For each cohort, the important factors in restructuring women's experiences (particularly in the labour market) are the maturity and departure of children and the decline and death of older kin.

The final strand is the displacement of the structural to the personal, the phenomenon whereby constraints arising from the social structure are perceived as personal problems or as choices which are made at the individual's own discretion. Such displacement can be a means of ideological control (Allatt, 1981), and any critique of the life-cycle approach to our understanding of social life must take account of its potential for ideological use by powerful groups in the legitimation and preservation of their advantaged position. It is this element which, perhaps, underlies the durability of the concept in conventional wisdoms, found in professional and academic theories as well as in lay understandings. Cunnison addresses the issue in her study of the constraints which surround women's participation and attempted participation in trade-union activity.

Selectivity and fragmentation are also key components of an ideology (Poulantzas, 1973; Williams, 1973), and the ideological power of the life-cycle concept lies in the apparently clearly delineated stages of the cycle; it is this delineation which renders the stages available for selective use. Cunnison identifies three life-cycle stages for women in employment: from leaving school to marriage; the period of settling down and childcare; and that following the leaving home or the adulthood of children. She argues that the ease with which male trade unionists were able to impose the middle phase as a stereotype (the most debilitating as far as trade-union activity for women is concerned) upon all women irrespective of their age and circumstances, arises from the fragmentary quality of women's identities, shifting between and straddling paid work and family. Unlike men's unitary identity in work, the fragmentation of women's identity, which earlier studies have shown can be underpinned by legislation (Allatt, 1981), places women from the outset in a subordinate position in their own eyes as well as in the eyes of male trade unionists.

The ideological component, recognised by the assumption of the 'naturalness' of any particular behaviour (Morgan, 1975), informs the work of Wimbush's chapter. She explores the ways in which becoming a parent marks the turning-point at which gender inequalities become 'more deep-rooted, or perhaps only more transparent'. She notes that these inequalities are often expressed in terms of the naturalness of the social transitions experienced by mothers. In the empirical study, particular attention is paid to the ways in which choice and control over personal time become limited both ideologically and materially. The inadequacy of the conventional distinctions between employment and leisure time led to a focus on the identification of the processes which shape recreational opportunities and define leisure options. The image of the 'good mother' shaped the respondents' priorities, often limiting their personal time, and tensions arose if 'self-motivation' produced a demand for free time, particularly where male partners influenced timetables. Single mothers frequently experienced greater autonomy and independence. She notes the importance of social class in the mediation of these experiences.

Brannen elaborates this particular turning-point by using the life-course perspective to illuminate how, at the major social transition of becoming a mother, structural factors mediate individual lives; it is one of the turning-points at which lifecourse trajectories collide. Focusing upon the employment careers of first-time mothers and how these are influenced by other careers (women as mothers, the consumption career of the household, and fathers' careers), Brannen provides more evidence of the power of ideology in both defining the situation and in influencing the allocation of resources at a critical life juncture when, theoretically at least, practices are open to negotiation. For even when women continue in full-time employment careers after childbirth, the traditional patterns of men's and women's paths are only marginally altered. Despite the economic necessity of continuing in paid employment, women see the decision to return to work as their own personal choice which can be revoked, leaving them room for manoevre at a later date. Moreover, even when a wife's earnings result in a net economic benefit to the household, the additional costs of parenting, both financial and in terms of responsibility for and management of childcare, are largely borne by women. This is illustrated by the way in which such costs are viewed as a wife's expenditure to be covered by the wife's earnings rather than acknowledging them as one part of total household expenditure. The effect is to allow the career trajectory of men to remain uncontaminated and simple.

Such structuring of the respective unitary and fragmentary character of men's and women's lives finds echoes elsewhere in this volume. From a study of the occupational career of approximately 100 women seeking to return to employment, one quarter of whom had no children under ten years old, Bird and West challenge the prevalent view that childbearing, rather than marriage, influences the continuity and direction of a woman's employment. They found that the 'marriage effect', that is husbands not children as the problem, was strikingly linked to what could be called secondary occupational mobility – a change in employment career induced by the occupational mobility or employment career of a spouse. For a woman this may herald an end to her intitial work phase or the start of downward occupational mobility. This was especially evident amongst the more educated women. Such mobility, they argue, is functional for the economy as a whole, serving to maintain the flow of women into the secondary labour force, as described by Barron and Norris (1976a).

Marriage also obscured structural and ideological influences upon women's employment careers. Thus the condition of the local labour market was more critical to a woman's success in obtaining employment than were her domestic circumstances; and ideologies associated with the life cycle rendered the husband's occupational move as a 'natural' break for the start of child-rearing. This interpretation of women's breaks in employment raises questions about social policies – for example, retainer schemes – designed to maintain women's participation in the labour market, resting as they do upon the assumption that childcare responsibility is the overriding deterrent to women's employment. The whole issue converges in the conventional curriculum vitae. The explanation of the 'gap' in paid employment or the, usually downward, shift in occupation is denied legitimacy, even by the women themselves, and these experiences, both domestic and occupational, were never presented as positive, legitimate and valuable attributes of a career profile. As the authors observe, for the professional CV reader this kind of movement 'suggests incompetence, mental instability or misconduct, and the gap of "nothing" suggests incarceration'. None of these explanations fitted these women; all that had happened to them was that they had married, or, in some cases, expected to marry. In sum, the authors argue, the occupational careers of men and women are very different.

Finally, Marsden and Abrams analyse women's cycle of caring for all dependants, both young and adult, the assumption of its inevitabilty and the ways in which it becomes a moral imperative.

Caring is seen as a duty by social policy agencies. This serves to reinforce and perpetuate the structured dependency of the elderly and the subordination of women. Yet such impositions of care can invoke a range of feelings amongst the carers which span love, rejection and hate, the latter being accorded little or no place in the structure of our society. These feelings and the physical demands made upon women have far-reaching consequences for the life trajectories of a not insubstantial proportion of our citizens.

In sum, these chapters show how the retention of two apparently competing frameworks of analysis enhances the appreciation of the complexities which accompany an individual's progression through life. They contribute to the elaboration of 'people work' in the sense used by Stacey (1981), provide more evidence of the ways in which established social structures can resist and deflect change, and raise questions about the influence of economic and demographic change upon the interdependent life trajectories of men and women. Finally the chapters illustrate the role of qualitative studies in revealing the substance of people's lives which should inform social policy.

Part 1

Social Categories: Exploring the Conventions

2 Gender and Generation: The Life and Times of Adam and Eve

Ann Oakley

The objective of this chapter is to chart some of the different meanings of the life cycle to males and females. This is not exactly unknown territory, but its geography is definitely patchy. Another difficulty is the personal nature of our involvement in issues to do with gender and generation. As Wittgenstein said, talking about the task of thinking *well* about problematic concepts:

> It is, if possible, still more difficult to think, to *try* to think, really honestly about your life and other people's lives. And the trouble is that thinking about these things is *not thrilling*, but often downright nasty. And when it's nasty then it's *most* important. (Wittgenstein, cited in Elshtain, 1981, p. xi)

Thinking about gender and how it influences our passages through life is not necessarily nasty, but it is undoubtedly important. There are a number of different routes that can be taken to explore the territory of gender and the life cycle. One strategy is to examine the differential impacts of *biological* life (and death) events on the lives of men and women. A second is to consider the gender-differentiated articulation between *production* and the life cycle; and a third is to consider the subject from the viewpoint of *reproduction*. This chapter makes some use of all three of these strategies. There is, throughout, a degree of emphasis on health issues, because health in the bravely holistic sense advocated by the World Health Organisation – 'a state of complete physical, mental and social wellbeing' (World Health Organisation, 1978, p. 2) – could be said to be the key focus in each. The other orientation of the discussion that follows is towards a focus on *families* and the life cycle. This is very much a consequence of the direction taken by most knowledge in the area of gender and the life cycle: we know a great deal more about the life cycles of individuals who live in families than we know about those of individuals who do

13

not, and who move in and out of family structures over time in ways that used to be thought of as unorthodox, and so have been less accommodated within the research paradigm.

A central idea behind the description of gender trajectories is that of 'status passage' which was discussed in some detail nearly a generation ago by Glazer and Strauss. Glazer and Strauss borrowed the idea from anthropological work, where it had mainly been used to explore movements between age-linked statuses: they extended it to look at other transitions, including those within occupations and organisations which 'may entail movement into a different part of a social structure; or a loss or gain of privilege, influence or power, and a changed identity and sense of self, as well as changed behaviour' (Glazer and Strauss, 1971, p. 2). Glazer and Strauss list twelve properties of status passages, ranging from their reversibility and repeatability to people's awareness of the fact that they are going through them, and the degree of choice they are able to exercise over whether they embark on that particular status passage in the first place. In applying these ideas to gender trajectories through the life cycle, my particular focus is the extent to which men's and women's passages through life are different in terms of three dimensions: their *inevitability*; the amount of *control* which can be had over them; and the extent to which transition from one status to another is *legitimised* by authorised agencies of one kind or another.

INTO THE CRADLE

From or before the moment of conception, quite obvious and also mysterious forces propel males and females into a different relationship with time. Many examples of these known and unknown forces could be quoted: one is that 'An increase in the sex ratio at birth is associated with insemination early or late in the menstrual cycle' (MacGillivray *et al.*, 1986, p. 372). It hardly needs saying that an *increased* sex ratio of course means proportionately more males. To unpack the medical sentence, then, more boys are more likely to be conceived as a result of intercourse which misses ovulation. More girls are conceived on time as a result of punctual intercourse, which fits well with women's idea of themselves as punctual creatures, even if it contradicts men's views of women as unreliable. There are also some interesting patterns related to the mother's age, with male babies becoming progressively less likely as the number of births increases. All of which must be counted as fascinating pieces of esoteric knowledge, given that we can only guess at the underlying reasons for these differences.

In their consequences, however, they are real. A large study in Scotland a few years ago showed that boys are more likely to be born early and girls late (Hall and Carr-Hill, 1982). Female babies are more likely to be the wrong way round (bottom first) when labour starts. With babies the right way round (head first) the boys are much more likely to be delivered by forceps or Caesarean section, and female babies are much more likely to deliver spontaneously without medical help. Since, on the whole, no one knows the sex of the baby until it is born (and they certainly did not do so when these data were collected), these differences cannot all be explained as due to gender-differentiated ideas in the heads of medical attendants (with doctors being, for example, in more of a hurry to get boys out, or, having detected a female bottom, being more inclined to let nature take its – or her – course). A more likely explanation is that the different perinatal procedures represent some biological input into the early sociology of the life cycle. For example, boys weigh more and have bigger heads, and for related reasons they generally have a considerably worse time being born than the girls, showing more severe fetal distress and accidental death (Macfarlane and Mugford, 1984).

Another piece of perinatal evidence is minor bad news for girls. Although they are not the focus of the same degree of medical intervention as boys, if their passages into the world are initiated by medical induction they are more likely to suffer because of it (Pocock and Turner, 1982). The drugs used to induce labour are undetectable in the blood of boys after birth, but significantly present in the blood of girls three to six days after birth, with an effect equivalent to mild jaundice and sedation. No one knows why this happens.

Once the birth is over the whole sorry business of gender socialisation begins. From the 1960s on, an immense amount of effort has gone into an exercise called 'spotting the gender difference'; if we are concerned to identify ways in which the experiences of the two genders may be different, the question is, what do we know about gender in infancy and childhood? Are there significant biologically or culturally shaped ways in which the lives and life events of boys and girls are different? (Naturally class and ethnicity also affect gender and generation, and a comprehensive picture would require all these perspectives.)

WORLDS OF CHILDHOOD

Everyone knows that Louis XIII wore a skirt, played with dolls and made innumerable insufferable references to his genitals. At least, we know that, if we believe Philippe Ariès's version of childhood (Ariès, 1962), and there are others (for example, Greenleaf, 1978). Our knowledge of gender transitions in British childhood is very much limited by the data available to us. For example, to ask whether there is any difference in the percentages of female and male babies that are breast-fed, is by and large to frame a new question. The large OPCS survey of Infant Feeding in 1980 by Jean Martin and Janet Monk looked at breast-feeding incidence and duration by birth order, social class, education, mother's age, mother's employment status, mother's reproductive history, her pregnancy, delivery and postpartum medical care and the child's birthweight – but it did not examine the hypothesis that the early feeding experiences of males and females might be different (Martin and Monk, 1982). There is evidence that boy babies are given solids earlier than girl babies (Guise, 1986). To assert the desirability of sex-differentiated feeding statistics is to make a prior assumption that any sex difference is interesting, and this is of course not necessarily the case. But there are other pieces of evidence which tell us that a sex difference in feeding would at least be consistent with what we know about nutritionally related patterns of health and disease in later life (Faulkner, 1980), and also with some of what we know about early parental behaviour towards boys and girls.

It is a rare study that reports no sex differences in parental behaviour. One, in 1972, found that mothers talked to and smiled at girls more, but spent more time feeding boys (Thoman *et al.*, 1972). Another, in 1976, disagreed and said that boys were smiled at more – though the greater talkativeness of mothers to girls persisted in that study (Chateau and Wiberg, 1976). Yet a third, in 1978, reported that mothers had more skin-to-skin contact with girls but, somewhat curiously, spent more time arranging clothes on boy babies (Hwang, 1978). Why mothers should touch the clothed parts of males babies more and the unclothed parts of female babies more, is not clear, and indeed may not be very interesting. (The mothers in question lived in Goteburg, Sweden).

Fathers, when researchers discovered them to be of interest, also discovered them to be behaving in strange ways. For example, when left alone with newborn babies they spent much more time looking at them than holding them, though they were more likely to hold boys than girls (Rodholm and Larsson, 1979). Another study showed a rather low incidence of smiling amongst fathers towards babies – a further gender difference; fathers also stayed in the delivery room with newborn sons on average for three and a half minutes longer than they stayed with daughters. At two months, fathers had a clear tendency to hold girls and boys in different positions; the favourite position for holding boys was so that father and child looked directly at one another, whereas girls were held crossways so the baby had to turn her head in order to look at her father (White and Woollett, 1981). (This finding is capable of several different and intriguing interpretations.)

The research on early parental behaviour followed historically hard on the heels of research on gender differences in infant behaviour, some of which was truly impressive on the subject of cradle chauvinism. However, like various other scientific discoveries, this was found in the early 1970s to be partly fraudulent, since it was realised that some of the excess aggression and irritability in male infants, previously hailed as a major sign of a biologically determined gender difference, was instead due to the fact that many of the male babies used in the research samples had just had their foreskins removed. The suggestion was subsequently made that research should only use female babies; however, this then posed something of a problem from the viewpoint of locating gender differences (Korner, 1974).

The point is, that even where we can see gender differences, we have to contend with a complex picture contributed to by cultural and historical artefact. The articulation between different portions of people's lives is partly a function of where and when they were born, and we can see this clearly in the limited but detailed perspective of the British cohort studies. For example, going back a little painfully for a moment to the example of circumcision, 17.5 per cent of boys in the 1946 cohort had been circumcised by the age of one, and this had dropped to 4.6 per cent by the 1958 cohort. There had also been changes in another elective surgery rate – tonsillectomy – with 12.3 per cent of children under the age of six having had their tonsils out in 1946 and 8 per cent in 1958. Between these years a particularly bizarre regional peculiarity also disappeared: in 1946 Scotland had the lowest level of circumcision and the highest level of tonsillectomy, while the pattern in Wales was exactly opposite. These inexplicable oppositions had been muted by 1958 according to the evidence presented in the National Child Development Study (Fogelman, 1983, pp. 215–16).

If we define the basic tasks of childhood as physical and emotional survival and integrity on the one hand, and the acquisition of literacy and numeracy skills on the other, then we can see that males are considerably more vulnerable and less successful than females, but that by the age of eleven or so these differences are beginning to even out. Returning to the National Child Development Study, the significant female superiority in reading-test scores at the age of seven had become sex equality in reading at the age of eleven in the 1958 cohort. The slight difference in favour of male mathematical ability at age seven was retained at eleven. By sixteen the boys were marginally ahead of girls both in mathematics and reading. Comparing these results with those obtained in the earlier cohort, born in 1946, it is clear that some things had changed, even if it is not immediately clear just what had changed and why. For the 1946 cohort, test scores at eleven showed girls to be ahead of boys in both reading and mathematics, whereas in adolescence the gender difference reverses itself in exactly the same way as it does for the 1958 cohort. Does this cohort difference suggest that girls born in 1958 were relatively *less* advantaged compared with boys than those born in 1946? If so, it goes against the evolutionary view of gender which says that equality increases, rather than decreases, with time. Although gender patterns changed between the 1946 and 1958 cohorts, social class differences did not, and both sets of data show a progressively larger social class gap from seven through to eleven through to fifteen (the 1946 cohort) and sixteen (the 1958 cohort).

Other factors, such as family size, have been shown to have a mysterious and complicated relationship with school attainment. Family size in the 1946 cohort had exerted its maximum influence by the age of eight; after that there was no increase in the disadvantage of coming from a large family. Conversely, for the 1958 cohort, between the ages of seven to sixteen, large family size exerts a progressively detrimental influence. However, more subtle analyses than those done on the 1946 data show that the truly hazardous aspect of membership of large families lies in the number of *older* children in the household rather than in the number of *younger* children (Fogelman, 1983).

Despite these differences, there is a sense in which it is true to say that these phenomena are not differentiated by gender. Control, as a dimension of status passage, is not much of a respecter of gender;

neither boys nor girls have much chance of affecting these early processes. In addition the impact of material disadvantage on the life cycle for both males and females stares at one out of every table with its relentless chi-square underneath. So far as legitimation as another crucial dimension of status passage goes, the extent to which gender differences in educational behaviour and attainment are *legitimated* by authority is probably much the same for boys and girls. 'Legitimated' may not be the correct term to use here, because the advanced sociological consciousness of the 1980s about public processes such as education reaching parts other processes cannot reach, tells us that making children gendered is a powerful hidden motif of schooling. There is some evidence that teachers do more explicit gendering with boys.

In two other areas of childhood the impact of life-events appears to distinguish quite markedly between the sexes. The first area is accidents, and the second is parental separation and divorce.

About a third of child deaths between one and fourteen years occur as a result of accidents or violence; and about one in five of hospital admissions in this age group fall in this category (Macfarlane and Fox, 1978). Since about 1950, accidents have been the commonest single cause of death in children aged one to fifteeen years in Britain, and accidental injury has itself been described as 'the most important epidemic in the western world today' (Jackson and Wilkinson, 1976, p. 1258). Boys have twice as many accidents as girls: these accidents are more likely to be fatal for boys and they also occur in different places. For example, 10 per cent of fatal accidents to boys aged five to fourteen years happen in quarries and industrial premises, but only 2 per cent of fatal female accidents happen in these places. As might be expected, girls are much more likely to have accidents at home. From ten to fourteen years there is a female excess of fatal accidents occurring in 'places of recreation' (Macfarlane, 1979) – the message of which is perhaps that girls would be better off not trying to enjoy themselves.

As with much of the other information we have, gender-differentiation is less marked in social classes I and II than at the other end of the social class spectrum. The accident rate for boys in social class I is about the same as that for girls from social class III manual households. If low social class is a risk factor, so is being in a one-parent family. Non-fatal accidents are twice as common in children from single-parent or stepfamilies than among children in two-parent families.

When we look at the impact on boys and girls of the life event of parental separation or divorce, we also see a difference, with boys appearing to be more vulnerable than girls. In fact, studies in the 1960s identified three areas where boys subjected to this ordeal excelled themselves, namely 'aggressive acting out', 'lack of self control' and 'disturbances of traditional sex role typing'. The effects of marital breakdown last longer with boys, who tend to adopt a 'feminine' pattern of low-level physical and high-level verbal aggression which makes them especially unpopular with their peers (Richards and Dyson, 1982).

Behind such findings lie a number of discrete points. First, boys seem to do less well when presented with overt parental conflict. Second, the result of marital breakdown is more commonly that boys 'lose' their fathers than that girls 'lose' their fathers, and the evidence suggests that father-loss for boys jeopardises the development of orthodox masculinity.

Studies of children's reactions to marital separation show that boys separated from their fathers before the age of five are more dependent, more feminine in self-concept and play patterns, and less aggressive than boys not separated from their fathers. Rising divorce rates on an epidemic level might therefore be expected to reduce male aggression – however, this faint hope disappears in the storm-clouds of adolescence where gender rears its ugly head again, a head made even uglier by the angry and inflammatory presence of sexuality.

THE BIRTH OF THE STEAM ENGINE

Although 'the adolescent' was invented at the same time as the steam-engine (Musgrove, 1964), this does not mean that the two are the same kind of phenomena. Indeed, Rousseau described this time of life as 'the second birth' (Rousseau, *Emile*, bk 4). So what kind of birth is this, the second one – and how do biological and cultural inputs shape the trajectories of females and males as compared with the first time round?

As Arnold van Gennep originally remarked in his *The Rites of Passage*, ' "physiological puberty" and "social puberty" are essentially different and only rarely converge' (van Gennep, 1960, p. 65). Physiological puberty is unusally easy to define in girls and unusually hard to define in boys. The average age at which menstruation begins in the UK is now about thirteen and a half years, and has shown a secular trend towards occurring at earlier ages. In the National Child

Development Study, 98 per cent of girls were menstruating and the pubic hair of 50 per cent of boys was considered 'adult' by sixteen (Fogelman, 1983). Van Gennep pointed out that even the neatly measurable physical event of first menstruation was fairly unhelpful as a guide to social puberty – first because of the enormous individual variation in its timing, and second because physical maturity is not necessarily a prerequisite for sexual experience, nor, of course, does sexual experience necessarily follow from the fact of physical maturity.

Van Gennep was interested in initiation rites as one example of rites of passage. He saw puberty initiation rites as similar to the cutting of the umbilical cord, in that they represented the separation of the individual from one world, and his or her incorporation into another. In the case of puberty, the individual is being taken out of an asexual world and into a sexual one. Van Gennep described this process as much simpler for girls than for boys since 'the social activity of a woman is much simpler than that of a man' (van Gennep, 1960, p. 67). However, the scholarship of the last twenty years has taught us that the opposite statement is much more likely to be true – a man's social activity is much simpler than a woman's.

Sylvia Plath described it well, albeit from a middle-class stand-point, in her autobiographical novel *The Bell Jar*. 'I saw my life branching out before me like the green fig-tree in the story', wrote Plath in the persona of her hero-person Esther Greenwood:

> From the top of every branch, like a fat purple fig, a wonderful future beckoned and winked. One fig was a husband and a happy home and children, another fig was a brilliant professor, and another fig was Ee Gee, the amazing editor, and another fig was Europe and Africa and South America, and another fig was Constantin and Socrates and Attila, and a pack of other lovers with queer names and off-beat professions, and another fig was an Olympic lady crew champion, and beyond and above these figs were many more figs I couldn't quite make out. I saw myself sitting in the crotch of this fig tree, starving to death, just because I couldn't make up my mind which of the figs I would choose. I wanted each and every one of them, but choosing one meant losing all the rest, and, as I sat there, unable to decide, the figs began to wrinkle and go black, and one by one, they plopped to the ground at my feet. (Plath, 1963, p. 80)

Sylvia Plath's vision of the blackening figs describes a real dilemma in the lives of young women today. This dilemma has to do with the selection of, or selection into, largely alternative pathways marked 'woman' and 'person'.

In order to understand the ways in which this happens, it is worth considering what kind of state adolescence is – or how prevailing ideologies describe it. In the index to the world-famous *Book of Childcare* by Hugh Jolly, we find listed under adolescence: 'acne in; and the adopted child; disturbance due to loss of parent; and drugs; fatness in; growth in; helping cope with problems of; physical changes; sex education; thinness in;' and 'see also puberty' (Jolly, 1975, p. 593). This unhappy list may echo commonsense views of adolescence, which paint it as an unhappy period of turmoil. It may be unhappy for adolescents, or for parents, or for both. On the whole the parenting of adolescents has received little sociological research attention.

When Frank Musgrove sampled adults' and adolescents' attitudes to one another in the Midlands in the early 1960s he found that 'The adults ... were far more hostile and critical in their attitudes to adolescents than were adolescents to adults' (Musgrove, 1964, p. 102). Two-thirds of the adults made wholly or mainly critical statements about adolescents, whereas only a third of the adolescents were nasty about adults.

Sigmund Freud's daughter Anna had this to say about adolescence:

> Adolescence is by its nature an interruption of peaceful growth, and ... the upholding of a steady equilibrium during the adolescent process is in itself abnormal ... adolescence resembles in appearance a variety of other emotional upsets and structural upheavals. The adolescent manifestations come close to symptom formation of the neurotic, psychiatric or dissocial order to merge almost imperceptibly into ... almost all the mental illnesses. (Freud, 1952, pp. 255–78)

Perhaps it would not be too far-fetched to suggest that the statement that a peaceful adolescence is abnormal, is like the statement (made a little further on in life) that women who avoid postnatal depression should really worry, because there might be something wrong with them (see Oakley, 1981).

Within this framework of necessary neurotic turbulence, surveys of adolescent attitudes show a remarkably rational grasp of social options, including those relating to gender role. However, adolescents' perceptions of gender seem to have a stronger link with the past than their other perceptions, which are quite consciously related to a world dominated by economic recession, unemployment, inept politicians, the scarcely comforting stars of soap operas, and the everpresent and increasing threat of nuclear war. Girls think about nuclear war more than boys (Solantaus *et al.*, 1984), but they are just as concerned about the threat of personal unemployment. In Simmons and Wade's study of 820 young people's answers to ten questions about themselves and their views of life, 'getting a job' was said to be 'the best thing that could happen to me' by 30 per cent of girls and 25 per cent of boys. (Passing exams was the best thing' for 18 per cent of girls and 17 per cent of boys, 'winning the pools' for 13 per cent of girls and 20 per cent of boys, and 'success at sport' for 1 per cent of girls and 10 per cent of boys (Simmons and Wade, 1984).)

This more-than-a-mere-suggestion of gender differences is entirely borne out by other studies. Millicent Poole, in her study of Australian youth, commented on the basis of her findings that:

> It would appear that the large majority of girls intended to work, then to marry, to have children and to return to the work-force as soon as their children were old enough. This was the typical sequence of anticipated life-transitions that the females in the sample saw for themselves in the future. More often than not females saw themselves after marriage in a part-time job, usually their former job. The same sequencing was not apparent for males. There was no mention of leaving the work-force during family formation. (Poole, 1983, p. 246)

Twice as many boys as girls were uncertain about marriage, and revealed in their comments the notion that marriage marks the end of life – for instance, these remarks of one boy: 'I will be working all the time and I will not be married till I have a lot of fun. When I have had all my fun then I'll get married' (p. 247). As expected, twice as many girls as boys wanted children, and could even be specific as to details of eye and hair colour.

So far as motherhood is concerned, the work of Shirley Prendergast and Alan Prout (1980) has illuminated the sense in which teenage girls can be said to know about the realities of motherhood. They know about these primarily from their own mothers' experiences with them. But when faced with the pervasiveness of social stereotyping (good mothers stay at home, children are women's fulfilment and satisfaction, etc.), this personal knowledge may be repressed in favour of the orthodox view. What this means is that adolescent girls may seem to espouse a sentimental image of motherhood which is different from boys' notions of parenthood. But behind the public declaration (and the answers given to social science interviewers) is the real experience of life with their own mothers which gives girls a different covert knowledge (Prendergast and Prout, 1980).

These different articulations around the themes of production and reproduction portray adolescence as a life stage high on the scale of gender-differentiation. And so, indeed, it is, in other ways. In the Simmons and Wade (1984) survey twice as many boys as girls ranked material possessions as important and twice as many girls as boys said friendliness is an important human quality (p. 46). Girls rated the family as one of the pleasures of life, three times more often than boys (p. 168). Nevertheless, some responses revealed boys and girls to be more alike. Asked to state 'the sort of person I would least like to be', the most frequent least-liked models for both sexes were (i) 'snobs and bigheads', and (ii) Margaret Thatcher (p. 52).

When we think about the reasons why adolescents should be prone to regard themselves and the world as gendered, biological and cultural explanations cannot be seen as competing. Becoming adult, getting married and having children are virtually synonymous activities in our society (Leonard, 1980). With high unemployment rates among school-leavers, marriage and parenthood may, indeed, increasingly substitute for that other potent symbol of adulthood – involvement in the world of work, at least for girls. The importance of heterosexuality and reproduction, and their differential importance to females and males, begins to be impressed on children in the early years of schooling – from 'the cult of the apron' (Spender, 1980) in the Ladybird books, to teachers' expectations, which surface even in apparently neutral subject areas. But children do not 'need' to act out the precise dimensions of these gender scenarios until they themselves are on the verge of becoming adult.

PARENTHOOD

The teenage girls who described a pattern of employment fitted around child-rearing knew what they were talking about. However, to talk knowledgeably in a statistical sense about the relationships between production, reproduction and gender in adult life is extremely difficult because of biases in the information collected. We know too much about men and production and also too much about women and reproduction. Both the official statisticians and the social scientists have inflated gender-specific links – between men and work and women and the home – so that key pieces of the jigsaw puzzle to do with women and work and men and the home are missing (Oakley and Oakley, 1979). Another difficulty is that official statistics may tell us very little about the quality and meaning of people's lives. For instance, if we say that age at marriage is rising and marriage rates are falling and that there is still a two-year-or-so gap between the average ages at which men and women marry, what does this tell us about the intimate experiences men and women have either inside or outside the institution of marriage?

Of course it tells us very little. Love, which is supposed to be the reason for marriage, may temporarily breach the gender gap in its guise of 'revolutionary' phenomenon, as the Italian sociologist Francesco Alberoni has described it (Alberoni, 1983). This 'collective movement of two individuals' sets up the other gender, at least for a while, as an unambivalent object. Men's views about women, and women's views about men, temporarily take a back seat, and the other gender, in the persona of the loved person, becomes what is most wanted. Indeed, the being-in-love stage (or stages) of life is probably the one in which the experiences of men and women are most nearly similar, which only makes the task of sustaining intimacy throughout marriage even more monumental.

Among the many important questions to do with gender, reproduction and production in the years from the early twenties to middle age, three critical ones are: How do people divide and use their time? What is parenthood like? How does parenthood affect men's and women's involvement in the public domain of labour?

In the *General Household Survey 1983*, the section on leisure contains a list of eighteen possible activities, only five of which show any sort of gender difference in people over 16. These five activities are: going out for a drink, gardening, home repairs (which men do more), and needlework/knitting and reading books (which women do more). Using other data to supplement this picture, *Social Trends 1985* reported that women watch about four hours more television a week than men, but men read more newspapers, in particular the *Sun* (32 per cent of men read the *Sun* in 1983 as against 26 per cent of women). To put these figures in perspective it is relevant to note that 3 per cent of men and 1 per cent of women read *The Financial Times* and 11 per cent of men and 46 per cent of women also read women's weekly magazines. Men are twice as likely to do the pools. If compensation for this is called for, women are twice as likely to play bingo (*Social Trends 1985*, pp. 150–3).

Quite large gender differences exist, then, in terms of the leisure component of adults' lives. One of the differences is that women's leisure interests take place in the home more than do men's. Perhaps we should not be too surprised by this. And we also know that when we think about work in the home rather than leisure in the home, this is a female speciality too.

Many centuries on it is still true that among cohabiting female–male couples without children, women do more of the housework. Indeed, it seems that, so far as appropriate time budget data are available, women's housework hours in this stage of the life cycle may have actually increased in recent decades. Canadian research shows that some of the larger gender differences in the proportions of total time allocated to work exist precisely in the categories of couples without young children (here defined as children under ten) (Meissner *el al.*, 1975). In other words, it seems that 'marital status' affects the extent of women's and men's involvement in household work. The proportion of time spent in this work goes up in both sexes with marriage, but it goes up much more for women than for men. At the same time, it is now true that marriage on its own does not affect whether or not women are involved in employment work, or it does so only to a very small extent. Whether it does so or has done so for men is an open question (Martin and Roberts, 1984).

Parenthood has an impact on both men's and women's work and leisure, but its effect on women is greater. The largest gender difference in time allocated to household work is in what is known as the 'active parenthood' stage of the life cycle, when the youngest child is aged 0–6 years. In other ways, too, the transition to parenthood is an entirely different status passage for men and women. Joel Richman in a chapter on 'Men's experiences of pregnancy and childbirth' captures and clouds the essence of these well, when he says that 'Fathers' pregnancy careers not only differ from mothers' by being more diffuse and opaque but they also have a greater resonance with their occupational careers' (Richman, 1982, p. 98). In other words, men do not get pregnant; those whose female partners are pregnant behave in very different ways from their partners. Neither pregnancy nor fatherhood stop the men working. However, these facts have not prevented researchers, and especially psychoanalytically oriented ones, from diligently searching for signs that fatherhood is a kind of crisis. The psychiatric literature notes that fatherhood may cause schizophrenia, alcoholism, lying, suicidal gestures and premature ejaculation. One paper in the *Psychiatric Quarterly* for 1972 noted that 'There appear to be some ophthalmological problems associated with fatherhood, mostly styes and cysts. Also of note is an increased incidence of toothache occasionally leading to multiple extractions of uninfected teeth' (Lacoursiere, 1972, p. 124).

But if parenthood means extracted teeth and continued employment for men, the employment indications, at least, for women are different. As Richman observes, 'the date at which pregnant women leave employment is legally mandatory and also often ceremonially observed'. But first childbirth carries other important connotations for women aside from (temporary) retirement from the world of work outside the home. It means institutionalisation – as all but 1 per cent of women in Britain give birth in hospital – and all the invidious stigma of institutionalisation as described by Goffman apply to mothers in hospital as much as they do to other 'inmates' (Goffman, 1961). Indeed, only the logic of denuding inmates of their personal identity can explain such bizarre practices as routine shaving of pubic hair, which has never been shown to have any medical advantage (Romney, 1980) but which nevertheless continues to be practised as a barbaric ritual in some places. Childbirth also frequently means surgery – not only the current one-in-nine risk of Caesarean section (Maternity Alliance, 1983), but the two-in-three risk of episiotomy (Macfarlane and Mugford, 1984), another barbaric ritual classed medically as a minor procedure but often with major implications for women themselves. The fact that childbirth equates with patienthood often escapes unnoticed, but the role of patient is a very particular one in our society, and it implies an ideal type of behaviour (passivity) which is notably at odds with that required for the role of mother (activity and responsibility). This contradiction may be one of those implicated in the genesis of that major epidemic of our time – postnatal depression. A cultural preference for boys probably underlies the fact that women have more trouble adjusting to the births of girls than to those of boys (Breen, 1975). The transition to parenthood is one of those aspects of life most strongly legitimated by an external professional authority – for women. It may also be one in which the dimension of control is most notably lacking. Contraception renders motherhood less inevitable than it used to be, but it remains true that the all-absorbing ideology of natural fulfilment to which, and within which, women are reared, means that few women feel they really can avoid becoming mothers.

If women run the risk of postnatal depression, the 'marital satisfaction' literature shows that, on the whole, children add to the reported happiness of women more than that of men. It is necessary to disentangle the effect of children on marital happiness from the effect of time. Over time, what happens is something called disenchantment. But the birth of the first child overlays this broad time trend with an abrupt drop in all indices of marital satisfaction. According to Jesse Bernard's aphorism about two marriages – his and hers – *she* may actually suffer more from childbirth, but *his* marriage actually suffers more from the entry of children into the household, because his marriage requires certain things of her that hers does not of him – for instance, a monopoly on her 'attentions and ministrations' (Bernard, 1973), p. 66). Slight clues to this process are provided by a study done in the late 1970s by Jane Chetwynd. The study involved showing 200 men and women drawings of six distinctive female physiques and asking them to evaluate these drawings on ten descriptive scales, including 'like a wife', and 'like a mother'. Results showed that:

> the men consistently placed a higher value on 'wife'. They saw her as more attractive, less prudish and less socially deviant . . . and saw the fatter and less attractive physiques as less likely to be wives. In contrast, the women consistently rated 'mother' higher . . . . They saw the mother role as more attractive, more like themselves and their ideal selves . . . in comparing the two roles the women saw little difference between 'wife' and 'mother', but the men saw a wide contrast. (Chetwynd, 1975, p. 145)

Men like wives, and women like being mothers – not perhaps a good recipe for conjugal happiness: it may even be a reason for depression. It is well known that women tend to get depressed more than men. They visit doctors more, are diagnosed as depressed more, given prescriptions for psychotropic drugs more, and admitted more to mental hospitals than men (Macfarlane, 1980). Some of this depression may be postnatal, but there is convincing evidence that the natality in question is the woman's own – that is, depression in women is related to their membership of the social minority category 'women'. Until puberty, boys are more often treated for mental disturbances of one kind or another; from 10 to 15 the sexes are equal; and by 15 the female excess is marked and consistent (Cochrane and Stopes-Roe, 1981). Almost as well known as the female specialisation in depression is the unequal effect heterosexual unions have on health. Marriage protects women less than men from the risk of entering a mental hospital. Single, widowed and divorced men are more unhappy in this sense than their female counterparts, but the gender difference reverses itself for marriage. Since most of the population gets married, the overall gender difference in mental health is largely accounted for by this fact. However, the usual caveat about the meaning of statistics applies here. One of the intervening processes seems to be that being married helps to keep depressed men out of hospital (because their wives look after them?), whereas it does not have this effect for women (because their husbands do not do so?).

If the area of mental illness enables us to see some of the manifestations of men and women's different relationship to reproduction, we can also see here some of the ways in which production is important. Being employed protects both sexes from depression. Unemployed men make their wives depressed, whereas unemployed women, although they are more likely to be depressed themselves, do not appear to make their husbands depressed (Cochrane and Stopes-Roe, 1981).

One impressive fact associated with being female is the different and problematic relationship women have with the world of 'productive' work – the domain of public labour. The OPCS survey of women and employment showed that 96 per cent of women who have children have a break in their employment. It has always been the case that a majority of mothers have taken up paid work again, but this proportion has been steadily rising, so these days, according to this survey, 'it is clear that the two-phase model of women's employment is increasingly a less accurate description of how a large group of women behave in the labour market' (Martin and Roberts, 1984, p. 187). Most women are now employed between births, whereas in the past it was more common to continue the break until the youngest child reached school age. Also notable in this research are, of course, the continuing occupational separation between men's and women's jobs and the poorer pay and working conditions of women. Childbearing for women is also more likely to bring downward occupational mobility than anything else. This is especially marked for part-time work. In the OPCS survey, 45 per cent of mothers returning to part-time work were downwardly mobile in the labour market. Thus motherhood, which still has the cultural meaning of promotion to full adult female status, means demotion in the world of work outside the home – another of the contradictions facing women, but not men, in their transition through the different phases of life.

INTO THE GRAVE?

The main biological event straddling middle and old age is the menopause, a process located in a more extensive and tangled web of myths and misogynist statements than any other similar biological happening. Like birth and death the menopause happens to both sexes, but unlike birth and death it is a cultural accretion; when life expectancy was short people did not survive to experience, puzzle and mythologise about this particular ageing of their bodies.

Robert Wilson's book, *Feminine Forever* (published in 1966), launched the present era of menopausal mythology. Wilson says that among the unfeminine consequences of the menopause (in women) are aching joints, itching skin, loss of memory, an inability to concentrate, and dryness of the mouth, nose and eyes; to which another doctor adds an inconvenient allergy to household detergents and floor polishes. But Wilson's major targets of attack are breasts, which he calls 'psychological organs' (because they are important to a woman's sense of self esteem: what count as nutritional organs at one stage of life thus undergo an important personality change at another). According to Wilson:

> After menopause, when estrogen and progesterone sink to a low level, the breasts begin to shrivel and sag. Once the supply of these two nourishing hormones is cut off, the breasts become pendulous, wrinkled and flabby. Often the skin of the breasts coarsens and is covered with scales. The breasts lose their erotic sensitivity and sometimes do not respond to pain stimuli. Only timely estrogen replacement therapy can prevent this premature decline of a woman's symbol of femininity. (Wilson, quoted in Delaney *et al*. 1977, p. 167)

As a corrective to this picture there is a study carried out in Oxfordshire in 1980 which looked at the incidence of various physical symptoms in men and women across the period from age 30 to 65. This showed that some symptoms such as Wilson's itching skin were equally prevalent in men and women. Others such as irritability and headaches were more common in women but showed no association with the menopause. Only flushing and night sweating showed an association, though 50 per cent of women never described the first symptom, and 70 per cent did not have the second, and some men complained of both these symptoms (Bungay *et al*., 1977).

Other research shows clearly that other life events are happening around the same time as the menopause, and women's reactions to these life events are being wrongly caricatured as part of the menopausal syndrome. The obvious event is children growing up and leaving home – the empty-nest syndrome. In a Scottish study done in the early 1970s this process proved to be causing problems before the time of the menopause itself (Ballinger, 1975). Perhaps this is not surprising since the average age of the menopause is 51 and children often leave home well before that.

According to van Gennep in his *Rites of Passage*:

> For groups, as well as for individuals, life itself means to separate and to be reunited, to change form and condition, to die and to be reborn. It is to act and to cease, to wait and to rest, and then to begin acting again, but in a different way. And there are always new thresholds to cross: the thresholds of summer and winter, of a season or a year, of a month or a night; the thresholds of birth, adolescence, maturity and old age; the threshold of death and that of the afterlife – for those who believe in it. (van Gennep, 1960, p. 189)

The *British Medical Journal* is much less poetic:

> Take 20,000 newborn babies, equal numbers of boys and girls, and apply current mortality rates: after 70 years there would be 5743 men and 7461 women still alive. Five years later the male survivors would be down to 4083, while there would still be 6256 breathing women. (*British Medical Journal*, 18 June 1977, p. 1605)

These 6256 breathing women, but also their breathing male predecesors, pose quite a problem. The problem arises because this historically unprecedented degree of longevity characterises a society which makes an extremely low level of provision for its elderly dependants. Not all elderly people need to be dependent on others for their daily care, but as the elderly get even more elderly, this is more likely; whereas 86 per cent of 65–69-year-olds can still cut their own toenails for example, only 43 per cent of those aged 85 and over are able to do so (Open University, 1985, p. 165). When the Equal Opportunities Commission carried out its survey of caring for elderly and handicapped relatives in 1980, it found that women made up 77 per cent of those caring for dependent adults aged over 65. One in four of these carers had been performing their caring role for ten years or more (Equal Opportunities Commission, 1980). The notion of 'caring' is itself problematic; at the very least a distinction needs to be made between 'caring for' and 'caring about' (Ungerson, 1983), though it is women who, historically, have specialised in both. The personal implications of caring work are profound. Again it was Jessie Bernard who pointed out an unfortunate conjunction in women's lives today, which is that at the same time as children leaving the nest, parents are liable to become dependent and lay claim to women's caring skills. Women are in the middle, caught between the dependencies of two generations (Bernard, 1975).

Some of the random strands of thought in this chapter could be summed up in three statements:

(1) Gender and generation both influence people's progress through life.
(2) Biology and the division of labour shape the impact of gender on the sociology of the life cycle.
(3) The cultural management and determination of biology is more pronounced for women than for men; women's lives are more medicalised, and so are some of their transitions.

These conclusions are much less interesting than the raw material from which they were drawn. A great deal more could be added – for instance about the social networks and relationships of men and women, which show quite dramatic and influential differences at all stages of life.

But the point is that everyone's vision is selective, and so was Milton's when in his *Paradise Lost* he described Adam and Eve leaving the Garden of Eden hand in hand with the world before them, absolutely free to choose what to do in it. In fact they took the original sins of gender and generation with them, and we are still dealing not too well with the consequences of this today.

3 The Social Classification of Women: A Life-Cycle Approach
Helen Roberts

There has been a considerable body of largely theoretical literature over the last decade concerning the social classification of women. Objections to the current conventional classification range from the ideological – that it is offensive to many that married women should be classified according to the occupation of a husband on whom they may or may not be dependent – to the straightforwardly logical – that to classify a woman in terms of her own occupation until the day she marries, but from then onwards to classify her in terms of the occupation of her husband (whether or not she is in paid work), is inconsistent. There is good evidence (Graham, 1984; Land, 1980) that the resources of the household are not equally shared, which weakens the case that the household is the appropriate unit of stratification (and the occupation of the male 'head of household' most useful for this purpose). Among objections to the classification of women using existing scales are the inability of these to distinguish sufficiently finely between women's occupations, problems concerning the manual/non-manual divide, and the concentration of a very large number of women in a very small number of occupations. Current conventions of classification do not distinguish between full- and part-time workers, and for those women whose labour is in the home and unwaged, there is no classification scheme at all.

While there has been a good deal of theoretical work, and critiques, counter critiques, and replies (for example, *Sociology*, volume 17, no. 4; volume 18, nos 2 and 4), far less has been achieved at a practical level, though a notable exception is the work of Arber, Dale and Gilbert (see Dale *et al.*, 1985). Not only have they developed the basis of a classification scheme which differentiates women's occupations more finely than do other scales, but they also distinguish between full- and part-time work. Their work, however, deals only with women in paid employment.

This chapter examines some of the literature on women and social class; addresses some of the problems in the derivation of classification schemes; and discusses a classification being developed on the basis of the Longitudinal Study (LS), a 1 per cent sample of the population taken from the 1971 and 1981 censuses and supplemented with information on live and stillbirths, cancer registrations, and death of a spouse between the censuses. This scheme is designed to classify women on the basis of their full- or part-time paid work, and their unpaid work entailing the care of children.

THE LITERATURE

Occupation, the universal measure of an individual's social class is in the case of women alone replaced by a completely heterogenous criterion: marriage. (Delphy, 1981, p. 116).

In each household there can be only one head of household and one housewife. So long as the husband is resident he takes precedence over the wife in being head of household. This means if you have a married couple living together, even if the wife owns the property, or has her name on the rent book, you count her husband as the head of household . . . When two people of different sex have an equal claim to be head of household, i.e. you are told ownership is joint, then you take the male of the two to be head of household. (Atkinson, 1971, pp. 116–17).

There are three main bodies of literature on women's social class classification: the sociological literature on stratification, which may give a greater or lesser attention to the position of women; a body of feminist literature looking at the theoretical issues of whether or not women themselves form a social class and whether domestic labour represents a distinctive mode of production (for example, Delphy, above); and an 'official' or semi-official literature on the way in which, *in practice*, classifications are (to be) made.

Early feminist critiques of the way in which social class classifications are made for women can be found in the work of Acker (1973) and Haug (1973). Acker discusses assumptions made about the social position of women in stratification literature, the central pivot of which is the view that the family is the unit in any system of stratification. As she points out, the inconvenient fact that some women are not married or living in the household of a male relative may cause problems.

Delphy (1981) argues that problems of social class classification should not be viewed simply as methodological errors or ideological biases. In other words, the present problems of the classification of women for social class purposes are not merely superficial flaws. One serious problem which would remain, even were all women to be classified in social class terms according to their own occupations, would be those women who have no paid employment.

In criticising work on women and social class from a Marxist perspective, Jean Gardiner (1975), among others, has drawn attention to the failure of Marxism to address theoretically or politically the implications of the relationship of women to the class structure through both waged and unwaged labour. Much of the domestic labour debate, to which Gardiner made an important contribution, was concerned with fitting feminism into the glass slipper of Marxism. Attempts to integrate women into existing social class classifications raise similar problems.

Mirza (1985) in her work investigating the ways in which gender and race affect educational outcomes for young black women, draws attention to the inappropriateness of classifying West Indian children by their father's occupation in families which are frequently headed by females. As Mirza points out, this convention is based on an ethnocentric assumption concerning the nature of family structure and the distribution of resources within the family. Mirza's Emperor and Clothes observation underlines the gap between data, theory and classifications.

In recent years, there have been substantial criticisms of major studies which have failed to look at women in terms of social class, and feminists in particular have argued that large-scale funding of studies which fail to take women into account is not money well spent. Neither the Oxford Mobility Group, which studied occupational mobility in England and Wales, nor the Scottish Occupational Survey included females in their samples, although the Scottish study did collect information on wives. But as the authors of the latter study themselves point out (Payne *et al.*, 1981), the wives of a random sample of men are not a random sample of women. They exclude single, widowed, divorced and separated women, and their selection is dependent upon the selection of their partners.

Responses to the feminist critique have borne a marked similarity to Billy Bunter's cry: 'I didn't take that cake. And it wasn't a very nice cake anyway.' John Goldthorpe writes:

Taken at face value, such [feminist] critiques may be thought cogent. However, they appear somewhat less impressive once more attention is given to their alleged target. For, on closer examination of the matter, it becomes clear that the conventional view which they seek to oppose occurs in more than one version. While it is true that most stratification theorists *have* treated the family as the unit of stratification, and have been crucially dependent on the location of the family head within the occupational division of labour, what needs also to be recognised is that this view has been arrived at through different and . . . sharply contrasting theoretical routes. (Goldthorpe, 1983, pp. 465– 6)

Stanworth (1984), replying to Goldthorpe, argues that the conventional approach which he defends both obscures the extent to which the class experience of wives differs from that of husbands, and ignores the extent to which the inequalities that divide women and men are themselves the outcome of the operation of the class system.

A useful classification of women is not, of course, merely a question of ideological niceties, though it may be noted that no man, whether in or out of employment, is classified according to the occupation of the woman to whom he is attached by marriage. Attempts which have been made so far to integrate women into existing categorisations are derived from assumptions about work (that is paid, full-time and continuous), which may work reasonably well for most men, but not for most women. Any serious attempt to look at the social classification of women needs to begin from the realities of women's lives rather than attempting to awkwardly fit them into pre-existing categories. A classification of women should derive from the sorts of lives women lead, and not from categories derived from the realities of the lives of working men.

THE CONSTRUCTION OF SOCIAL CLASS

In *The Social Grading of Occupations*, Goldthorpe and Hope draw an interesting distinction between the procedures which one carries out in an attempt to produce a valid and reliable measuring instrument, and the evidence one is able to bring forward for the degree of validity and reliability that the instrument actually possesses. Drawing an analogy, appropriately enough, with the building industry (in which women occupy much the same position as they do in the work of Goldthorpe and Hope) they write:

the scaffolding may contribute to the erection of a sound and imposing structure, but the final judgement of the critical onlooker will be passed on the building when the scaffolding is no longer in view. (Goldthorpe and Hope, 1974, p. 1).

The following looks at some aspects of the scaffolding behind occupational classifications. Women, according to feminists, may hold up half the sky, but as far as the structure of the occupational classifications is concerned, they are rather less evident.

In constructing occupational scales, scholars have purportedly been concerned with validity and reliability. The validity of failing to take into account rather more than half of the population, has apparently been of rather less concern than the weighting to be given to a particular occupation. How has the problem of making decisions about social class allocation been approached? Is it a matter of asking five of one's best friends for their ideas, making judgements based on one's own expertise (or prejudice), or is there some 'objective' way of measuring just where people are in the social structure? Given the very large sums of money (by social scientific standards) spent over the last twenty years on investigations of social class and social mobility in Britain, one would expect a high degree of virtuosity from the publications resulting from this research, and on the whole one would not be disappointed.

Perhaps the most interesting and intricate investigation in recent years has been that of Coxon and Jones (1978; 1979; 1980), who adopted a novel socio-linguistic approach. They were interested in occupational judgement and in investigating the extent to which differences exist in the perception of occupational structure. They considered three factors:
(a) socio-economic status (and/or the formal educational require-
    ments of an occupation);
(b) people-orientation;
(c) stage in the life cycle.

In order to go about their task, the authors employed a mixture of painstaking attention to methodological and statistical data, and a curious lack of reflection about some of their procedures. They write, for instance: 'We chose to study men from the Edinburgh area' (Coxon and Jones, 1980, p. 2). The justification for not using a national sample is dealt with by a one-liner on cost. The justification for using men only is not dealt with at all.[1]

Coxon and Jones were not concerned with reconstructing an occupational scale, however. What of those more directly concerned with that enterprise? A recent contribution to this area has been that of Erikson (1984), whose article lucidly discusses some of the principles in the construction of a class index, and then discusses some possible alternative indices. Explaining that the division into social classes results from the organisation of production in societies, he goes on to say that 'a class assignment . . . then, should as directly as possible be based on . . . positions in the system of production . . . i.e. . . . occupations (Erikson, 1984, p. 502).

He apparently takes it as unproblematic that occupations (rather than, for instance, work) are indicative of positions in a system of production, and does not refer to – even to reject – Delphy's argument that domestic labour is a distinctive mode of production. Arguing for a 'family class', Erikson suggests several ways of arriving at a class position for the family. These are:

(1) Trying to find some 'average' of individual positions.
(2) Deciding 'in one way or another' that one of the members is the head of household, and using his or her individual position as the class position for the family.
(3) Letting various combinations of the different members' positions form the different categories.
(4) Ranking the individual positions in the family in a dominance order and letting the family position be equal to the individual code that is the highest in this order.

It is this fourth position which Erikson favours. Having promised us principles for the construction of a class index, it is instructive to see the way in which, in practice, Erikson arrives at his scale. He writes:

> The *assumption* [my emphasis] behind this method is that the market situation of the family is more dependent upon the work position of one of the parents than of the other, provided the positions are different. (Erikson, 1984, p. 503).

In this, he assumes that it is the family, rather than individuals within it, who have a market position; an argument which is not supported by much of the material on the distribution of household income. In constructing his family class system, Erikson writes that a quarter of families are 'unproblematic' because 'man and wife' (or 'woman and husband' as we feminists like to say) work in the same occupational category. The problem, he says, is caused by families where husband

and wife are in different occupational categories. One might well
argue that 'the problem' is not those unhelpful families where
husband and wife are in different occupational categories, but that it
lies with social scientists who construct scales which are fundamentally at variance with social reality. In order to construct his index:

> We have to *decide upon* [my emphasis] a dominance relation for every
> pair of work positions. This means that we have to *make an assumption*
> [my emphasis] about which of the two categories has ... the greatest
> impact upon ideology, attitudes, behaviour and consumption patterns
> of the family members. (Erikson, 1984, p. 504)

He goes on to spell out various assumptions, from which he
constructs a ranking order of dominance between work positions,
from lowest to highest. Among his assumptions is the view that
higher educational qualifications dominate lower; self-employment
(since it spills over into personal life) dominates employment; and so
on. The problem about these assumptions is that they *are* just
assumptions, as are his assumptions about full-time work dominating
half-time work, and half-time work dominating part-time work.
Finally, he introduces an empirical component comparing indices
based on husband's occupation, wife's occupation, own occupation,
'dominance' occupation, and 'household' occupation (based on a
further index he constructs for household type). He then comments
on the fit, or lack of it, between these various scales. The problem, of
course, is that a rather large burden of the weight of his work falls on
his assumptions, which, on the face of it, seem not at all
unreasonable. But precisely the problem with reasonable-seeming
assumptions is that they are likely to reinforce our commonsense
views, being drawn, as they usually are, from similar value systems.
One might take an altogether different set of assumptions, not based
on the conventional view, and from which one might draw rather
different conclusions. If we were to assume that it was not occupation
which was important in devising indices of class from which one might
draw various conclusions about, for instance, mortality and morbidity, but the presence or absence of a full-time nurturer, our
assumption would rightly be questioned. One of the rather large
number of assumptions made by Erikson is that in his 'individual'
index of classification, housewives continue to get their index value
from their husbands' positions, and retired persons from their own
previous main occupations. 'This index,' he writes, without apparent
irony, 'we call INDIVIDUAL' (his capitals). Even if we do not

question his assumptions about occupation, we might wonder whether 'housewife' may have given up her job only last week, and 'retired' thirty years ago. If this were the case, would it make any difference?

Perhaps the most important scale in recent years has been that devised by Goldthorpe and Hope (1974). This involved drawing two randomly selected samples of voters in Oxford. One of these samples was given a fairly conventional grading test on the basis of forty occupations; the other asked to look at those same forty occupations on the basis of four criteria, namely, standard of living, power and influence over other people, level of qualifications, and value to society. On the basis of their findings, the authors suggest that:

> While the results cannot ... conclusively confirm the interpretation that we would give to occupational prestige scales – that is, that they represent a composite popular judgement of the 'general desirability' of occupations – they are at all events highly consistent with it. (Goldthorpe and Hope, 1974 p. 16)

On this basis, the authors suggest that such a scale 'offer[s] the best guarantee against the drawing of unwarranted and possibly misleading inferences when such a scale is being applied' (Goldthorpe and Hope, 1974, p. 16).

In constructing their scale, Goldthorpe and Hope first needed to find some way of handling the very large numbers of occupations identified by the Office of Populations Censuses and Surveys (OPCS) whose coding procedures they had decided to employ. By crossing unit group and employment status from the OPCS classifications, Goldthorpe and Hope arrived at what they call the 'basic atoms' of their classification system. The task of formation of the scale categories came next. Four experts were enlisted to help with this. The selection of occupational titles for empirical grading, which was the next step, was done on the basis of three rules, the apparently arbitrary application of which would have given Piaget food for thought. First, all the titles selected had to be likely to be known to the majority of respondents in the sample. Second, subject to Rule One, the titles selected should cover the range of occupations comprised by the category, taking into account all occupational attributes known to be regularly associated with assessments of 'general desirability'. Third, where Rule One allowed and Rule Two made it desirable, ten occupation titles were selected from each category; otherwise, five titles were selected.

Now for the interesting part. Proceeding in this manner, Goldthorpe and Hope were able to produce sets of representative titles for all their categories except one. This was a category made up of a single occupation grading unit and covering domestic housekeepers with the status of employee. 'In this case, we were unable to find any occupations falling within the category which were typically engaged in by males. We decided therefore that this category should be excluded from our scale' (Goldthorpe and Hope, 1974, p. 46). So much for rules. If the data don't fit, change the rules.

THE CITY CLASSIFICATION SCHEME

The classification scheme currently being developed using the LS does not meet all of the criticisms of current classification schemes, but it does go some way towards meeting them, and offers a way forward which, since it is based on routinely collected data, is widely applicable.[2]

The basis of current classification schemes is occupation, which according to the 1980 classification of occupations concerns 'the kind of work' performed by an individual. Our scheme is based on the same principle: that the kind of work done by a woman is crucial in the development of a classification scheme. Where we depart from the 1980 Classification of Occupations is in our evaluation of household work (an important component of the kind of work performed by most women and some men). The Classification of Occupations defines housewives as 'inactive' (economically speaking) along with 'all persons who have never been in employment and are not now seeking employment and those who have spent more than six months in a prison and are returned as out of employment' (OPCS, 1980, p. x).

We cannot claim that ours is an entirely novel approach. Hakim reports that:

> Unpaid household work was included in the definition of economic activity from 1851 to 1871; from 1881 onwards it was excluded as the primary concern with work done for pay or profit began to emerge. (Hakim, 1980, p. 88)

We are using data on women's occupation and status from a 1 per cent sample from the 1971 and 1981 census to classify women on the basis of the work they do, paid or unpaid, full- or part-time.

Roger Thomas (1984) has pointed to three problems with the current system. First, the nature of the classification scheme may not adequately distinguish between jobs done by women. Second, women's levels of skills may not be adequately reflected in an occupation-based classification historically devised with men's occupations in mind, and finally there is the problem of the referencing system where the 'head of household' acts as the reference point for the whole household. Our work does not challenge, and indeed is necessarily based upon, the current Classification of Occupations. This means that we are unable to subdivide the larger occupational groups, such as clerks and cashiers, except in terms of variables other than occupation. Should modifications be made to the existing classification, however, they can be incorporated into our scheme. Our scheme does overcome the problem of the 'reference person', since any woman, in or out of paid employment, will be classified on the basis of the work she does.

In looking at the kind of work done by women, an important influence has been the Martin and Roberts (1984) *Women and Employment* report and the work now being done by others on secondary analyses of their data (for example, Dex, 1984; Joshi, 1984), which has provided valuable empirical material, including material on work histories, full- and part-time work and domestic responsibilities.

Our first step in attempting to derive this classification was to look at the jobs in which women are most highly represented. As Thomas (1986) has pointed out:

> a high proportion of women in employment are assigned to a small number of Occupational Unit Groups (OUGs) . . . almost a third of all the jobs done by women coded as part of the 1981 census 10% sample fell into the three OUGs roughly defined as 'clerks, typists and shop assistants'. (Thomas, 1986, p. 7)

Using sample data from the 1981 census, we took the forty-four occupational unit groups in which women are most highly represented. Of women in paid work, 83 per cent are in one of these forty-four OUGs. We allocated the remaining 17 per cent of women in paid employment to five residual groups on the basis of occupational order. These five groups comprise: first, others in orders 1, 2, 3 and 4 (i.e. professional and related); second, others in orders 5 and 6 (e.g. managerial, clerical); third, others in orders 7, 8, 9 and 15 (e.g. selling, security, catering and transport); fourth, others in orders 10,

11, 12, 13, 14 and 16 (e.g. farming, processing, painting and construction); and, finally, those in order 17 (i.e. occupation not stated or inadequately described). This makes forty-nine groups, which are each divided into four sub-groups:

(1) those working full-time with domestic responsibility;
(2) those working full-time with no domestic responsibility;
(3) those working part-time with domestic responsibility;
(4) those working part-time with no domestic responsibility.

Those women not in paid work are allocated to a fiftieth group. In allocating these women into sub-groups, we also considered the kinds of work they do, bearing in mind that women's unpaid work tends to change as their children get older. Those women who are not in paid work are therefore divided into five groups:
(1) those with no children;
(2) those whose youngest child is 0–4;
(3) those whose youngest child is 5–10;
(4) those whose youngest child is 11–16;
(5) those whose youngest child is over 16.

Our present definition of 'domestic responsibility' in terms of the care of children is not an entirely satisfactory one, since one might want to include, as dimensions of domestic responsibility, care of husbands, care of the elderly or care of the handicapped. An Equal Opportunities Commission report on the care of the elderly and handicapped points out that: 'The OPCS survey of 1968–9 . . . found that approximately 80 per cent of handicapped adults were living with others and so would presumably be receiving some care from members of their own households', and 'on the basis of [Hunt's] 1967 survey of the home help service, she estimated that "between the ages of 35 and 64 roughly half the 'housewives' can expect at some time or another to give some help to elderly or infirm persons"' (EOC, 1982, pp. 9–10). As the EOC points out, since then the number of very elderly has grown quite significantly and so the proportion may now be rather greater.

One aspect of our further work in this area will be to investigate the use of other dimensions of domestic responsibility, though these other dimensions are likely to be more difficult to assess, since we would not want to assume, for instance, that the presence of an elderly person in the household was always a 'domestic responsibility' when that person might be a positive asset in sharing the responsibilities of the household. Martin and Roberts (1984), for instance, showed the important role played by grandmothers in caring for the children of working mothers.

For the present, however, the forty-nine groups of women in paid work are each divided into four sub-groups, and the fiftieth group of women who are not in paid work are divided into the five sub-groups described above, giving 201 'work positions' in all. These 201 positions have been ranked according to various characteristics, including the social class distribution of husbands, access to one or more cars, and distribution in the housing market.

A woman's work position is therefore derived on the basis of personal information. Is she in paid work? Is it full- or part-time? Does she have domestic responsibilities in terms of children? The *rankings* of the work positions which will enable us to develop a hierarchical scale derive from the characteristics of *all* women in a particular work position. How likely are school cleaners, for instance, to own their own homes, or be married to men in social class I? Without categorising individual women according to the work performed by their husbands, we recognise that the work done by their husbands does influence the ranking of their own work positions. As Delphy (1984) points out:

> If we compare the standard of living to which a woman can aspire if she remains single, and the standard which she can reasonably expect from being married ... relative economic deprivation will be experienced by married women as time goes on. We are confronted with a paradox: on the one hand marriage is the (institutional) situation where women are exploited; and on the other hand precisely because of this, the potential market situation for women's labour (which is that of all women, not just those who are actually married) is such that marriage still offers them the best career, economically speaking. (Delphy, 1984, p. 97)

Having ranked the 201 work positions according to various dimensions, we have taken an average rank, though at a later stage multivariate and clustering techniques will be used. On the basis of these average ranks, a hierarchical scale has been provisionally constructed. The following four methods have been used as bases for dividing this scale into five 'classes':

(1) quintiles of numbers;
(2) quintiles of ranks;
(3) breaks in the graph which occur when work positions are plotted against husbands' social class and housing tenure;
(4) following the same distribution as that for men, using the registrar general's classification.

While the fourth choice has many disadvantages, among them that of continuing to predicate women's classifications on males, it does have the advantage that in looking at father/children mobility, the mobility of sons and daughters will be able to be more sensibly related.

The current exercise is being carried out with 1981 data. For comparative purposes we are repeating the exercise using 1971 data, and in due course hope to repeat it with 1991 data. As Baker and Cunnison (1986) point out, many women may be thought of as having a variety of working lives, which change with what may broadly be seen as life-cycle stage. Dale (1986) draws attention to changes in occupation, income and household assets over the life cycle. A classification scheme based on longitudinal data is able to show these changes over time.

The scheme is still at a relatively early stage, and requires development, but it does seem to have the potential of classifying individual women according to the work they do. Because of the way that we have used domestic responsibility, such a classification could not be used for fertility studies, nor is it a houshold classification – it classifies individual women relative to other women. In principle, there is no reason why a similar classification could not be used for men, but, in practice, since less of their work is within the home, the 'domestic responsibility' dimension would be misleading.

Perhaps the most important conclusion which can be drawn at this stage is that it *is* possible to develop a classification for women, on the basis of routinely collected data, that meets some of the criticisms of current practices. Such a classification can take into account the work of waged as well as unwaged women, full- and part-time paid work, and domestic responsibilities. The next stage of our work will involve exploring in a preliminary way the gradients which are obtained using the classification. It remains to be seen how well the classification works once the scaffolding has been removed.

NOTES

1. More recently, Coxon and Davies, with Jones (1986), have suggested that, 'A study of occupational belief systems extended to cover all aspects of . . . women's work would, in our view, be extremely valuable in the feminist debate over the reimportation of women into the sociological mainstream' (p. 206). Professor Coxon has also pointed out (personal communication, 1987) that the Edinburgh sample did actually include a number of 'naturally occurring' women in occupations such as social worker. 'More to the point, we had wanted deliberately to include women's occupations in our Occupational Sampling Design, and had intended to include women naturally in our "Combing Sampling" . . . but we were expressly told by our funding agency (SSRC) that we would not be funded to do so since this widened the focus unnecessarily.'

2. I am grateful to Raymond Barker for providing technical support for this study, to John Fox who has provided constructive advice and criticism, and to colleagues who have attended the meetings on women and social class in the Social Statistics Research Unit at City University.

Part II

Historical Time and Private Lives

4 Adolescent Girls: Transition from Girlfriends to Boyfriends?

Vivienne Griffiths

INTRODUCTION

In this chapter, I shall examine what happens to girls' friendship groups when adolescent girls start going out with boys, referring to some research which I carried out in West Yorkshire. Rather than emphasising the breakdown of girls' friendship groups with the onset of girl–boy relationships, as some previous studies have done, I shall stress the positive strategies which the girls I worked with used to resist pressures to drop their girlfriends.

STRONG FRIENDSHIPS

I spent a year in a mixed-sex comprehensive school in an industrial town in West Yorkshire, following a group of sixteen working-class girls aged 13–14 (thirteen white, two Afro-Caribbean, one Asian) through from their second to third year of secondary schooling. At first I spent most of the time observing lessons, but over the year more and more time was spent with the girls at break, lunchtime and after school. I gradually got to know their friends from other classes, which brought the total number of girls I mixed with regularly to thirty-four. I also talked to sixteen white girls in the fifth year, ten of whom I met again six months after they had left school.

As I got to know them, a strong, positive picture of the friendships between the girls emerged. The girls' friendships were intense and long-lasting, providing emotional and practical support, and exemplified by trust and loyalty. The girls enjoyed going round together, 'having a laugh' or a 'right good doss'. Some of the girls were virtually inseparable: they would call for each other on the way to school, walk to school together, and spend the day together as far as possible. If they had different lessons, they would wait for each other outside the classrooms, ready to walk home together again at the end of the day. In the evenings, the girls would call for each other again, go round to each other's houses, or hang around the streets. I wondered how much of this would last once the girls started to go out with boys.

FINDING BOYFRIENDS, DROPPING GIRLFRIENDS

The cultural and ideological pressures on girls to get a boyfriend are enormous and have been well documented (McRobbie, 1978a and 1978b; Griffin, 1981 and 1985b). For instance, Christine Griffin writes, 'Getting a boyfriend was seen as proof of young women's "normal" heterosexuality and more "grown-up" femininity' (Griffin, 1985b, p. 59). Within this context of 'compulsory heterosexuality' (Rich, 1980), to continue close relationships with girls without a corresponding interest in boys might be regarded as abnormal or deviant. Finding a steady boyfriend may also be a way of protecting a girl's reputation from the label 'slag' (Lees, 1986).

One way in which heterosexuality may be presented as the norm is through the media. Angela McRobbie's analysis of *Jackie*, a magazine for young women, shows that:

> the stories consist of isolated individuals, distrusting even their best friends and in search of fulfilment only through a partner . . . *Jackie* stories . . . elevate to dizzy heights the supremacy of the heterosexual romantic partnership. (McRobbie, 1978a, p. 17 and p. 20)

Here the friendships between girls are undermined; young women are divided in competition with each other to get a man.

Although there are a growing number of accounts, particularly from feminist researchers, demonstrating the importance of friend-ships between girls (Ward, 1976; McRobbie, 1978b; Griffin, 1985b; Lees, 1986), much of the literature states that girlfriends take second place or are dropped altogether as girls start going out regularly with boys. The model which emerges is a polarised one: girlfriends *or* boyfriends. The two are seen as incompatible, and inevitably the boyfriends win in the end – just like the *Jackie* stories.

However, there are some important differences in emphasis between these studies. Some accounts, usually those written in the 1970s,[1] state that girls drop their girlfriends unquestioningly. For example, Dorothy Hobson writes:

When they began 'courting', they [the girls] abandoned their spare-time activities and their girlfriends. There is an acceptance that women 'give up' their freedom, there was no sign of assertion of their right to continue their own leisure activities. (Hobson, 1981, p. 137)

The picture which comes across is that young women are passive victims of ideological pressures, totally taken over by the cultures of femininity and romance.

In contrast, other usually more recent studies present the process as more complex. Whilst the final outcome is the same – that is, boyfriends eventually take over from girlfriends – girls do not drop their girlfriends without some resistance. For example, Christine Griffin stresses:

Most young women are well aware of the threat posed by 'deffing out' to supportive female friendships and feminine cultures in 'leisure' and the school. They take steps to avoid the loss of these collective female networks. (Griffin, 1981, p. 8)

Diana Leonard notes a strategy by which girls resisted the breakup of their friendship groups:

Should one girl start seeing too much of one boy she was drawn back into the group by her friends ridiculing her choice, by their ignoring her (e.g. by not calling for her), or by their whispering about her in front of her. (Leonard, 1980, p.80)

At the end of *Typical Girls?*, Christine Griffin lists a number of positive strategies, such as two-timing or taking 'blokes for a ride' (Griffin, 1985b, p. 192), which girls adopt to resist the pressures to 'get a man' and abandon their girlfriends. Young women here are presented as taking a direct and active role in their own lives.

In my research, I expected to find a relatively unproblematic transition from girlfriends to boyfriends. I was surprised to find considerable evidence of the kind of resistance illustrated above and, unlike most previous studies, friendships between girls being largely maintained alongside relationships with boys. In the rest of this chapter I shall describe and elaborate on the strategies the girls I worked with used to keep their girlfriends. The pressures on young women to 'break friends' are undoubtedly strong – all the studies are agreed on this – so I shall also try to pinpoint what causes those pressures and at what stages they are strongest.

AGES AND STAGES

The girls' relationships with boys were divided into clear stages, according to their age and how well they knew them. From 'going round with' a boy, usually in a mixed-sex group at the age of about 13 or 14, the girls 'progressed' to the more clearly delineated 'going out with' a boy from about 14 or 15, and from there to more regular boyfriends and 'courting' which might lead to engagement. The girls were very clear about the boundaries which existed between one stage and the next. Whilst largely taking for granted that they would end up getting married, they were nevertheless able to use the stages to keep control in relationships with boys and to maintain their friendships with their girlfriends.

2nd-Years: 'Going Round With' – Mixed-Sex Groups and Boyfriend Swopping

Studies of younger girls show the strength and closeness of friendships between girls persisting alongside boyfriends (McRobbie, 1978b; Lees, 1986), and I found this to be the case in my own research. At this stage, boyfriends posed little threat to the friendships between the girls.

Most of the girls either went out with groups of girlfriends in the evenings or in mixed-sex groups. The mixed groups were usually two single-sex peer groups who started to hang around together, a pattern reported in other studies of early adolescence (Ward, 1976; Leonard, 1980). The mixed group was at first just an extension of the all-girl group. The ritual of the girls calling for each other was still maintained, and the boys were something of an afterthought:

> Mandy: There's normally about ten of us, about five girls and a few boys.

The boys were not necessarily considered as boyfriends:

> Elaine: They're just good mates.
> Carol: Have a good laugh with 'em.

However, it was from these groups that the first boyfriends came, rather than an individual girl meeting an individual boy, as I had assumed. For example, when I asked Karen, 'How did you meet him?' she replied, 'Just went round with him', and this was typical of other girls too.

I also assumed that when the girls started talking about having a boyfriend, that this meant going out with a boy on an individual basis. The girls soon made it clear that I was jumping a stage:

Pam: I didn't go *out* with him, I just sort of went *with* him.

Having a boyfriend to these girls usually meant being nominally attached to a boy within the group, but still hanging around with the rest of the group at the local park or disco.

Relationships with boys formed through these mixed-sex groups were very brief, lasting from one night to two or three weeks at most. I found it hard to keep up with the girls' boyfriends, they changed so quickly. Speedy turnover of boyfriends is something that I remember vividly from that stage too. These temporary attachments to boys were a great contrast to the intense, long-lasting friendships between the girls themselves. The girlfriends formed what John Ward calls a 'social anchor' (1976, p. 53), a stable point in the ever-shifting configuration of boyfriends.

There was a sense in which the girls were keeping a deliberate distance in relationships with boys, 'trying out' several before they felt prepared to get more involved with one, as Jane explained:

before you do [go out with a boy], got to decide whether they're right for you first.

A strategy which helped the girls do this was boyfriend-swopping, which I experienced myself during early adolescence. Going round in mixed-sex groups meant that the girls could actually rotate boy-friends until they had all gone round with all the boys in the group. One group of girls all liked a particular boy, and virtually passed him round from one to the other.

Boyfriend-swopping enabled the girls to keep control over their relationships with boys. The girls could compare notes amongst themselves about the boys, and this was important in some cases: for example, to warn each other about a boy who 'lied to everyone', and particularly about which boys 'tried it on'.

The picture which emerged from this stage was very different from the usual stereotype, perpetrated by girls' magazines and popular belief, that girls compete with each other for boys, and fall out with their friends because they both like the same boy. I found that this might happen between different girls who were not friends, but between girlfriends there was a co-operative supportive approach, as exemplified a this stage by the boyfriend-swopping, and later in a very different way, by a code of practice not to poach each other's boyfriends, as I shall describe.

3rd-Years: 'Going Out With' – Foursomes and Chaperoning

At this stage, many girls were still hanging around with boys in mixed-sex groups rather than going out with a particular boy, and some girls were not mixing with boys at all, but only seeing their girlfriends, so there was considerable variation. For example, a group of black girls who did not have boyfriends were most scathing about the white girls who were 'always mooning around after boys'. There is some evidence that black girls may experience less pressure to get boyfriends than white girls (Griffin, 1985b). Certainly these black girls seemed quite satisfied with each other's company.

For those girls who did have boyfriends, relationships with boys were sometimes longer lasting than they had been the previous year. For instance, Elaine had had the same boyfriend for three months. Some of the girls were beginning to go out individually with a boy on occasions, though still meeting in the mixed group too, as Vicky described:

> We usually go round together, but now and again if there's something good on at t'pictures, we usually go there or something like that.

I had to be careful not to assume that *seeing* a boy meant the same as *going out with* him on an individual basis. For example, Carol said that she saw her boyfriend four times a week. However, on closer questioning, it emerged that she rarely went out with him alone. She either saw him in a large group, or more usually in a foursome:

> cos Elaine knows him as well, cos she's been out with him, and she's going out with a lad now as well, who is his friend sort of, so we can go round together . . . and Karen, her boyfriend Wayne, if we see her, we sometimes go round with her, so we still see schoolmates.

There is still the sense in Carol's description of the close-knit mixed group, where girls and boys swopped partners. Foursomes of this kind were a frequent pattern, and usually a way in which the girls were able to maintain their close girlfriendships too.

However, in one or two cases, the foursome was founded more on the boys' friendships than the girls'. For example, Jane told me:

> And now I go round with him and his friend Alan ... we go to each other's houses and to the park and up to this girl called Christine up Hayton ... and to town sometimes.

Christine was not one of Jane's usual friends, and she did not see her outside the foursome. Some studies report that going out with a boy and *his* friends seriously undermines girls' own friendships and interests (Griffin, 1985b; Lees, 1986). In my research, I did not find this happening to any great degree: Jane still saw her close girlfriends at other times, whilst another girl, Jenny, enjoyed extending her friendship group in this way:

> We see a lot of other lasses, girls, through going out with these boys ... you kind of chum up with some others because they happen to be around at that time.

Nevertheless, I recognise that there may be a real danger for some girls of dropping, or being forced to drop, their own friends.

Some of the girls did their best to resist this possible breakdown of their friendship groups by adopting a strategy I shall call 'chaperoning'. For example, even when girls went out with a boy alone, they sometimes started the evening with their girlfriends and met them again later:

> Lizzy: We set off together ... then [after] about half an hour we'd leave 'em to go off to us boys, then we'd come back ... to go home.

This was true of the fifth-year girls too, even when they had regular boyfriends:

> Jenny: When I'm going to meet him she walks me, don't you?
> Sarah: I walk around until he comes and then we might chat a bit –
> Jenny: Then she goes.
> Sarah: – and then I go missing.

Like boyfriend-swopping, chaperoning enabled the girls to maintain their close girlfriendships, and to assert solidarity and control in relationships with boys. The girls were able to keep their pattern of calling for each other and to compare notes about what had happened with their boyfriends afterwards.

It is important to stress that even the girls who were beginning to pair off with boys or go out in foursomes still saw their girlfriends separately. Any reduction in time spent with girlfriends was largely due to the onset of winter, and the fact that many of the girls' parents would not let them go out with just girls once the evenings were darker. Without necessarily wanting to, the girls therefore found themselves in mixed-sex company more often in winter than summer.

5th-Years: Steadies and Courting – Girls' Talk and Girls' Times

By the age of 15 or 16, some girls had regular boyfriends and these relationships were tending to last longer; for instance, Sarah had gone out with a boy for five months. Two of the girls had been going out with their boyfriends all year and were deemed to be 'courting'. There seems to be general agreement in the literature that a steady boyfriend or courtship constitutes the greatest threat to girls' friendships (McCabe, 1982; Hobson, 1981; Leonard, 1980; Griffin, 1985b). I found that while courtship did pose a serious threat, regular boyfriends did not, and the girls clearly differentiated between the two stages.

Even when girls were going out regularly with a boy, most of them saw their girlfriends frequently, not just in school, but in the evenings too. This happened particularly when the girls lived close to each other. For example, Sarah and Jenny saw each other every night, as Sarah said:

> I'm always popping round to her [Jenny's] house ... I see her more than I used to see me boyfriend didn't I?

These two girls were part of a larger group of seven white girls who went round with each other all the time at school. There was no question of fitting their girlfriends into hairwash night (as *Jackie* suggests) for most of these girls; boys were fitted into a busy social life with their girlfriends rather than the other way round. Their leisure activities seemed much closer to the male pattern described by Annie Whitehead, who writes about men in rural Herefordshire:

Boys and men do not give up the old pattern of going out with their
mates when they are courting, but often reserve special nights – Friday
and Saturday – for their girlfriends. They spend the other evenings
drinking with their peers. (Whitehead, 1976, p. 195)

The girls too had clearly allocated girls' times and boys' times. School
and most of the weekends were for girlfriends. On Saturdays, those
who did not have Saturday jobs would go round the shops together;
Saturday nights were spent with their boyfriends (if they had one),
and Sunday nights they would all meet at the local chippy. The
Sunday night meeting anticipated the more institutionalised 'Friday
night girls' night' which developed after they had left school.
Boyfriends were definitely restricted to evenings, but some evenings
were for girlfriends too, as I have said. Even when the girls were
going out with their boyfriends in the evening, they often chaperoned
each other (see previous section), so girls' times could spill over into
boys' times.

Talking about what had happened with their boyfriends was
something the girls looked forward to, as Sarah described:

As soon as we come up to school in t'morning we're all walking up
going, 'Oh! This happened and this happened', aren't we? ...
Especially after that party on Saturday, all t'gossip were flying round!

Sarah made it clear that the pattern of calling for each other on the
way to school was still being maintained, and introduced the point
that the girls sometimes saw each other on a 'boyfriends' evening', for
example at parties. Talking through what had happened actually
seemed to add to the excitement, as though experiences with boys
were incomplete until they had been relived with their girlfriends.
Talking about their relationships with boys was just one part of a
general sharing of experiences, which provided the girls with
emotional feedback and mutual support. Talk as a central feature of
girls' relationships has been found by other research too (Ward, 1976;
Johnson and Aries, 1983; Lees, 1986).

Confiding and comparing notes may have helped build up trust and
loyalty, and prevent the rivalry between friends over boys which
Jackie and other magazines present as commonplace. Like Sue Lees
(1986), I did not find girlfriends competing for men to any great
extent. Indeed, an informal code of practice had evolved among
some of the girls to prevent this occurring:

Sarah: That's never happened!
Jackie: Not yet!
[All laugh]
Jenny: Yeah, we've all got different tastes ... if we knew that
someone liked him [the same boy] tho', we wouldn't go flirting
or owt would we?
Sarah: Oh no, no we wouldn't would we?
[All laugh]

The girls' laughter and self-mocking suggests that they were well
aware of the possibility of rivalry but, as with the younger girls, this
only occurred between them and girls outside their friendship groups.

Courtship presented a far stronger threat to the girls' friendships,
and the girls were aware of this:

Jackie: If you've been going out with a boy for a long time, and you
don't see them [your friends], quite often they just reject you.
Jenny: *We* don't tho'. No.
Jackie: No, but you know, other people do, other groups.

As with the rivalry issue, there were vehement denials that this might
apply to them. Nevertheless, there *were* severe tensions in this group
because two of the girls were courting and seeing less of the others.
This was not fully admitted until I spoke to the girls six months after
they had left school. Then I discovered that Marje and Tricia, whilst
still at school, had been seeing their boyfriends 'all t'time', not just in
the evenings but impinging on the girls' times at school, at weekends
and summer holidays. However, even in this case there was evidence
of resistance against the breakup of the girls' friendship group.
Whilst Marje had started seeing her boyfriend during the day
without any qualms, thereby following the more traditional pattern,
Tricia had been extremely unhappy about the situation and had
eventually withstood the pressures from her boyfriend to spend all
her time with him.

Even six months later, Tricia talked vividly and at great length
about what had happened. She was aware that because she was
encroaching on the girls' times she might lose her girlfriends, and felt
absolutely torn between wanting to be with her boyfriend and her
girlfriends:

I wanted to [see my boyfriend] but I didn't if you know what I mean,
cos I thought, well I'll be seeing him tonight anyway and I won't see
me friends tonight.

Tricia's eventual solution was to restore some balance in the allocation of time, so that 'School was friends' time and then night was boyfriends' time.' In order to do this, she had to employ some extreme measures, such as hiding under the table at dinner time so that her boyfriend would not see her.

Much of the motivation to see less of her boyfriend during the day came from within Tricia herself, because she valued her girlfriends and felt bad about neglecting them. There was also some teasing from the other girls to get her back into the group; as Tricia put it, 'It'd be more of a joke but to get it over', and this obviously had its effect. As Diana Leonard found (1980), the girls were not going to let their friend go without a struggle. However, in Tricia's case it was less drastic for the remaining girls than it would have been had she been in a pair of best friends. As Sue said:

> Well you realised there were one missing but – but you know it didn't
> – it wasn't as if you were left on your own because she was gone off
> with her boyfriend.

I shall describe the impact of courting on a best-friend pair in the next section.

In contrast to this example, it is important to stress that some girls in the fifth year did not have regular boyfriends and spent their time almost entirely with their girlfriends.

After Leaving School: Steadies and Courting – Keeping in Touch and Girls' Nights

After leaving school, the girls went on to college (sixth form college, Tech, Art college), jobs (bank clerk, secretary, shop work), YTS schemes, or the dole. The pressures on young women to lose touch with their girlfriends may be particularly strong at this point, especially when the daily contact at school has gone (Griffin, 1985b). Diana Leonard (1980) found that this is when a steady boyfriend is most likely to take over from girlfriends. However, my research indicates the persistence of many previous friendships, particularly between best friends who lived close to each other. Large groups of friends were harder to maintain and were being replaced not by boyfriends, but by the formation of new friendship groups among young women at work and college. My findings accord most closely to those of Kris Beuret and Lynn Makings (1986), who describe a group of hairdressers with steady boyfriends whose friendships with other young women were still important. In my study, friendships between girls also existed alongside regular boyfriends.

Sarah, Jenny and Jackie had kept in touch most easily because they had moved together to the local sixth form college and were therefore still seeing each other every day. Sarah and Jenny were still following the previous year's pattern of seeing each other most evenings too, in spite of the fact that Sarah had a boyfriend whom she had met at college. As Jenny said, 'She sees me more than him'.

I would suggest that one reason for this was the less sex-divided atmosphere of college life. The girls mentioned that one of the things they liked best about college was that, unlike school, they could 'get friendly with lads without anybody making silly jokes about it'. Girls and boys mixed more naturally in the day, without necessarily being girl and boyfriend. Even at night, mixed-sex groups were informal: parties were frequent occurrences and girls were not expected to go with a partner. All this added up to a very different atmosphere from the polarisation of school where you were either with your girlfriend *or* with your boyfriend. The girls who had gone to Tech and Art college also valued the informality and felt that the pressures to courtship were diminished.

Paradoxically, Beuret and Makings (1986) suggest that the 'freer' culture of college life may lessen the importance of all-women groups as young women mix more freely with men. This raises the important question of whether a strong female friendship group depends on, or thrives best in, a polarised situation. However, age and class background may be crucial factors. The students in Beuret and Makings's study were aged 19 to 24 and middle class; whereas the girls at college in my study were 16–17 years old and working class, and there were no signs at this stage that their friendships with each other were being undermined.

The 'developing primacy of the heterosexual couple' (Griffin, 1981, p. 8) posed more of an obvious threat to the friendships between girls who had gone straight from school to work. Marje, who had been courting since before she left school, was now very much following the stereotyped pattern, seeing her boyfriend

> nearly every night . . . We mostly meet in each other's homes but we go out sometimes.

She only rarely saw her old schoolfriends, and only occasionally went out with girls from work. However, some of the young women who were now at work were still strenuously resisting this pattern. For example, Tricia, who was also courting, had been seeing her boyfriend every night,

> but I just got bored with it, just arguing all the time, so I don't see him so much now.

This gave Tricia the chance to go out with girlfriends on some evenings.

In another case, Anne's relationship with a boy had nearly caused the breaking-up of her best friendship with Michelle. Michelle had felt left out: 'she'd be going out with her boyfriend at t'weekend and I didn't want to stay in'; so she had started going round with another girl. This was the closest I found to the examples of 'deffing out' given by Christine Griffin (1981; 1985b), where best friends take second place to boyfriends. The emotional impact on Michelle of Anne's courting was much stronger than Tricia's had been on the large group. However, Anne and Michelle had not split up for good: Michelle had not got on with the other girl, and when the friends realised that they missed each other's company, they made things up. Although both girls now had regular boyfriends, they were retaining time for each other, as Michelle explained:

> I see her twice a week now usually ... We usually just stay in, watch a bit of telly and talk.

For the young women at work, there were not so many opportunities to socialise in the day as there had been at school. However, there was evidence that the girls were still maintaining time for their closest previous friends and also making new friends at work. Apart from the kind of arrangement Anne and Michelle had made, groups of girlfriends tended to go out together on a Friday night and see their boyfriends on Saturday evening. According to Tricia, 'All the girls I know' did this. It was most noticeable that the streets in town on Friday night were full of groups of young women, all dressed up, arms linked, talking and laughing, and off to have a good time. They presented a strong, positive image and contradicted my expected finding that female peer groups would disappear when the girls left school. 'Lasses nights', as they were known, are mentioned in other research (Westwood, 1984; Beuret and Makings,

1986), which suggests that this is a widespread custom for young working-class women.

However, keeping in touch with girlfriends may not be so easy for young unemployed women, as Christine Griffin stresses (1985b). For example, Mandy had been unemployed since leaving school. In the end she moved away from the area to try and find work. Her best friend Pauline was upset that they might lose touch. Neither of these young women had boyfriends.

AFFIRMATION OF FRIENDSHIP

Contrary to my expectation and the findings of much previous research, the friendships between the girls in my study did not break down, but were largely maintained *alongside* boyfriends. I have identified strategies such as boyfriend-swopping and chaperoning which the girls used at each stage to prevent the breakup of their female friendship groups. As I have mentioned, I did not always ask the right questions, and sometimes made faulty assumptions about the degree to which boyfriends might be taking over from girlfriends, but the girls were always ready to put me right.

It is important not to underestimate the very real pressures the girls faced to 'break friends'. Courtship presented one of the strongest threats to the girls' friendships, especially after they had left school and did not necessarily see their friends during the day. But by means of girls' times and for those in work the more institutionalised girls' nights, all but one of the young women maintained close relationships with girlfriends. I was particularly heartened by the reassertion of friendship which occurred when girls who had split up or nearly split up with their girlfriends renegotiated a relationship which persisted alongside boyfriends. This seemed to me to be a real affirmation of the strength and value of friendship between women.

My emphasis throughout this chapter has been a positive one, reflecting the girls' attitudes themselves. Most of the girls I worked with held traditional views about the future: they took it for granted that they would get married and have children. Nevertheless they still hoped to have women friends. How far they would be able to achieve this in practice I can only speculate. I should like to end on a hopeful note by giving the last word to one of the young women. Jenny, of whom it was said by one of her friends, 'never loses touch with anybody', may have derived some of her sense of the importance of women friends from her mother:

> Me Mum says that it's best to [keep in touch with your friends], cos she tried to, and she lost contact with her schoolfriends, and she were you know a bit unhappy about it . . . but luckily she has now [met up again] with two of them, and it's two of her best ones . . . and she won't break up again, so it's all right.

NOTE

1. For a fuller account of feminist research on girls and subcultures in the 1970s, see Christine Griffin, 'Broken Transitions', Chapter 6 in this volume.

5 'I've Got Used to Being Independent Now': Women and Courtship in a Recession

Kristine Beuret and Lynn Makings

A great deal of previous sociological research on working-class girls and young women has stressed the central importance of love and marriage, both in their current lives and in their expectations about the future. For cultural, social and economic reasons 'getting a man' and getting him to the altar seem to dominate thoughts, conversations and social activities during the years between puberty and marriage.

For girls still at school, having a steady boyfriend is primarily valued for the status it gives them with their girlfriends, and because it guards against them being labelled 'slags' or 'lessies' (lesbians) (Cowrie and Lees, 1981). Once out at work, these concerns seem to be at least partially replaced by economic considerations. Given their generally low wages as compared with young men of their own age, their present spending power is enhanced if they have a steady 'fella' to take them out regularly and quite literally 'pay court' (Westwood, 1984). On a broader level, men pace the relationship, make the decisions and generally dominate (Leonard, 1980).

As to their future, the 'male breadwinner' myth is still widely believed. To have comfort, security and a home of one's own depends on getting a husband. Coupled with this is the cultural importance of love and romance. Several studies (for example, Pollert, 1981) have pointed out the considerable degree to which workplace conversation revolves round courtship, with the younger women swapping stories about their boyfriends and if and when he will 'pop the question', and the older married women showing interest and dispensing advice. An engagement occasions a whole set of elaborate rituals second only in importance to the send-off for the bride-to-be.

Young working-class women, it seems, do not make a positive

choice about whether to marry – there is simply little or no alternative. Economic considerations and social expectations pull in the same direction. Marriage is their career, and its fulfilment is to be achieved as soon as possible. They are locked into a socio-economic 'dependency syndrome'.

Much less research has been done on middle-class girls and young women (but see Sarsby, 1983), but conventional wisdom suggests that, again for a mixture of economic and cultural reasons, they are less 'obsessed' by romance and marriage. Working towards educational qualifications and a career is seen as an important goal, and the presence of a steady boyfriend at an early age might threaten its attainment. The impact of feminism has been greater here and girls are becoming more socially independent. Their greater future earning power also holds out the possibility of economic independence.[1]

The implication is that such social class differences are based on differential economic power as between men and women which affects the balance of power in personal relationships. Detailed empirical investigations have focused on the links between the 'public' world of paid employment, and the 'private' world of domestic economy, and the complex ways in which sources and allocation of money both affect and are affected by the balance of power within the family. To date, this research has largely been confined to married or cohabiting couples (for example, Edgell, 1980; Pahl, 1983).

> In societies in which money is a source of power, and income and wealth are central expressions of advantage, the relative economic positions of husband and wife must be reflected in their relationship. Conversely it is likely that the balance of power between husband and wife will be reflected in their control over economic resources. (Pahl, 1983, p. 238)

Recently, as a result of economic recession, sociologists' critical re-evaluation of the 'myth of the male breadwinner' (Land, 1983) has raised questions about whether women's dependence on men within marriage is being altered, particularly in families where the man is unemployed. This is the question that McKee and Bell raised at the beginning of their research:

> Does increased male unemployment herald a breakdown in patriarchal structures and enhance wives' spheres of authority? (McKee and Bell, 1984)

Our research was designed to explore such questions. In particular we wished to extend this interest to the study of dating behaviour and courtship. If indeed economic changes are having an impact on the relationships between women and men at this stage of the life cycle, it might have important consequences for marriages and families in the future.

Recent research on married couples warns us against making the assumption that economic factors inevitably lead to changes in social relationships and behaviour between husbands and wives; money may be a source of power in our society but old habits die hard. Women and men might cling to the ideology of male breadwinner/ dependent wife even when (or perhaps especially when) it no longer describes their economic situation (Makings and Saks, 1983; McKee and Bell, 1984). Indeed, husbands' unemployment might actually strengthen traditional attitudes about 'appropriate' roles for wives and husbands, and reduce the relative independence of the former; as, for example, when his loss of earnings means that she has to spend much more time in careful shopping and elaborate food preparation to make ends meet, or when his greater confinement in the house means that she is less able to go out or have her friends round.

Similar strategies to preserve or even intensify the status quo might be characteristic of employed unmarried women dating unemployed men. To the extent that this is not the case, then the very tentative hypothesis could be suggested that superior economic status for the woman, if achieved *before* marriage, might carry over into the marriage relationship.

Our interest in these questions derives from a wider study of courtship (Beuret and Makings, forthcoming) which includes middle-class women students on economic parity with the men students they were dating (Beuret and Makings, 1986). Twenty-five students and twenty-five hairdressers were interviewed early in 1986. The hairdressers, the focus of this chapter, were aged between sixteen and twenty-seven; all were unmarried and had current boyfriends who were unemployed. Interviews were conducted in Leicester and the North East of England, both areas of relatively high male unemployment.

THE RESEARCH

All the hairdressers came from a working-class background with, typically, the father in a skilled and the mother in a part-time semi-skilled manual occupation. In a number of cases the father was self-employed as a plumber or builder etc. It was noticeable that most of the hairdressers' parents were economically active, well above the norm in both Leicester (where registered unemployment in 1985 was 12.5 per cent) and in the North East (where it was 18.9 per cent) (Income Data Services, 1985). This was also reflected in such factors as car ownership and housing tenure.

The general impression gained from the interviews was that these families were weathering the recession more successfully than many of their neighbours and had either acquired or aspired to a higher standard of living. It is possible that the economic security stemming from this sort of family background makes the choice of hairdressing as a career more likely, given the low or non-existent wages during training.[2]

Many hairdressers mentioned that their choice of hairdressing had resulted, at least initially, in loss of earnings, and though this was frequently partially offset by generous financial support from parents and other relatives, the decision to follow such a career had been made in the knowledge that pay-offs would come in the future, and they realised that this distinguished them from many of their ex-schoolfriends. Most had career plans for the long-term future with the ultimate dream of one day owning their own salon.

They were deliberately selected on the basis of having boyfriends who were unemployed, since we were interested in the effects of their having greater spending power than their boyfriends. There are no studies known to us that examine the behaviour of young women in this situation, and yet it is an increasingly common one in the UK. Tentative contrasts can be made with the young women in Leonard's study of courtship in Swansea, where none of the womens' boyfriends were unemployed, and where it seemed to be generally assumed that the boyfriend would pay on dates, except in very unusual circumstances (Leonard, 1980). It should be noted, however, that her research was carried out over fifteen years ago, and the very marked contrasts between her findings and ours might well be partially due to this.

The hairdressers were very aware of the impact of their boyfriends' unemployment on their dating behaviour. The following quotation is fairly typical:

Yes, well of course Barry only gets his dole money plus a bit he makes on the side helping out at the Club, whereas since I changed salons

I've been coming home of a Friday with £130 clear. My mum won't take more than £10 so I'm sitting pretty. It makes going out with Barry a bit awkward. Up here [the North East] everyone expects the fellows to pay. When I'm out with me mates I drink Bacardi and coke but when I'm with Barry I have lager. He saw me drinking with the girls once and got upset when he saw the shorts, but I said it was Linda's birthday and we were having a treat.

Other more contrived ways of 'saving face' were also mentioned:

I like my man to look good on a Saturday but Mike is a bit touchy if I buy him anything pricey. So I pretend that one of the customers works for 'Next' and gets seconds cheap. I got him a smashing jumper last week, it cost me £39 but I told him it cost £5. He insisted on giving me the fiver too, poor sod. Men have no idea do they?

Many of them mentioned holidays as something that they liked to save and plan for, and talk about. Apart from the ease with which they could 'treat' their boyfriends without embarrassment, holidays abroad seemed to offer escape from the reality of their boyfriends' unemployment:

I let him pay for the everyday things like drinks when we do go out, but I pay for the larger items, especially holidays. We're going to the Canaries in May and I've already paid for both of us. It's all in, meals as well, so this won't leave him much to find for drinks and that when we go out.

These and similar strategies for handling the financial aspects of the relationship were designed to preserve the appearance, both to the boyfriend and to other outsiders, of him being in financial control. To this extent they can be interpreted as attempts to maintain the man's traditional provider role. However, it is noticeable that the women felt themselves to be in charge of these situations. The various economic subterfuges were of their own devising; they frequently involved duping their boyfriends (the comment above; 'Men have no idea do they', was by no means atypical), and their purpose was often to make sure that the woman achieved *her* desired goal – a foreign holiday, a smartly dressed boyfriend, favourite drinks, or whatever – rather than deny herself these things as a consequence of his straitened circumstances.

In terms of their overall leisure patterns, when they were not out

alone with their boyfriends they either spent the evening at home, or
went out with a group of girlfriends. They rarely seemed to go out in
mixed-sex groups.

Nights out with 'the girls' were seen as very important and were
usually maintained even when steady boyfriends raised objections:

> Well before I started going out with Neil, I always went around the
> pubs in the centre with the girls I was at college with. Five or six of us
> would troop about from one place to another eyeing the talent. Not
> that we were desperate about that, we have a good time anyway. We
> take a half bottle of gin with us and top up on the quiet. We've had
> some good laughs over the years. Anyway, when I met Neil, he
> wanted me to go out only with him. 'No way' I told him, and I still see
> the girls at least once a week. He knows he won't stop me. Bloody
> cheek anyway!

When out with other women, they said they laughed and joked
more, swore, and generally behaved differently.

The importance of all-women groupings to these women with
steady boyfriends contrasts with Leonard's findings that female peer
groups tend to collapse when girls leave school, and that this makes it
more important to find a steady boyfriend to avoid social isolation,
whereas boys retain social ties with a group of mates (Leonard,
1980). Griffin finds this too in her study of girl school-leavers
(Griffin, 1985b). Our findings more nearly match Westwood's when
she mentions the importance of women going to town as a group on
Friday and Saturday nights, 'at the pubs and discos, dancing, flirting
and getting pissed up' (Westwood, 1984, p. 105). She also mentions
the ways in which the shared night out provided the basis for talk and
general hilarity at work the next week. Another study finds that
women who retain their all-women friendship groups are more likely
to self-assured and assertive at work (Pollert, 1981).

The hairdressers were, however, similar to Leonard's sample in
the central importance of home in their lives, and their enjoyment of
leisure time spent with their families. It was also noticeable how
unusual it was to visit the boyfriend's home. When probed on this
point a number offhand comments were made: 'Well I've got my
ironing to do', or 'His mum doesn't like me', or 'His house is bloody
chaos'. Behind such sentiments might be the desire to 'call the shots'
and to organise things on *her* terms. Indeed this seemed an extension
of the manipulative aspects of economic arrangements described
above. Leonard also mentions this tendency however, and here it is

difficult to define it in these terms. It might merely reflect particularly
close relationships between mothers and their adult daughters.

During the interviews, questions were raised about taking the
initiative in courtship. We were particularly interested to see if there
was any evidence to suggest that women were becoming more
assertive, both in making the first approaches, and in pacing and
organising subsequent dating activities. Most existing research
presents a picture of male initiatives in these respects. The response
to such questions was overwhelmingly to describe ways in which they
very consciously manipulated the men so that it appeared that the
men were taking the initiative:

> Well I saw him going into the betting shop next door but one, and I
> thought 'H'm, tasty'. So when his sister came in to have a blow-dry I
> dropped a few hints that I'd be in 'Mr C's' Friday night and Bob's your
> uncle. In he strolls, buys me a drink and so that was it. Six months later
> and I fancy him more than ever.

It was clear that although slightly abashed by this kind of behaviour,
in general these ploys are pursued with confidence and seen as
necessary. 'You can't let on what you're up to but you've got to give
them a bit of a push haven't you.'[3]

This leads on to a second aspect of courtship, i.e. the way in which
dating is organised once the couple are 'going out together'. Clearly
decisions about how frequently to go out, and often where to go,
were predominantly made by the women. There were obvious
explanations for this, given their boyfriends' unemployment.

> Well you can understand it from Jo's point of view, he's hanging
> around all day bored. He sometimes meets me from work and he
> always gets here too early. He gets on my nerves actually, keeps
> walking past the shop. He used to come in but Rose doesn't like men in
> the shop and I don't either. He would like to see me nearly every night
> but I like a few evenings in, and one out with me marras [women
> friends].

Neither their devious strategies to initiate the process of 'going out',
nor their control over its pace thereafter, should be interpreted as
meaning that they were unromantic. Quite the reverse; the experience of 'being in love' was often referred to as the explanation of why
they understood if their boyfriends were over-dependent, either
emotionally or economically:

It's bloody hard for Mike being unemployed. Sometimes my heart goes out to him when he says he'd like to buy me a nice present or take me out for a nice meal. To tell you the truth I love him more than ever at those times.

John can get a bit depressed but not often because we've got such a fantastic thing going between us. Sometimes when I'm working, even when we're really busy, I suddenly think about him and I get this trembling in my stomach and I almost have to sit down. It's fantastic, especially as he obviously feels the same way about me.

This last quotation demonstrates the strong association which often emerged during the interviews between being in love and physical attraction. They were very outspoken about this, introducing the subject themselves, and were often observed discussing such matters with customers as well. In the all-woman atmosphere of the salon, quite explicit details relating to sex were discussed. For example:

The main attraction is that he really knows how to turn me on; when I think of the pathetic shoot, bang, fire, blokes of my past, well, I'd never put up with that now.

There were strong indications that sexual attraction, and their own sexual satisfaction, were very highly valued aspects of their relationships, perhaps more so than shared interests; but such impressions are very tentative and further research is required.

Questions were also raised about how they perceived the future, both in their relationship with their boyfriend and in more general terms. It was quite clear that few were keen on early marriage, and indeed some were positively wary about the very idea of marriage:

When I left school I couldn't wait to get married. I used to stick pictures of wedding dresses in my bedroom even. But now I'm thinking twice.

I've got used to being independent now. I do love John but I prefer seeing him rather than living with him. I work hard at this job and I want to start my own business soon. Marriage could put paid to all that. One day but not now.

There was no evidence that they did not plan to marry eventually, and some specifically said that they would like to marry if things were different.

> If I ever do take the plunge it will definitely be with Jo, but I can't see it for a bit until he gets himself a job. I wouldn't like to keep him on my wages.

Some showed detailed knowledge of the costs and benefits involved:

> I hear a lot from my customers. It seems that unless you find a man with a good job you're worse off getting married.

Conclusions at this stage are very tentative. Our research is continuing with studies of the courtship behaviour of other groups of young women. In particular we are aware that women from working-class backgrounds who choose hairdressing are atypical, in that they forgo current economic advantages in the interests of building a career. They are also older than women in most relevant previous research. We are also conscious that numerous other variables such as class, level of education and training, occupational environment and region can act in different combinations to influence results (Silverman, 1970).

We can suggest that the recession and male unemployment *are* having an impact on courtship, and in the situation described here – employed girlfriend, unemployed boyfriend (one that is becoming increasingly common) – the effects seem to be weakening the dependency syndrome of women.

The attitudes of the hairdressers must in part be due to their economic independence of their unemployed boyfriends, reinforced by a wider cultural recognition that in some areas of the UK, high unemployment, particularly among working-class men, is here to stay for the foreseeable future. Hence making oneself economically dependent on a male provider by getting married may be financially disadvantageous, even if it is still seen as the ideal, enshrined as it is in current government policies and prevailing ideology.

Even before the full effect of the recession was experienced, many have argued that the 'dependent woman family model' was inappropriate to describe the situations of most women. For example, married women as a proportion of the labour force have increased steadily from 11.8 per cent in 1951, 23.1 per cent in 1971, to 25.9 per cent in 1981. Over the period 1971–83, the economic activity rate for men declined by 7.2 per cent whilst that of women increased by 8.4 per cent (*Social Trends 1985*). Of all women between 16 and 59 years of age, 64 per cent are now economically active, compared with 33 per cent in 1951 (Equal Opportunities Commission, 1985). The proportion of women heading one-parent families increased from 7 per cent in 1971 to 12 per cent in 1982–4 (Office of Population Censuses and Surveys, 1985). The majority of families with children have a mother in paid employment. Of the new jobs being created, full-time jobs are increasing by only 1 per cent, compared with part-time jobs which are increasing by 7 per cent, and two-thirds of the latter are taken by women. In 1985, the female unemployment rate was estimated at 9.8 per cent compared with 16.3 per cent for males (although unofficial estimates put both, but especially female rates, much higher) (Department of Employment, 1986). We could quote many other figures which demonstrate the changes.

These changes create a paradox. On the one hand the government is attempting to support and even enhance the 'dependent woman model'. Examples which demonstrate this are: the decision of the DHSS to oppose the payment of Invalid Care Allowance to married women (*Guardian*, 23 January 1986); the barring of married women from the Community Programme (*Guardian*, 9 September 1984); and most recently the proposed transferable tax allowance which if introduced would amount to a subsidy to husbands with non-earning wives and a deterrent to women on low wages to work outside the home (Lawson, 1986). Yet, on the other hand, these and other attempts to 'encourage' women to leave the labour force and perform 'caring roles' for free, seem remarkably ineffective in deterring women from paid work. The reasons for this are complex. One explanation is that many of the jobs available are low-paid, part-time and in traditional 'women's' employment sectors. It is also because more and more women like the variety and interest that work outside the home brings to their lives.

Governmental policies based on the 'dependent woman' model have only ever 'worked' if the male partner is able to fulfil the 'breadwinner' role. With deepening recession this is ever less likely to be the norm. If the man is unemployed, then in many respects it could be argued that the working woman is better off not marrying him. For example, she will then retain independent tax status (presently (1986) worthwhile only if a married couple's joint income is over £25 361). If living at home with parents, contributions to household expenses may be modest. In addition, her household duties will be less onerous if she has no man to 'service'; there is evidence to show that women work much harder on household tasks even when both partners are in paid employment (Oakley, 1974; Fawcett and Piachaud, 1984). Even if a woman decides to set up home with a man, by not marrying, their mortgage tax relief allowance will double from £30 000 to £60 000. Should there be children, it is possible to argue that still in some ways single women will be better off, especially where the potential husband is unemployed. The additional allowance for children in one-parent families is one advantage. Also, single mothers can claim an allowance for children, unlike the married mother who can only claim if her husband is 'incapable of supporting himself and is likely to remain so' (Federation of Claimants' Unions, 1985). If an unmarried woman stays at home to care for a dependent child or relative she – unlike a married woman, even one paying National Insurance contributions – can claim the Invalid Care Allowance. Pro rata, a woman alone gets more supplementary benefit and/or pension than a couple. She can also be considered as the claimant for supplementary benefit, whereas married women need their husband's permission. Unmarried women can also earn more before money is deducted from supplementary benefit. Finally, there are additional benefits such as concessionary fares, entrance fees, educational fees, holiday schemes, priority for nursery places and on housing waiting lists, which may be available to the single parent and not the married couple.

The fact that hundreds of Liable Relative Officers are employed by the DHSS to enforce the cohabitation rule is testament to the government's determination to prevent cohabitation becoming more advantageous than marriage. New proposals are constantly suggested by all political parties 'to give the advantage squarely to marriage' (Rimmer *et al.*, 1983). This is not to say of course that life for the single parent is a 'bed of roses'. Whilst commenting on the tendency for young women to have 'babies on the dole', often not getting married and staying with their parents and quite soon getting a council house, Campbell also concludes:

> Their dissidence is confronting the conservatism of Labourism and the patriarchal principles of women's dependence which is embedded in the old labour movement's codes of behaviour, in housing policies and the distribution of incomes. But their dissidence is cauterised by their isolation and poverty. (Campbell, 1984).

To summarise, most existing marriages took place before the recession prevented so many men from fulfilling their 'breadwinner roles'. Even before the recession the 'dependent woman family model' was inappropriate. Since unemployment, especially amongst young men of marriageable age, has risen so rapidly, it has become even more inappropriate, as has the 'dependent girlfriend model'.

Yet women's dependence on being married is still reinforced by government thinking, largely endorsed by other political parties. Furthermore, dependence on being one of a couple, especially for working-class women, is stressed in a number of other ways. The ideology of 'falling in love, getting married and living happily ever after' is still a very powerful one, transmitted through the expectations of parents and peers, and through the mass media and commercial interests. For working-class women in particular, not to be going steady by a certain age, and thereafter married and 'settled down', is widely regarded not merely as unusually, but as socially deviant. Remaining single is not a socially acceptable alternative. A recent study confirms that fifteen-year-old girls already recognise this (Lees, 1986). Though many of the girls were less than starry-eyed about love and marriage, they accepted that they would get married themselves. As one girl put it, you only stay single 'if you are really ugly or in a right state or something' (Lees, 1986, p. 91).

So, socially, women are still expected to marry, even when male unemployment makes it economically disadvantageous to do so. However, the recession could well be affecting *when* they marry. As previously mentioned, the hairdressers were aware of the costs and benefits of marriage, and frequently decided to delay it. Admittedly they were in the financial position to be able to do so, and their career aspirations gave them an additional incentive. However, in Lees's sample too there was considerable emphasis on having fun and being socially independent first, and the mid-twenties or even later were mentioned as the ideal time to marry. One girl said 'I don't want to get married until I've had my life' (Lees, 1986 p. 84). Many of these girls probably *will* marry soon after leaving school, but it clearly is not their current central goal. Like the hairdressers, marriage is not a career – on the contrary it can threaten career plans.

Economic independence and the experience of having more money than their boyfriends is also likely to affect the kind of marriage that women like the hairdressers will eventually have. In a variety of ways they were used to organising their dating and courtship behaviour. They were certainly not the passive recipients of their boyfriends' decisions, and it seems rather unlikely that these lessons will be totally unlearnt on marriage.

NOTES

1.   Results from our wider research on middle-class students suggests that many of these assumptions are stereotypical. They reflect in part liberal hopes about a 'steady march of progress' led by the middle class, which had its parallels in the model of the symmetrical middle-class family, similarly found to be overstated (see, among others, Edgell, 1980). Moreover, the use of conventional class analysis to locate women's position in the class structure is intensely problematic and the subject of a great deal of current debate (see, for example, Crompton and Mann, 1986).

2.   Until recently, there were two routes to qualification as a hairdresser (MSC, 1983). First, there was salon apprenticeship. This lasts for three years with pay rises at the end of each year (as a rough guide, from £22 per week in the first year to £60 in the third year). Apprentices go to their local college for one day a week off-job training, giving the opportunity to qualify in City and Guilds hairdressing exams. The second route is a two-year full-time course at college. Such courses offer more opportunity for the study of theory than do apprenticeships. Although they lack the day-to-day work experience, many people on these courses supplement their full-time courses, and their incomes, by taking a Saturday or holiday job in a salon. More recently the YTS has offered an alternative route into hairdressing, although the opportunity to obtain the City and Guilds qualification has only arisen since April 1986, when the one-year YTS was transformed into a two-year Training for Skills Programme. Before the introduction of the YTS system a very large percentage of the total apprenticeships taken up by girls were in hairdressing.

3.   It is interesting to note that it was only in our middle-class student sample that anybody raised feelings of anxiety of hostility to the idea of women taking the initiative in dating, and these women mentioned the risks to reputation if they should be labelled 'pushy' or 'fast'. This seems strange given that the 'slags vs drags' distinction has previously been associated only with working-class subcultures (Willis, 1977; Cowrie and Lees, 1981).

6 Broken Transitions: From School to the Scrap Heap

Christine Griffin

Some recent British studies of youth unemployment have argued that many young people, and especially working-class youth, are now facing a 'broken transition' to adult status (for example, Willis, 1984). This work is part of the considerable research literature on youth which has developed since the discovery of 'teen-agers' after the Second World War. Its antecedents lie in G. Stanley Hall's comprehensive study of adolescence, in which nineteenth-century social Darwinism provides the foundation for the ideological construction of adolescence (Hall, 1904; cf. Cohen, 1986). Research in this area has spanned sociological studies of 'youth' and psychological investigations of 'adolescence', including work on juvenile delinquency, youth cultures and sub-cultures, the transition from school to work, and adolescent moral and sexual development. The recent sharp rise in youth unemployment has led to a marked increase in research on or around youth. Some researchers have reproduced dominant themes in the study of unemployment, whilst others have reassessed existing assumptions about youth and adulthood, work and leisure, as well as prevailing analyses of young people's experiences and the transition to adult status (Griffin, 1985a). On another level, recent research on youth unemployment has retained some key features of earlier studies, notably the focus on young men's experiences as the norm, and the perception of young people (especially white and Afro-Caribbean males) as potential problems, or alternatively as sources of important cultural and political resistances.

This chapter looks at recent developments in youth research, making connections and tracing discontinuities with the constructions of youth and adolescence in previous studies. The treatment of gender relations and young women's experiences is particularly important in this respect. Much of the research on youth cultures and sub-cultures, for example, has retained an almost obsessive interest in young (mainly white and working-class) men's lives. This is something of a paradox for an approach which is presented as an apparently 'radical' critique and development of mainstream youth studies. I shall be examining this phenomenon in the context of changing patterns of youth research and shifts in ideologies around youth, looking at those studies which have (whether by accident or design) attempted to break out of this 'boys' own' approach.

YOUTH RESEARCH: SOME COMMON THEMES

The extensive research literature on youth and adolescence has not been characterised by its theoretical coherence or sophistication. One review suggested that this work has been held together more by a series of common themes than by any shared theoretical framework (Cockram and Beloff, 1978). These common themes reflect dominant ideologies around youth and adolescence, which Cockram and Beloff describe in terms of the 'Storm and Stress' model; the life-cycle approach; the focus on adolescent alienation and anomie; and the emphasis on major role transitions.

The Storm and Stress model views adolescence as a period of intense physiological and hormonal turmoil and profound social change. It usually relies on a biologically based explanation for what is seen as an inevitable and universal phenomenon. The life-cycle approach sees youth as a distinct phase in a linear series of life-cycle stages, which move in a cumulative path from infancy to old age. The social and physiological changes which take place during adolescence are assumed to be irreversible, and part of the move towards responsible, mature adulthood.

The alienation and anomie perspective sees youth as characterised by a psychological and/or social disaffection with the status quo as represented by adult society. This is part of a 'natual rebelliousness' against the establishment and a questioning of dominant values. The role-transitions approach views adolescence as a confusing period between the relative dependence of childhood and the expected financial independence of adulthood. It involves a series of major role transitions or status shifts, including the move from school to the job market.

These four themes overlap and they have each been viewed from biological, psychoanalytic and social perspectives. They share a perception of youth as a distinct period during which crucial physiological and social changes must occur. Youth is allowed to be a time of turmoil *because* it is seen as a 'passing phase' which will progress towards the 'normal' end-point of adult maturity.

These themes have much in common with the four 'bio-political' premises described by Phil Cohen, which 'constitute youth as a specific type of population and as a site of particular political interventions' (1986, p. 6). These dominant ideological premises view youth as 'a unitary category, with certain psychological characteristics and social needs common to the age group'; as at 'an especially formative stage of development, where attitudes and values become anchored to ideologies and remain fixed in this mould later in life'; as part of 'the transition from childhood dependence to adult autonomy', which 'normally involves a rebellious phase, which ... is part of a cultural tradition transmitted from one generation to the next'; and as 'young people in industrial societies [who] experience difficulty in making successful transitions and require professional help, advice and support to do so' (1986, p. 6).

The prevalence of these dominant ideologies around youth has meant that even where researchers reject the biological determinism inherent in the Storm and Stress model for example, they might still view adolescence as synonymous with immaturity, emotional tur- moil, and irresponsibility, albeit caused by social rather than physiological factors (Cockram and Beloff, 1978; Rapoport *et al.*, 1975). Few studies have moved a stage further to examine the relatively powerless position of young people in western societies, and the implications of inconsistent messages about their status for young people's positions in education, family life, and the job market. The primary emphasis of most youth research may have shifted from physiological upheaval to social and psychological trauma. But the underlying assumptions about youth and adolesc- ence remain fundamentally unchanged. This is most noticeable with regard to the treatment of adolescent sexuality, an area which has also been crucial to debates about age, class and gender relations (McRobbie, 1978b).

The dominance of biological explanation in psychological research on adolescence has resulted in a tendency to focus on changes at puberty and especially on young people's sexuality. A typical example here is John Conger's popular psychology text, *Adolescence*, in Harper & Row's Life Cycle Series (Conger, 1979). One aspect of adolescence is presented as universal despite cultural variations: 'the physical and physiological changes of puberty ... and the young person's need to adjust to and master these changes' (p. 17). The main driving force behind these physiological changes is assumed to lie in the development of a 'normal' mature adult heterosexuality. Conger must then explain adolescent homosexuality as mere 'sex play' and a 'passing phase' distinct from 'true' (i.e. adult) homosexuality. Conger makes special mention of the 'so-called schoolgirl crush', which is assumed to be less sexual than its male counterpart, since boys are supposedly 'more conscious of specifically sexual impulses than girls, and find them harder to deny' (p. 52).

Most sociological youth studies would not share Conger's biological determinism nor his almost voyeuristic obsession with adolescent sexuality. Sociological studies do mainly share the view of heterosexuality as the normal adult sexuality, and the 'natural' precursor to marriage and parenthood (for example, Schofield, 1965). Most research with an interest in young people's sexuality has been shaped by the prevailing treatment of such a 'sensitive' topic.

Thelma Veness's influential study *School Leavers* in 1956 came up against the constrained moral climate of the period. This research spanned the border between sociology and social psychology, using a combination of structured questionnaires and autobiographical essays from 14- and 15-year-olds in English schools. Veness was concerned to demonstrate that 'the average youngster' was a 'non-delinquent adolescent', in an attempt to allay fears about 'the teenager rampant' (1962, p. 9), and to investigate the nature of British ambition.

The objections of two out of the five headteachers who took part in Veness's study led to the removal of two 'controversial' items from the questionnaire. One asked young people at what age they would like to marry, and the other asked them how many children they would like to have. Presumably such questions might have given young people ideas about those two great British unmentionables of the 1950s: (heterosexual) sex and childbirth. Whereas most biologically based studies of adolescence were able to discuss the onset of puberty and sexual behaviour (for example, Ford and Beach, 1951; Mussen and Jones, 1958), those with a more 'social' approach, such as the Veness study, could not stray into these taboo areas. Marriage and parenthood had to be presented as 'natural' and inevitable.

Despite the omission of these two questions, over one-third of these young women's autobiographical essays described the early deaths of their imaginary husbands, either coinciding with the birth of their first child, or with the last child leaving home. In most cases the husband's death left the young woman as female head of an extended family group or household (cf. Griffin, 1985b).

Veness's study exemplified a shift away from the biologically based assumptions of psychological research on adolescence towards a more 'social' analysis of youth. By the mid-1960s, studies of the so-called 'transition from school to work' began to develop a more critical and explicit analysis of class inequalities, and to move away from an emphasis on the individual towards an examination of the education system and the job market. The wasted potential of unqualified working-class youth became a major theme, and there was considerable concern that this group were receiving inadequate preparation for their entry to the full-time job market (for example, Carter, 1962, 1966).

Like Thelma Veness, Michael Carter focused on the 'low job aspirations' of school-leavers, but his main concern was with the position of working-class youth. Carter had little time for the psychological approach to adolescence, preferring to examine the emerging 'teenage culture', and paying minimal attention to gender relations. He did have something to say about 'racial strife', and his comments about the possible consequences of rising youth unemployment (in 1966!) are revealing:

> There are insufficient jobs, and, at the same time, many school-leavers are not equipped – because of faulty homes and schooling – to hold down such jobs as there are. These boys and girls have been described as 'social dynamite': they might blow up at any time .. Many of the unemployed are actual or potential delinquents: an added complication is the danger of racial strife *inspired by* coloured children without jobs against white children with jobs, and vice versa. (Carter, 1966, p. 175, emphasis added)

As the debate over class analysis raged in sociological circles, the post-war economic boom of the 1960s was coming to an end. By the 1970s, a more radical approach to youth research had been imported to Britain from the USA with the National Deviancy Conferences: the analysis of youth cultures and sub-cultures (see Brake, 1984). Paradoxically, young women and gender relations became increasingly marginalised, even invisible, within this 'alternative' approach to youth research.

FROM TRANSITIONS TO RESISTANCES

Throughout the 1970s, most psychological studies of adolescence continued to examine moral and sexual development within a biological framework, or searched for the causes of 'juvenile delinquency' using a deficit model of individual inadequacy (Reicher and Emler, 1985). Sociological analyses of youth became increasingly polarised into mainstream studies of the school-to-work transition and youth cultures research. The former looked at those potentially disaffected working-class youth who were assumed to have difficulty in moving smoothly through the school-to-work transition, such as 'job changers' and 'the careerless' (for example, Ashton and Field, 1976). Most researchers expressed a liberal concern for these school-leavers, but it was usually asssumed that young people would have to shape their expectations to meet the demands of the labour market, and not vice versa.

Youth cultures research presented itself as a radical alternative to these approaches, with a different methodology and a critical theoretical analysis. Most studies in this area used qualitative ethnographic techniques based on informal interviews and participant observation. Youth cultural studies aimed to start from young people's perspective, no longer presenting working-class youth as potential problems for the education system and the job market. On the contrary, the latter institutions were seen to impose oppressive structural and ideological constraint on these young people's lives (see Hall and Jefferson, 1975).

Whereas mainstream research focused on formal institutions such as the education system, most youth cultural studies were more interested in young people's leisure activities. The emphasis shifted away from fitting young people into the demands of employers and the education system, towards the identification of young people's resistances to these demands. As developed at Birmingham's Centre for Contemporary Cultural Studies, this work took a special interest in the collective cultural forms of white working-class male youth in Britain's inner cities, employing an explicitly Marxist analysis (Hall and Jefferson, 1975). The youth cultures approach in general, and the work of CCCS in particular, has not been without its critics (for example, Jenkins, 1983; see Brake, 1984, for review). However, this work did provide an important and influential attempt to develop a critical analysis of young people's lives, which challenged some of the dominant ideological assumptions about youth.

One of the most remarkable aspects of youth cultures research is the treatment of gender and sexuality. This new and apparently radical approach seemed to provide an ideal means of examining the construction of gender, race, class and age relations in school, family life, leisure and the job market, and the ways in which different groups of young women and men negotiate the transition to adult status. Here was a valuable opportunity to combine a Marxist (or at least socialist) analysis of class and race relations with a feminist examination of gender relations and sexuality, and to look at the development of 'normal' adult heterosexuality using a critical social analysis rather than a psychological focus on biological and physiological factors. Unfortunately, many (male) youth cultures researchers showed a marked antipathy to feminist critiques and analyses of gender relations, and few studies examined the construction of heterosexuality as the compulsory and 'natural' form of sexuality for young people (Griffiin, 1985a; McRobbie, 1980).

The most common means of ignoring gender relations was to focus on young men's experiences, omitting any discussion of masculinity, sexism or gender in the process. The overwhelming majority of youth cultural studies are about the lives of young white working-class 'lads', providing a prime example of the 'boys' own' approach (Dorn and South, 1983). Feminist researchers objected to this gender-specific focus, arguing that it should be possible to look at gender and class at least, and that youth studies which paid minimal attention to sexuality, relationships between young women and men, domestic work and family life were limited and unsatisfactory (McRobbie, 1980).

The playing and watching of football has been a major theme in most youth cultural studies. The lads' participation, especially as spectators, is usually presented as an expression of collective working-class strength and pride, in contrast to the recurring media panics over 'soccer hooliganism' (for example, Clarke, 1978). The existence of young female fans, and the significance of the lads' racism and their macho posturing have seldom featured as a major theme in these analyses. Far fewer studies have looked at sports with a predominantly female following, such as gymnastics, skating, hockey or even dance (Talbot, 1981; McRobbie, 1984).

Young women dominate in one of the most widespread forms of collective crowd activity for young people in contemporary western societies: the pop concert. Youth cultures research has not looked at such forms of collective behaviour among young women, working-class or otherwise. A few studies have examined 'fandom' as a focus for white working-class female youth cultural activities which tend to be based in the home rather than on the streets (for example, McRobbie and Garber, 1975). Yet young women's involvement in larger public events, as fans of Adam Ant, Boy George or Wham!, have not received the same attention compared with young men's activities as football spectators. Such was the vocal and visual impact of the young female fans at one recent Duran Duran concert, that the *New Musical Express* critic devoted an entire review (including photos) to the audience, arguing that they were the real stars of the show, and they knew it.

Those studies which have looked at young women's experiences and gender relations are faced with a difficult dilemma. Most of the theories in this area have developed from analyses of young men's lives, and they do not necessarily apply to young women. There is an unavoidable pressure to 'fit' young women's experiences into these gender-specific models, and it can take considerable confidence to recognise and admit when this is not feasible (Davies, 1979; Griffin, 1985b; McRobbie 1978b).

During the early 1980s, I worked on a study of the 'transition from school to work' for young working-class women, which was funded partly as a female version of Paul Willis's influential work with young white working-class lads and 'ear'oles' (Willis, 1977). I was unable to identify any obvious female equivalents to the pro- and anti-school cultures of the 'ear'oles' and the lads respectively (Griffin, 1986).

There were several reasons for this. First, the social structure of female friendship groups did not necessarily conform to the prevailing 'gang of lads' model. Second, there were considerable differences between the meanings associated with conformity and deviance for young working-class women and men both in and out of school, and for young white, Asian and Afro-Caribbean women (Griffin, 1985b). Third, there was no clear relationship between the class and gender dimensions of specific occupations for young working-class women and men. Finally, there was no smooth cultural connection between young women's friendship groups, their attitudes to school and job expectations, and their eventual destinations in the labour market. There were also considerable variations between the experiences of young white, Asian and Afro-Caribbean women due to racist assumptions about 'suitable' jobs for young white and black women (Griffin, 1985b).

This does not mean that Paul Willis's analysis is totally worthless, any more than it invalidates the numerous studies of male experience to be found in youth research. However, these analyses cannot be applied to young women's lives in any straightforward manner. I would prefer to view young women as moving through simultaneous points of transition in the labour market, the marriage market and the sexual marketplace, balancing social and financial pressures to get a good job and a boyfriend (eventually a husband).

Learning to Labour did at least acknowledge the lads' racism and sexism, examining the close relationship between masculinity and specific working-class male forms of pride and solidarity. Willis's analysis reflected the social and economic pressures which constrained these 'lads', as well as their creative negotiations of and objections to their class destinies. These young men were not presented as 'hooligans', 'delinquents' or 'low ability' problem pupils. The analysis began from their perspective, rather than from the viewpoint of teachers, careers advisers or employers. Willis also shifted his research focus away from 'spectacular' youth groups such as bikers or punks, towards 'everyday' working-class youth cultures in school, on the street corner, and in the workplace. Since he was concentrating on young men's lives, there was minimal mention of the home as a site of cultural reproduction or resistance (cf. McRobbie, 1978b; Griffin, 1985b).

Mainstream sociology did not welcome this Marxist cultural analysis with open arms. Criticisms included queries about the representativeness of such a 'small sample'; accusations of 'political bias'; objections to Willis's tendency to romanticise white working-class male youth culture; his use of the concept of cultural resistance; and the less detailed consideration of the 'ear'oles' compared with the 'lads' (Hammersley and Atkinson, 1983; Walker, 1986). Feminists objected to the male focus of the study, and its relatively superficial analysis of the lads' racism and sexism (McRobbie, 1980). Despite these reservations, Willis's approach has proved more valuable than many mainstream sociological or psychological analyses as a means of appreciating the implications of rising youth unemployment.

BROKEN TRANSITIONS: YOUTH UNEMPLOYMENT IN THE 1980s

The 1980s have brought many fundamental changes in young people's positions in education, training and the job market. There has been a rapid expansion of the Manpower Services Commission and their various youth training programmes; tougher policing strategies and a stronger law-and-order lobby; repeated uprisings in Britain's inner cities; and the increasingly hysterical representations of these events in the predominantly right-wing media.

Long-term unemployment is still increasing, and in many inner-city areas over 50 per cent of young people, and especially working-class and black youth are without jobs. Youth research has been compelled to consider what happens when the transition from school to work becomes a move from the classroom to the dole queue. It is no longer possible to define 'work' simply in terms of paid labour, or 'leisure' as 'free time' (for example, Parker, 1971; see Griffin *et al.*, 1982, for critique). Prolonged periods of enforced leisure without the financial lubrication of the wage are unlikely to be spent making carefree journeys to play squash at the new Sports and Leisure Centre, or in a spending spree at the local DIY Superstore.

The economic and social conditions which produced the highly distinctive youth sub-cultures of the past three decades are rapidly disappearing. American-owned multinationals have moved in to commercialise pop and rock music on a vast scale, and to sell youth cultural styles on record, compact disc, cassette, video and in feature films and TV series (Street, 1985). Young people, and especially working-class youth, no longer provide a large and lucrative market of 'teenage consumers' (cf. Abrams, 1959).

Psychological research on adolescence has been the least affected by these changes. The main focus was never on young people's entry to the job market, and unemployment has been treated as one contributory factor to the rising incidence of depression, suicide and drug abuse among young people within a clinical context (for example, Stokes, 1984). Relatively more social psychological studies have focused on the psychological and social effects of youth unemployment. Unsurprisingly, the main findings here are that prolonged unemployment produces increased levels of depression and a lowering of self-esteem (for example, Banks *et al.*, 1984). The predominantly quantitative methods used in these studies reflect only limited aspects of young people's experiences, and they tend to be more descriptive than analytical (though see Ullah, 1984, and Fryer and Payne, 1983 for exceptions).

These studies have attempted to avoid some of the conceptual errors of previous research, taking care to differentiate between 'work' and waged labour, so that unemployment and housework do not become synonymous with 'leisure' or 'free time'. However, most studies retain a focus on men's experiences, giving minimal attention to 'sex differences' or gender relations (for example, Warr, 1983; see Griffin, 1985a). Although recent psychological studies of youth unemployment have focused on social rather than biological factors, they still tend to concentrate on individual differences and inter-personal relations, rather then collective or inter-group behaviour. One potential hazard with the former approach, especially when tied to a deficit model, is that it becomes extremely difficult to avoid blaming young people for their own unemployment. Nor is this tendency confined to psychological research (Roberts, 1984).

Some researchers have identified structural factors such as the economic recession, and/or Tory government policies, rather than young people's supposed inadequacies or intransigence, as the major causes of rising youth unemployment (for example, Bates *et al.*, 1984). Paul Willis has developed his analysis of the school-to-employment transition for 'the lads' in a speculative article which argues that most working-class young people now face a 'broken cultural apprenticeship' to the job market and therefore to adult status (Willis, 1984).

Willis suggests that the traditional transition from school to waged work has all but disappeared in most of what were once Britain's key industrial areas, and that most working-class youth are trapped in a social, cultural and economic limbo, unable to reach the adult status associated with a full-time job. If unemployment undermines working-class masculinity, it may strengthen the position of young working-class women. Unemployed young men present a less attractive financial prospect as potential boyfriends, husbands and fathers, and young women may prefer to join the increasing numbers of 'single-parent families', rather than set up their own nuclear family of husband, wife and 2.5 children. Unemployment may lead young men to do more housework and childcare, and to take more of an interest in family life. However, all the evidence indicates that youth unemployment has tended to trap an increasing proportion of young working-class women in the home doing housework and childcare, so the picture is less optimistic than Willis suggests (Griffin, 1985b).

Unfortunately, Willis still tends to focus on young men's position as the norm, and to use 'work' as synonymous with waged labour. Capitalism remains the main driving force behind his analysis, so that the transition to adulthood depends on getting a job: 'no wage is no keys to the future' (1984, p. 19). The move from education to the full-time job market is a crucial mark of adult status, and of course prolonged unemployment blocks that transition. Willis tends to minimise the importance of managing adolescent sexuality via pressures to get a girl- or boyfriend for the transition to adulthood.

For most young women, and especially young white working-class women, 'getting a man' is a major sign of 'normal' adult femininity and of 'growing up'. Any analysis of 'transitions from youth' must consider the effects of social and economic pressures to get a job and to get a 'steady' for young women and young men.

Claire Wallace has tried to do just that in her recent analysis *Masculinity, Femininity and Unemployment* (1985). Reviewing the male bias of previous research on youth, Wallace proposes a 'new conceptual framework'. This rests on 'an analytical distinction between three dimensions linking the public and the private spheres': the material, the social, and the symbolic (1985, p. 9). In Wallace's terms, 'these material, social and symbolic relationships between gender and reproduction vary between social classes' (p. 10). Avoiding the male focus of the youth cultures approach, Wallace aims to bring some theoretical coherence and clarity to the analysis of youth unemployment, and especially young women's unemployment.

Claire Wallace elaborates her conceptual framework in relation to a study of working-class young people on the Isle of Sheppey. She concludes: that 'the "traditional" model of the family and of work roles lives on in the imagination of young people, even when this model is increasingly difficult to fulfil in practice... Rising unemployment appeared ... to make such traditional expectations even more entrenched' (p. 24); that 'social expectations are out of phase with labour market conditions' (p. 25); and that 'some of the male sub-cultural activity which has been interpreted as a response to class positions could also be seen as a means of bolstering an increasingly insecure sense of masculinity' (p. 25).

Claire Wallace's conclusions confirm the less optimistic aspects of Paul Willis's speculations on the cultural and social consequences of mass youth unemployment. Unemployed young men do not cling to the traditional cultural sources of masculine pride and adhere to 'rigid sex roles' simply because they are stupid, apathetic or unaware of their new situation. Their responses, however reactionary, reflect the potential benefits of creating mythical macho exploits involving 'gang bangs', or marathon drinking sessions for young men – if not for their female peers. Although Claire Wallace and Paul Willis have developed their ideas from rather different theoretical perspectives, they both suggest that contemporary youth unemployment has had a profound effect on family life and gender relations, as well as on young people's position in education, training and the job market (see Presdee, 1986, for an analysis of 'broken transitions' among working-class youth in Australia).

In conclusion, research on youth has experienced a sort of 'broken transition' itself over the past five years, or at least a minor theoretical and conceptual (not to say financial) crisis. The sharp increase in youth unemployment levels, combined with marked reductions in social science research funding, has lead to a reassessment of prevailing approaches to the study of youth. Several factors differentiate the current situation from earlier research on mass unemployment in the 1930s, and from youth studies during the more prosperous 1960s and 1970s. Explicitly feminist critiques and analyses have challenged the overwhelming focus on male experience as the norm, and examined young women's position, as well as covering domestic work, family life and pressures to 'get a man' (McRobbie, 1980). The second major development has been the increasing emphasis on white racism and on the different experiences of young white, Asian and Afro-Caribbean women and men (Gilroy, 1981; Amos and Parmer, 1981).

Young people are relatively powerless in western society, especially in the 1980s, as the official end-point of youth moves past the age of majority (whether 18 or 21) towards 25. Rising youth unemployment levels and the increasing of the length of MSC schemes only delay the transition to adult status for many more young people. Current research on youth has tended to concentrate on unemployment for obvious reasons. These studies need to move beyond the theoretically muddled descriptive accounts of most previous youth research; to start from young people's experiences rather than simply reflecting dominant assumptions about 'apathetic' or 'delinquent' youth; to drop the determinedly male focus of most youth research; and to develop a more critical understanding of young people's lives.

7 A Bed of Roses? Women, Marriage and Inequality in Later Life

Jennifer Mason

INTRODUCTION

Many commentators have demonstrated that inequality within marriage, in terms of the social and economic dependence of wives on their husbands, is part of the condition of gender inequality in our society, and that marriage is thus a structurally unequal relationship. For example, women's relative structural disadvantage in education, the labour market and social welfare provision help to ensure that they will be responsible for domestic labour and childcare within family-households; this in turn reinforces their structural disadvantage and makes it all seem reasonable and inevitable. Gender inequality, and with it an ideology of familism, are thus constantly developing and being negotiated through a dialectical process: constraints in the apparently separate spheres of 'public' and 'private' are used to legitimate practice in each other, and practice then in turn reinforces the constraints (Allan, 1985; Barrett, 1980; Collins, 1985; Hunt, 1980; Land, 1981).

This means that within marriage generally a common pattern has developed whereby women become and remain responsible for childcare, the servicing of household members and domestic labour. For each married couple this seems logical and 'in the circumstances' reasonable, hence illustrating that a common pattern can be produced by a process involving negotiation as well as constraint. However, negotiation is rarely explicit in the sense of 'sitting round a table' because constraints help to make certain choices and decisions seem obvious. Rather it is implicit in that married couples feel that they have individually worked out their domestic organisation to suit their own situation. In practice, therefore, gendered responsibilities form the taken-for-granted fabric of married life which itself is never renegotiated but within which negotiations occur.

This process is clearly one which is worked out both in practice and analytically in relation to young married couples, because of its heavy emphasis on female disadvantage and male structural advantage particularly in the labour market, and concomitantly on the significance of childcare for the formation of marital responsibilities. However, one cannot assume that domestic relations between husbands and wives remain constant over their lifetimes. Indeed, it is often supposed that marriages can become more companionate or 'equal' in later life, if also more boring, when the trials, tribulations and inequalities associated with breadwinning and the rearing of children have apparently passed; when men have more time to help out at home because of retirement or its anticipation, and when the general absence of children from the parental home means that there is less household servicing to be done and more time for couples to be alone together again (Roberts and Roberts, 1980; see also the retirement magazine *Choice*).

These sorts of optimistic assumptions are evidently far too simplistic. We need a closer understanding of what happens to marriage relationships once structural aspects supporting the dialectical process are disrupted, for example through exit from the labour force, departure of offspring from the parental home, birth of grandchildren, death and/or illness of elderly parents and other relatives. In this chapter I set out to show that a fundamental renegotiation of gendered responsibilities and relations between husbands and wives is unlikely to occur in later life. Using data from an intensive study of eighteen long-married couples in the age range 50 to 70, I will argue that these very sorts of 'structural disruption' result in a repatterning of forms of domestic organisation which serves to reinforce traditional gender responsibilities.[1] By analysing the ways in which the couples concerned were making sense of structural change through their domestic organisation, it is possible to say something of the ways in which gender inequalities were being created, interpreted and maintained or changed.

RESPONSIBILITY AND CONTINUITY

To be responsible for something means that one is liable to be called to account for it. Within the marriages of the couples in the study, the women had always been, and remained, responsible for the servicing of household members and for seeing that the housework got done; the men were responsible for seeing that structural and outdoor maintenance of the house was done, and that the family was provided for and protected.

Despite vaguely optimistic views about companionate marriages in later life, this continuity of responsibility is not really surprising given the importance of the general climate of gender disadvantage and advantage for marital inequality; this climate clearly does not cease or reverse at age 50. Women's employment disadvantage does not disappear (Dex, 1984) and in fact becomes reflected in their pension rights (Groves, 1983; Land, 1986). Women over 50 remain constrained, albeit usually informally, from entering public leisure environments such as pubs and clubs without an accompanying man, and men over 50 are nearly three times as likely as women of that age to have driving licences (Allan, 1985; Deem, 1982). Therefore women do not take on a strong marital bargaining position at this time.

But if the absence of renegotiation is unsurprising in the light of a continuing climate of gender inequality, we must add to this a consideration of what exactly such a fundamental reappraisal of the taken-for-granted fabric of married life would have meant for the eighteen couples in the study. Their pasts had in part conditioned the disruptions which were occurring and the ways in which the couples were dealing with them. Sixteen of them had been married to each other for over 25 years, the other two for over 15 years, and during that time they had developed, practised and rationalised particular methods of domestic organisation. They each had a *shared biography,* having premised their married lives on a traditional gendered division of labour and responsibility, lived against a specific period of historical time. The women had formed part of the post-war upsurge in married women's employment, all but one of them having been in paid jobs for most of their married lives. Yet their employment had been seen as secondary, voluntary and supplementary in a way that their husbands' had not. Indeed the women *had* tailored their employment around the servicing requirements of their families, negotiating absence from the labour market following the birth of children, or during family crises. Seventeen of them had taken *part-time* employment once their children were of school age or their daily care could easily be arranged. In all the cases it had been taken for granted that the women, not the men, should consider the domestic, health and servicing requirements of their children, husbands and sometimes elderly relatives in deciding whether or not to take paid employment and what type of employment would be appropriate.

The fact that their biographies showed that the women had done this, apparently having made *choices* about employment, meant both that their jobs could be reconstructed as non-essential and that their consequent employment histories were more intermittent than those of their husbands. One woman expressed very clearly the common view when she told me that: 'I've had various little jobs, that's all, to fit in with the children and that.'

This view formed the cornerstone of a tradition of gendered domestic responsibility, apparently developed and negotiated by individual couples within their own 'private' marital pasts, yet in fact common to all of them. Every respondent had at least fifteen years of training in their respective responsibilities, and had developed standards and expertise accordingly. All of this had developed within the context of a relationship normatively based on the long-term, intimate commitment of husbands and wives to each other, which was now also becoming imbued with a particular sense of timing. Thus in their discourse the couples persistently betrayed their perception of being in the final stages of life and the consequences of this for domestic practice. One man typically explained that: 'it's too late to change things now anyway, at our time of life, not that we'd want to'. The couples each had a great deal invested in their own traditional way of doing things, and the initiation of renegotiation – by definition a proposal for radical change – by either party to this type of relationship would have appeared impractical, pointless and confrontational.

Changes were occurring though, forming not a renegotiation of domestic responsibilities but rather a repatterning of what those responsibilities meant in practice.

PATTERNS OF CHANGE

Domestic Labour

Despite a commonsense assumption that there is less housework to do in this 'stage' of life owing to the relative absence of children from the parental home, few of the women in the study were in a position to experience a period of domestic ease. Five had offspring currently living with them, none of whom did much housework. Furthermore, for many of the women the care and servicing of their own children had been replaced by or combined with care for others: all of the sixteen women with grandchildren were involved to varying degrees in their care or entertainment; one woman took in student lodgers; fourteen were currently or had at some time in the recent past been involved in caring for elderly infirm people (mainly parents and parents-in-law); and all of the women remained married to and resident with their husbands. Equally, ill health and advancing age can make housework more arduous even if there is less to do (Deutscher, 1959) and despite the ever-increasing availability of supposedly labour-saving equipment (Thomas and Zmroczek, 1985). Thirteen of the women (and eleven of the men) made reference to their own limiting ill health.

However, the fact that at least some of their children had visibly grown up and left home helped to support the commonsense view that, as one woman put it, 'there is so little to do now that really either of us could do it, there's no point in making an issue of it'. What she and the others were implying was that the *division* of domestic labour was somehow less relevant than it had been in the past; because there was apparently not much to do, it did not seem to matter who did it. In practice though the women tended to do most of it. Ten of the husbands in the last five to ten years had begun to do more housework – mainly washing up, vacuuming, helping with the preparation of food and accompanying their wives to the shops – but they rarely took responsibility for those tasks. Husbands spoke to me about *helping* their wives with the housework and wives tended to respond with comments like 'he's very good really'. What this means is that in the actual process of modifying task divisions, domestic labour was being reaffirmed as the wives' responsibility. The assumption that husbands were, or had been, chief workers in another sphere was maintained, thus legitimately excusing them from domestic responsibility. Blurring of task divisions was never so fundamental or routine as to challenge overall responsibilities, and, indeed, couples felt it necessary to justify deviance from, but not maintenance of, such divisions. Because this was all being worked out from within a framework which assumed traditional gender responsibilities, the negotiation of change was actually reinforcing those responsibilities.

Money Management

A similar form of continuity in the face of change was observed in relation to the management of the domestic budget. Changes centred around the decrease in income or its anticipation, but also a decrease in expenditure for most of the couples. The exact nature of these changes was complex, and is less relevant here than their tendency to provoke a conscious reflection and sometimes reassessment of budgeting procedures amongst the couples. Most of them actually began to talk about the principles of money management, where they had rarely done so before, and some had developed new budgeting strategies. In general the effect was for husbands to become more involved in the day-to-day household budgeting than they had been in the past, although this usually took the form of their overseeing what was spent rather than a daily involvement in domestic spending.

However, changes in the *sources* of income – most significantly from wages or salary to a pension – meant that the economic dependency of the wives on their husbands was becoming even more firmly established. In seventeen of the cases the men already had, or were anticipating, better pensions than their wives. None of the women either received or anticipated state pensions in their own right based on employment after marriage, and only two were anticipating some kind of occupational pension as compared with eleven of the men.

Thus, although the wives technically had a share of the married couples' state pension and where applicable their husbands' occupational pension, both of these had most visibly been earned by the husbands. Women's intermittent employment and continuous domestic labour became virtually invisible in a system rewarding 'real' paid work – i.e. full-time and continuous – with 'real' pensions. Paradoxically, what this means is that although in some senses income after retirement becomes more 'joint' through 'shared' pensions, it simultaneously becomes more wholly the husband's property. The wives retained responsibility for creating the best possible standard of living for the family, but the implication was that they did this with the husband's money. One man in the study gave a clear, if extreme, illustration of this issue:

> I've got my wife here and she's very good with money, and always has been, so I leave it to her. She handles it marvellously I think. I don't know how she does it, I don't want to know really, you know. I'm lucky, I mean a lot of chaps couldn't trust their wife with any money, but I mean only yesterday wasn't it she brought 30p from the bedroom, says 'Here you are, you must have dropped some money out of your pocket.' 30p under the bed. What worry have I got? I'd never have known if she'd put it in her pocket.

The main observation to be drawn from changes in domestic labour and money management is that negotiations were continuing to take place within a clear framework of traditional gender responsibilities, never challenging the assumption that men were providers and protectors and women were servicers and carers.

THE RELATIONS OF DOMESTIC SERVICING AND PROVIDING

Indeed it is within the overall context of the relations of domestic servicing and providing that the significant dynamics of change and continuity in responsibilities must be sited. Servicing a provider involves more than housework. It involves taking responsibility for the health, happiness and comfort of the family-household. Hilary Graham's work with younger women has documented the extent to which they take responsibility for family health in this sort of way (Graham, 1985). The women in my study had always done this, but the responsibility was beginning to involve a different set of meanings and practice for them. For example, they continued to subordinate their employment to the requirements of the family but this subordination now centred around questions concerning departure from, rather than entry to, the labour market, and the 'family' tended now to mean husbands. It was taken for granted by the couples that the wives would either retire before their husbands or at the same time; they would or should not continue in paid employment longer than their husbands. In fact six of the wives had retired prior to their husbands and two had retired simultaneously even though their employers had not required them to do so. Five of the wives reported that they would be retiring with their husbands within the next five years, again even though they would not officially be required to do so. It was assumed that the end of employment for the couples should be defined by the husband's departure from the labour market, and that retired men should not be at home on their own while their wives were out at work. In the remaining five cases the husbands had in fact left the labour force before their wives and couples clearly saw this as problematic and something they wished to justify in the interviews. Yet in the thirteen other cases no explanation was deemed necessary.

This helped to confirm that the women's employment was secondary and their income supplemental to that of the husband-providers, and was also both expression and confirmation of women's responsibility for servicing and caring for husbands. Thus if husbands were at home then the wives should be there to look after them. One woman actually retired from her job as a senior housing officer voluntarily, because her husband was seriously ill and she knew that he would not retire from his job as a prison officer if it meant being at home on his own. He did retire shortly after his wife, but her action illustrates what was a general theme for all of the women: namely that servicing included responsibility for worrying about the health and comfort of husbands and engaging in strategies to ensure their maintenance.

Changes in what this aspect of their responsibility meant in practice for the wives, due to the actual or anticipated increase in the amount of time husbands were spending in the home, raised two sets of issues. The first centred around finding things for their husbands to do, or for structuring their husbands' time; the second around problems or constraints imposed when this was difficult or impossible.

As far as structuring their husbands' time was concerned, it appeared that this became particularly problematic in relation to how much time husbands spent indoors. Most of the men actually talked with gusto about their outdoor activities, but they also spoke of frustration when the weather was bad or during the winter when they were unable to work outside. This affected men who were still in full-time employment as well as those who were not, although it was a problem of greater magnitude for the latter. It was a problem for the wives too in so far as they were responsible for the 'entertainment' of housebound husbands. Other researchers have noted that women often nudge their husbands into home improvement activity (Pahl, 1984), and indeed the women in the study often pointed out to their husbands the need for such work to be done. Routine and everyday structuring of husbands' time thus became part of the wives' servicing responsibility, and an activity in which wives who were worried about husbands' self-esteem or post-retirement stagnation became particularly assiduous.

It was not always possible for wives to find things for their housebound husbands to do, and on these occasions the women generally felt bound to modify their own activity. Several of those whose husbands had left full-time employment explained that they no longer called in to see friends for a coffee as they had before, because it meant leaving their husbands at home alone. One woman told me that she used to visit a friend once a week and they would go for a walk; she still visits since her husband's retirement but now they no longer go for walks. Instead, she told me, 'he makes the tea and listens to our talk'. Another woman, whose husband had recently retired, told me that she no longer feels able to go 'mooching around the shops on my own', a once favourite activity. Now she finds that her husband wants to join her; yet to say 'I don't want you to come' would see confrontational. Hence she no longer mooches, instead going to the shops only when she has something to buy, and generally being accompanied by her husband. Another woman expressed what seemed to be the common sentiment: 'You can't just go and do things like you used to. You're not free. You have a conscience.'

There is a parallel here with McKee and Bell's study of the effect of male unemployment on family life, where housebound husbands often severely curtailed both the extent and quality of their wives' social lives (McKee and Bell, 1985). This problem is enlarged by the structural constraints on women's leisure mentioned earlier, because there are few legitimate 'escapes' from the home. Furthermore, only two of the women in my study as against seventeen of the men were able to drive, one of these having her own car and the other sharing a car with her husband. Casual, unaccounted or apparently purposeless absence from the home was thus not easy for the women. The men were not subject to the same accountability. Because these women had always had the domain of the home as theirs, and because their husbands had generally been excluded during the day, it had never in the past been necessary to structure in opportunities for personal time or space. The increasingly permanent presence of husbands in the home simultaneously made this more important yet more difficult.

So on the one hand structural constraints and a 'conscience' made it difficult for the women to excuse themselves from their husband's presence in the home, whilst on the other hand this presence was doubly problematic precisely because the women routinely worried about and felt responsible for their husbands' well-being. It was the wives, therefore, who had become attuned to the social situational dynamics of daily life, picking up cues about whether people (and particularly their husbands) were happy, getting along with each other, seeing enough friends and so on. This is not to suggest that women have a biological predisposition to do this, or that men cannot do it too, but merely that these wives had grown accustomed to doing it as a matter of daily routine through years of childcare and domestic servicing. The husbands, for their part, had come to rely on this; they depended upon their wives' concern for them and on their caring for family health and domestic comfort. It is important to note that this did give the wives some control, for whilst they remained largely economically and socially dependent on their husbands, the men were in turn dependent on their wives. Most of the women felt that their husbands would not be able to manage without them and expressed something between pity and guilt about this dependence. As one wife said, 'I watch him trying to cope and my heart goes out to him.' It was, after all, a dependence partly cultivated by the women. Domestic and emotional dependence had become bound up together and assumed a new priority in the light of the women's and men's sense of timing. They perceived that soon one spouse would probably die and the other would be left to cope alone.

DOMESTIC CONTROL AND 'NAGGING WIVES'

This dependence of husbands on their wives helps to highlight an important contradiction. We have seen that the structures within which men and women construct their lives do not somehow become more 'equal' at this 'stage' of life and in this particular historical time; these women were not beginning to gain the right to admittance to the public domain on equal terms with men, and the men, however much they may have wanted to, could not individually give up the right to their domain and its attendant privileges – even on retirement – because it was a social right. This meant that for these couples *exchange* of responsibilities was not a possibility, and issues of negotiation were increasingly focusing around the domain of the home. There were negotiations, and even struggles, taking place in these couples' lives, and the women were active participants in these, but the process involved two contradictory elements for them. On the one hand, the women were trying to get their men to lessen the domestic burden by helping more at home, but, on the other, the women were keen to direct their husbands' help thus very clearly maintaining its definition as 'help', and retaining both the responsibility and control of the domestic domain. The fact that they had over the years developed an expertise in family servicing, so that their husbands were at one level dependent on them, was a part of this which helped them to retain control. The contradiction was therefore arising between wanting help, but not wanting too much of it. This sort of contradiction has been observed by Lydia Morris in her research on redundant steelworkers and their families. She points out that:

> The home is their [women's] personal environment and the running of it something which they simultaneously resent and value. It is their domain, and the location of their identity. The very presence of their husband at home during the day is seen as disruptive. (Morris, 1985, p. 411)

The contradiction gains a new priority for women over 50 because their husbands are likely to be re-entering the home on a permanent and almost full-time basis. To renegotiate responsibilities at this stage could only result in women losing control in their domain without being able to gain the social privileges of their husbands, and therefore this contradiction is at the basis of the absence of renegotiation. The women in the study did not want to renegotiate; they wanted to retain domestic responsibility and control, and they were active participants in the process which ensured that this happened. All of the interviews were full of evidence for this ambivalence between wanting to negotiate for more help, and for superficial change, but not wanting to renegotiate responsibilities. The women used and displayed domestic power in these negotiations; simultaneously expressing the contradiction whilst also creating the impression that they were ultimately more powerful than their husbands.

It is important here to establish that spouses' relative responsibilities were clearly not considered to be of equal value. Servicing was not felt to be the real 'nitty gritty' of what life was about. Hence breadwinning and providing were talked about and dealt with as fundamentals, housework and servicing having to fit around their strictures. However, paradoxically, the home was spoken of as the pleasant and comfortable sphere of life. Hence responsibility for that sphere in terms of servicing its members and creating a happy home environment was simultaneously *less fundamental*, but *nicer*, than responsibility for providing. Women's sphere of responsibility was implicitly recognised as depending upon men's; the provider and protector is the prerequisite of the servicer and carer. Indeed there is a framework for the articulation of men's sacrifices for wife and family, as providers, where women's sacrifices for husband and family are concealed because their lives and responsibilities are about sacrifice and service anyway. Largely as a consequence of existing social inequality, women appear not to miss much through devotion to home and family. Men, on the other hand, can be seen actually to have given things up or to have missed opportunities on behalf of the family, because their responsibilities more readily give them legitimate life and access to privilege outside the home. The status of breadwinning and providing is part of this. For example, the husbands in the study were not reticent on the topic of their own employment, nor about the 'hard graft' it had involved. Although they did not necessarily do this in a belligerent way, the point about hard graft was made by men in most of the interviews in some way. For example, one man explained that: 'We've got more financially comfortable. You don't work 68 hours a week and not have some benefit'. It was he, not his wife, who had been employed for 68 hours a week. In a similar vein other husbands made it clear that they had not enjoyed their jobs, only working through financial necessity, and a common theme was regret about job opportunities forgone because wives had been reluctant to move house. The men were thus easily able to articulate sacrifices they had made 'for the family', but the wives were not similarly able to do so. In a fundamental sense the wives *were* 'the family' for whom the sacrifice had been made.

Consequently responsibilities were constructed in such a way that the women appeared to have had the better deal out of life than their husbands. This was at the basis of the contradiction for them – between valuing their domain and resenting it – and is important for an understanding of issues of control of the domestic arena. There was an implication not only that women controlled the home, but that they were lucky to do so. This was underlined in the extent to which husbands were able to make a ritual of their wives' apparent power – for example, in complaining of how their wives were bossy or 'always nagging'. In all of the interviews was an assumption that in some sense wives were generally in charge, and this was often reinforced in ritual fashion through joking or ridicule. For example, in the cases where the husbands had begun to help more with the housework, this help was clearly not seen as being up to scratch, sometimes as a result of a carefully cultivated incompetence on the part of the husbands. Men either tended to do things the 'wrong way', or 'at the wrong time' and 'in the wrong place'. One husband told me that: 'I put things that are supposed to drip dry in the spinner sometimes, or so I'm told.' One of the women said that she would rather be out when her husband helps with the housework because he does not do it properly:

I notice that he doesn't clear up the boiler ash properly and sort of things like that you know. They'll wash up and go away, then you take the washing-up bowl out of the sink and you find all tea leaves round it because they haven't cleared up after themselves. And sort of splashes down the fronts of cupboards and things. They don't see those . . . *I* wipe it up after me you see. The men don't notice it so . . . all the bits are still there.

Yet another of the men told me that his wife is 'far too fussy with housework. She's a maniac.' He told me that his wife has a ritual of tidying up the house before they go to bed at night 'in case a burglar breaks in and thinks she's untidy'. Thus, although many wives wanted help in the home, they struggled actively to retain the power to direct that help, hence the consequent image of bossy wives and helpful but clumsy husbands who 'can't do a thing right'. It is not insignificant that these types of statement were generally made in the presence of the other spouse, and indeed often form part of an apparently good-humoured marital banter whose effect is to construct an image of women in this age range as dominating rather than submissive husbands.

Various commentators have noted that women do, on the whole, have control of the domestic arena. However, it has also been pointed out that this control is in a sense delegated to them by their husbands; it involves the servicing of others, and is therefore dependent upon women's subservience to men (Bell and Newby, 1976; Davidoff, 1976; Johnson, 1975; Pahl, 1983). As one of the men I interviewed rather aptly put it: 'I wouldn't want to be lord and master of the house. I'd rather *let her do that*' (my emphasis). This is rather paradoxical, because having been made a manager, and having been delegated responsibility for day-to-day domestic matters, the wife through subservience has seized a form of circumscribed autonomy; an arena from which she can legitimately exclude her husband. The home is her domain; she is in charge. Hence we can appreciate the development of popular images of the nagging wife or mother-in-law (see Harris, 1969) and the trammelled, downtrodden husband, which seem particularly pertinent at this 'stage' of life. The point is that by their nagging and their husbands' complaints, both wives and husbands are celebrating the legitimacy of the woman's control of the domestic sphere. Through the payment of lipservice to women's domestic power, the ultimate 'orchestration' power of husbands over their wives, stemming from their socially advantaged position, can be concealed whilst also being reinforced. Domestic power appears to be more immediate and vital.

Therefore a wife's domestic nagging is not threatening for her husband although he may find it very irritating, because by vocalising and symbolising her domestic power through nagging the wife is helping to conceal the unequal social position she has with her husband. Furthermore, a result of the construction of women's domestic power as nagging is to trivialise what it is that women do. The implication is that what is being nagged about is not a necessity at all but just one of the wife's idiosyncracies. Indeed, in the face of retirement some husbands in the study carried this through to suggesting a reordering of their wives' priorities. They tended to develop a renewed interest in 'doing things together', and often tried to persuade their wives to defer some of the housework in favour of joint leisure activities, or to do things in the house a bit less thoroughly so that they could go out together. The husbands made it known that if *they* were in control of domestic organisation they would have different priorities. Thus in losing a bid to reorder his wife's priorities a husband could legitimately avoid the 'fussy details' of housework, whilst setting her up as a nagging wife. If he were to win the reordering bid, the wife would feel that her control of the domestic sphere had been challenged and, as others have noted (Oakley, 1976), she would still have the housework to do tomorrow.

But given that negotiations for these couples were centring on the domestic domain, how far did husbands start to nag their wives about housework? Some husbands did begin to take an active interest in the daily routines of the domestic sphere but, as mentioned, this did not involve taking full responsibility. In fact, rather than taking over all the labour involved, husbands' interest in domesticity tended to take the form of monitoring or overseeing the work of the wives: helpfully suggesting 'more efficient' ways of doing things. With a few of the husbands this almost took the form of a professionalisation of domestic labour, whereby they installed and developed expertise in new household technology such as microwave ovens, which their wives felt unable or unwilling to use. However, the wives did not trivialise their husbands' interest in domesticity as nagging, but rather perceived that they were encroaching, criticising or 'taking over'. The women were beginning to have to be accountable to their husbands in a way that they had not been in the past, and this was partly because the women's sphere at this time was becoming observable to the men in a way that men's public sphere never becomes fully observable to women. Given the structure of social inequality, and given the women's perception that they could only lose control in one sphere without ever gaining power in the other, it is perhaps easy to understand why men nagging women about domesticity is more threatening, although probably no more irritating, than women nagging men.

The main point is that nagging is only nagging as opposed to monitoring, interfering or taking over in so far as it is considered to be talk about something inconsequential rather than the really 'nitty gritty' of what life is about. It is therefore significant that the women were seen to be 'nagging' when the men were 'taking over'. Those who have the power to say that others are nagging are in the process of helping to define the agenda and priorities of marriage by determining what is and what is not important.

CONCLUSION

There clearly had been changes in the married lives and domestic organisation of these couples over time, but gendered *responsibility* was an important area of continuity. What responsibilities actually meant in practice had changed for the couples, and particularly important was the extent to which domestic servicing relations involved different types and amounts of work as well as new conflicts and negotiations. Struggle or negotiation for these couples had become centred around the domestic domain, and women appeared on the face of it to be more powerful because they continued to direct the help that husbands gave in that domain, whilst asserting their authority over it and resisting any potential takeover bids. Men and women both ritually reinforced this notion, through men treating women as domestic 'bosses', and through women nagging their husbands. However, by keeping marital dialogue at the level of domestic power, attention was being directed away from at least three major characteristics of gendered responsibilities.:

(1) First, these women had been disadvantaged *vis-à-vis* their husbands throughout their lives in employment, pay and social and cultural inequality, and this remained the context for the marriage relationship.
(2) The domain which the women were hanging on to was actually one giving responsibility for *servicing* the needs of others. Thus the women's power was dependent on their subservience to their husbands.

(3) The husbands were in a position to be able to trivialise what the women did at home by saying that they were far too fussy and nagged too much, or even by reordering their priorities.

Negotiations, then, for a variety of reasons took place within a taken-for-granted fabric of responsibility supporting existing gender inequalities. The ways in which couples negotiated the changes in their lives actually helped to sharpen the boundaries of responsibility, and hence negotiations never actually became renegotiations.

NOTES

I would like to thank Graham Allan, Claire Buck and Janet Finch for their constructive comments on an earlier version of this paper. Special thanks also to Caroline Dryden for many invaluable discussions on some of the issues developed here.

1. This age range was chosen to exemplify the period of disruption. Couples selected for interview formed a social class mix. Three semistructured tape-recorded interviews were conducted with each couple during 1985; one jointly and one with each spouse individually. The research was funded by the ESRC and is currently being written up for submission to the University of Kent as a Ph D. thesis.

8 'My Husband Says I'm Too Old for Dancing': Women, Leisure and Life Cycles

Rosemary Deem

IS A LIFE-CYCLE ANALYSIS OF WOMEN'S LEISURE WORTHWHILE?

It is virtually impossible to study women's leisure without setting it in the context of their lives as a whole. Life-cycle stage has an important effect on the what, when and why of sport and leisure. Nowhere is this more evident than in the analysis of sport, where participation starts to decline after age 19 more rapidly for women than men (*Social Trends 1985*). Other leisure interests of women and the time devoted to them also change as women's life-cycle stages alter; hence the leisure patterns of teenage girls and that of mothers with school-age children are frequently very different.

The concept of life cycle in the study of women's leisure does not simply refer to age as Clarke and Critcher (1985) suggest, but also to life events, status transitions and attitudinal changes (Rapoport and Rapoport, 1975). Some life-cycle stages involve both cultural and biological factors (childbirth, old age) while others (like divorce) are mainly shaped by socio-economic variables. It is, however, important to remember that in taking life cycle as a major aspect in the study of women's leisure, other social divisions like gender, ethnicity and class, continue to be important.

USING THE LIFE-CYCLE CONCEPT

An important endeavour to use the concept in relation to leisure (Rapoport and Rapoport, 1975) explored how life-cycle changes affected and shaped family leisure revealing also important intercon-nections between work, family and leisure. In this analysis the life cycle is conceptualised as encompassing cultural preoccupations arising out of psycho-biological maturation processes; preoccupations give rise to interests, concerns and motivations and subsequently activities. However, the fit between these levels is not always perfect. Young adults, preoccupied with their social identity, often develop a fairly privatised lifestyle within a heterosexual relationship: for women this may result in them having relatively few out-of-home leisure activities. Whilst not necessarily a problem at this stage, a home-based existence may subsequently fail to provide a fulfilling social identity and the advent of children may indeed make home life constrained and conflictual.

As used by the Rapoports the approach is relatively limited, failing for instance to take fully into account the struggles women engage in over leisure entitlement. The study emphasises family, not individual, leisure. It does not easily encompass non-age-related events like divorce or redundancy. There is a tendency to assume that personal incomes increase up to retirement. Tensions in family life are glossed over in the emphasis on the coalescence of work, family and leisure; work is treated as paid. employment only. Class differences are given insufficient consideration. Women are assumed to be an homogenous group; those who remain single and childless, those who marry late or are widowed early, and black women, are thus to a large degree excluded. So, although pioneering, this study has drawbacks.

More recent studies of leisure have also made use of a life-cycle approach. For example, Dixey and Talbot's 1982 study of Armley (Leeds), part of their research on women and bingo, used life-cycle stages as one way of analysing activity diaries and other data. Young single women were rarely interested in bingo, but married women in their thirties and forties and fifties and pensioner women showed a considerable interest in the game. This use of life cycle also allowed Dixey and Talbot to pick out other patterns in women's leisure: for example, that mothers of school-age children stay in more than mothers of under-fives. Green, Hebron and Woodward (1985) have also used life-cycle stages as one of the ways of analysing leisure in their recent survey of over 700 women in Sheffield.

Utilising the life-cycle approach conveys the message that leisure is not static over a lifetime, but changes to reflect not only life events, shifting preoccupations and interests, but also new circumstances, opportunities and constraints. The meaning of leisure also alters over time – leisure may be a central focus for single teenagers, but much less central to mothers with young children. Activities too can pall, although in some cases old enthusiasms can be renewed later in life. Constraints on leisure can also alter or diminish; older women may gain more confidence in their ability to negotiate over leisure time, although Mason (1986) in her study of long-married couples suggests women over 50 have a *weaker* bargaining position than younger women. A single woman from a small town may marry and move to a large city, where she experiences both her husband controlling her leisure and collective male social control over her freedom to be in the city alone. In the rest of the chapter I explore the usefulness of the concept of the life cycle as a social construction.

YOUNG WOMEN AND LEISURE: GOING OUT AND STAYING IN

Who count as young women? Here I confine it to teenage girls up to age 20. A major feature of this phase is being single and childless, although a minority will already be married or mothers. Most teenagers view leisure as very important, although being unemployed dramatically affects this (Wallace, 1986). Having time hanging on your hands all day when unemployed is very different to having free time after work. Men, and male forms of control, are also central to teenage leisure. Whether it be anxious fathers restricting their daughters' visits to pubs and discos, boyfriends trying to control where their girlfriends go, the problems of sexual harassment, or dressing up to go to a nightclub to meet men, males and patriarchal control are omnipresent, a process which begins while at school (McCabe, 1981; Lees, 1986).

The leisure preoccupations of teenage girls often focus around relationships with boys (although this is obviously dependent on sexual orientation), clothes, records, tapes, and activities like dancing (McRobbie, 1978b; McRobbie and McCabe, 1981; McRobbie and Nava, 1984). Unfortunately research has not always taken fully into account variations based on ethnicity nor culturally specific notions of femininity which may produce different constraints and leisure experiences. Same-sex friendships are also important to teenage girls' leisure, although these may disintegrate if serious relationships with boys develop (Griffin, 1985b; 1985c; Leonard, 1980). However, Griffiths (1986) and Beuret and Makings (this volume) suggest that same-sex friendships can co-exist with such relationships.

Teenage female leisure is often relatively unvaried. Griffin's (1985b) study of female working-class school-leavers in Birmingham found a common leisure activity was 'dossing' – that is, groups of girls hanging around together in their immediate neighbourhood or (at weekends) going into the city centre. At home, leisure may consist of talking, playing music, trying on clothes and make-up, watching TV or videos, and reading teenage magazines (McRobbie, 1978b; McRobbie and McCabe, 1981; Brown, 1985; Griffin, 1985b). The pub may be a source of entertainment, even though illegal for under-18s, because other places intended for the young usually require an entrance fee. In Griffin's study the parents of girls living at home often tried to stop their daughters going to places where boys and alcohol were to be found (1985b). Griffin (1985b) and Brown (1985) found youth clubs were unpopular; boys often dominate the facilities and may be noisy and physically aggressive. Sport is rarely part of adolescent leisure, being already discarded as unfeminine, childish or boring, (Scraton, 1986; 1987). Only swimming, keep-fit, walking and pop mobility are likely to be popular (Brown, 1985).

There are a number of constraints on teenage leisure; black girls in Griffin's study faced not only sexual but also racial harassment, both of which were major constraints on their leisure time. Girls without friends living near to them found that it was difficult to become involved in out-of-home leisure. Unemployed girls living at home can often become socially isolated as a result. Girls in employment have more money and social contacts and do less domestic labour (Griffin, 1985b).

Both working- and middle-class girls face similar problems of male control over what they can or cannot do. As girls grow older the agent of that control may shift from fathers to boyfriends. Studies have shown that many more women than men over 16 have a regular partner; in such cases social life tends to revolve around that partner (Brown, 1985). My own research suggests that cohabiting and married women under 20 may be more restricted in their leisure than single women (Deem, 1986). Leonard's (1980) study of young engaged couples in a Welsh town suggests that, for the women, leisure was fairly limited compared with the social life enjoyed in pubs, clubs and dance halls prior to the development of a steady relationship. Leonard's study also shows that teenage leisure may be achieved at the expense of older women's free time; in return for affection and 'staying close', parents whose daughters lived at home 'spoiled' their offspring with domestic services, money and emotional support.

Leisure for women in their late teens, then, consists mainly of a relatively small range of activities. Dixey and Talbot (1982) call this 'the big three of drink, boys and discussion ... about adults, themselves, jobs and sex' (p. 41). Whilst 'going out' is something widely associated with teenage girls, this is less the case if there is a regular boyfriend or unemployment. Teenage women generally spend more leisure time at home than their male peers. But for those teenage women who are already mothers, their leisure opportunities and experiences are likely to be further curtailed and changed.

THE TWENTIES AND THIRTIES: SOCIABILITY AND DOMESTIC RESPONSIBILITY

This age-group covers a wide range of possible employment and household situations, and is considerably influenced by the presence or absence of marriage, dependent children and employment. A single childless woman may have a social life comparable to a teenager, but more money and not parental restrictions. Young married mothers may be highly constrained by their husbands intent on protecting their own leisure, be financially dependent, take sole responsibility for the house and children, have few friends living locally and be without personal transport. Although these are stereotypes, they bear considerable resemblance to the actual situation. Obviously not all women conform to them. But marriage, pregnancy and childbirth can be a crucial watershed for leisure activities, particularly sport.[1] They herald new forms of male control (Green, Hebron and Woodward, 1985) and bring new responsibilities. Furthermore, childbirth may be accompanied by physical changes such as increased body weight and decreased fitness, which affect leisure choices and confidence, and this is a crucial stage at which those women still interested in sport decrease their involvement.

In my Milton Keynes study the majority of women in this age-group were married or cohabiting mothers, with their leisure time spent mostly in the home. The gap between them and single women was considerable. Evening classes, clubs and sport were all activities done frequently by single or childless women but very infrequently by young mothers and married women. Mothers spent much of their leisure time with their children; both a pleasure and a tie. Shared leisure with partners was mainly confined to watching TV or videos, relaxing at home, having friends or relatives round for meals, and occasional visits to pubs or restaurants. Other in-home leisure was often linked to domestic chores – baking, sewing, knitting. Single mothers didn't have to negotiate their leisure with another adult, but with little money they also had little out-of-home leisure. Activities already given up (not always regretfully) by this age-group included dancing, going with female friends to pubs, restaurants or night clubs, and many kinds of sport.

I found some women who really missed their freedom and previous leisure activities. For example:

> I did keep fit through classes and exercise until I got pregnant – but then I put on loads of weight and I'd look silly now. (Woman, 28, ten-month-old baby).

> I used to love going out dancing on a Friday night with all my mates from work – I used to spend the whole week preparing, buying and trying on clothes and make-up, thinking who I'd meet, what I'd say, what I'd drink... I really do miss dancing, but ... [husband] would never let me go, he'd be worried I might meet someone else and the kids misbehave if he has them in the evening. (28-year-old part-time cleaner, two children).

Another woman who had won prizes for disco dancing as a teenager said sadly, 'My husband says I'm too old for dancing – but he just doesn't want me to go.'

Dixey and Talbot's (1982) Leeds findings are slightly different, emphasising the importance of regional variations, placing high emphasis on 'socialising': women in their twenties, married and mothers, or not, went out more often than any other group except teenagers. But women in their thirties with *school-age* children went out much less often. Dixey and Talbot argue that it is not the twenties but the thirties which is the decisive watershed for leisure. Women of between thirty and forty in Armley spent fewer nights out of the house than any other age-group, and two-thirds of them felt dissatisfied with this state of affairs: favourite ways of spending evenings were "reading quietly", "relaxing when possible", "with a good book and some chocolate", and "drink at home listening to music"' (Dixey and Talbot, 1982, p. 43).

Other studies see the advent of children as having a major impact on leisure (Green, Hebron and Woodward, 1985; Wimbush, 1986b). Mothers of young children face considerable restrictions on their leisure, especially as this is when they are likely to have withdrawn from the labour market. It is a period in their lives when domestic responsibilities peak (Graham, 1984) and the sexual division of labour between mothers and their male partners sharpens (Hunt, 1980). It is also a point at which the power of male partners increases, whether manifested in refusals to babysit or help with the housework, arguments over money or disputes over access to the household's car. Wimbush (1986b) found that her 'recreationally active' Scottish mothers often had to overcome disapproval not only from husbands, but also from relatives, who felt leisure outside the home was something mothers should willingly sacrifice. Children themselves too quickly develop their own leisure needs, and women may begin to live vicariously through their children's leisure and spend considerable time escorting children to leisure activities.

There is also a shift to family-oriented leisure for women as mothers, resulting in all those visits to stately homes, leisure centres and parks, fairs and seaside resorts which *Social Trends 1985* says are increasing in the UK. The notion of 'family leisure has a cosy, harmonious sound, although it is often conflict-ridden and beset by struggles between men, women and children over where to go, when, and with whom, who cuts the sandwiches, who drives the car and who escapes to the nearest pub when it all gets too much. No prizes for guessing who usually wins these struggles. The foremost example of tension-ridden family leisure is the holiday – often a breeding ground for arguments and family conflicts and where domestic labour for women may actually increase, especially if 'self-catering' or camping holidays are involved.

This stage of heavy domestic labour, little money, and family-oriented leisure doesn't last for ever. But as Mason's (1986) study of long-married couples observes, subsequent renegotiations of a lifestyle in which particular tasks and divisions of labour have been invested with considerable emotional and other significance, isn't very likely. Although patterns of life and responsibilities may alter with age, new responsibilities – for example, grandchildren, or adult 'children' living at home – may replace the previous ones. More dramatic status changes such as divorce or widowhood may also alter leisure, although Burgoyne and Clarke (1984) in their research on stepfamilies in Sheffield found that remarriages often follow similar patterns to first marriages.

THE FORTIES AND FIFTIES: THE REGAINING OF FREEDOM?

There are a number of distinctive features which separate this age-group from younger women. They are much less likely to have young children and are much more likely to be in employment than the twenties and thirties age-group. They form a significant proportion of women active in out-of-home leisure in a variety of women-only and mainly-women organisations and clubs (Deem, 1986). This age-group is one of the mainstays of women-dominated activities like adult education and bingo. They may also, according to social class (Rapoport and Rapoport, 1975), be heavily involved in couple-leisure. Couple-leisure, like family-leisure, isn't always enjoyable for women, especially if it consists of entertainment linked to a male partner's employment: 'Is ... cooking a meal for your husband's business colleagues leisure?' (women in discussion at branch of Business and Professional Women's Club (Deem, 1982)). Couple-leisure can mean also people you don't like coming into your home.

Dixey and Talbot's (1982) Armley study sees the forties and fifties as the 'best period for leisure' (p. 43). But Edgell (1980), Hunt (1980) and Mason (1986) have all shown that the removal of dependent children from the home and re-entry to the labour market do not always bring about real changes in the sexual division of labour within the household. Even if the tasks lighten, Mason points out that the fifty-plus age-group can expect more ill-health. More involvement in employment too leaves less time for what domestic labour must be done. Teenage children, whether living at home or not, continue to make domestic demands on their mothers. Moreover, when they themselves have children they may expect their mothers to undertake their care. Nor does male control over women's leisure necessarily lessen with time (Green, Hebron and Woodward, 1985; 1987).

At-home leisure is still important to the forties and fifties age-group, with emphasis on crafts, music and creative pursuits rather than the 'sit down and relax' leisure engaged in by younger women. In my study I found this age-group had the largest number of in-home leisure activities of any group. Out of the home they were noticeable not just for their involvement in voluntary groups and clubs, but also for taking on leadership roles in those groups. Sometimes this was seen by middle-class women as a substitute for a job. For instance, one woman, when asked why she got involved in the WI committee, replied:

My children were growing up and I found myself with time on my hands. My husband's one of those old-fashioned types who don't like their wives to work, so I decided I'd get more involved in the WI. I've also recently become a parish councillor but without the WI I'd never have had the confidence. Also I've learnt an enormous amount from being in the WI – it really isn't just jam and cake making. I've done photography, calligraphy, local history and how to run a meeting and speak in public. (Woman in late forties, three teenage children, husband civil servant)

Whilst sport is not a major preoccupation, yoga, keep-fit, walking and rambling are popular with more-active women.

Despite the continuing constraints of domestic labour and the increased involvement in employment, women in their middle years do enjoy much more leisure than at any other time since their teenage years. Yet the needs and interests of this group are often forgotten by policy-makers and commercial providers, despite Featherstone and Hepworth's (1981) argument that for both sexes the later years of middle age are a major focus of consumerism. Gender stereotyping often (groundlessly) sees ageing women as having little sexual or personal appeal, whilst men of a similar age (also groundlessly) are seen as having great sexual attraction and personal charm. Hence it is older *men* who form a major target group for goods and services and are a focus for sport and leisure policy-makers.

THE SIXTIES, SEVENTIES AND BEYOND: A STEADY DECLINE?

It is at this point in their lives that women begin to reap the consequences of a lifetime of subordinate roles. Low-paid employment, no proper pension entitlement, the likelihood of living longer than men, and poor health all contribute to a situation in which many women of over sixty have few financial or other resources for leisure. Yet leisure for the over-sixties is enormously varied. Some women are very active in a variety of clubs and organisations, bingo, evening and day classes and at-home interests. Others are socially isolated, have few interests and ironically have too much 'leisure time'. Once women are sixty they are eligible for senior-citizen activities. These, especially clubs, are hated by some: 'They're for *really old* people: the only time I went to anything like that they all kept mistaking me for the helper' (Milton Keynes woman aged seventy-one). Others are more appreciative, especially of things like cheap travel, although many women are apprehensive of travelling even short distances on public transport alone.

Physical well-being and friendship are crucial to leisure at all ages but especially so for this age-group. Those in poor health may find their leisure consisting of radio and TV, with only occasional visits from relatives to break the monotony. The social isolation of old women (for example, death and poverty reduce their friends) is not the only factor that makes their lives more difficult. The loss of many of their social roles may mean that they feel their lives lack purpose. As one woman said to Dixey, 'Well yes, you've had your life' (Dixey and Talbot, 1982, p. 45). A recent widow may find it difficult to adjust after a lifetime of housework and economic dependence on a man. Jerrome (1983), in a study of unattached women in their fifties and sixties seeking companionship through friendship clubs, found that some women in such clubs lacked the social skills necessary to make new friends.

The later years of life for women, then, may initially be full of activity, but circumstances can change rapidly. The 'time on my hands' syndrome may surface for many elderly women, especially the widowed or lonely, and unoccupied time, far from being a scarce resource, comes to be dreaded. Ageing thus brings in its wake restricted leisure and an over-abundance of 'spare time'.

LIFE CYCLES AS AN APPROACH TO WOMEN'S LEISURE: DOES IT HELP?

This chapter has tried to show how using the notion of life cycle can assist the study of women's leisure. It is certainly an important antidote to the belief that what we need to do is to concentrate on those women (for example, mothers of young children) who have least leisure and are most constrained (Hobson, 1981; McIntosh, 1981). Focusing on such experiences alone can paint a very misleading picture. It is crucial that women's leisure is set in a broader context of their lives as a whole, so that both changes and those things which remain constant in women's leisure can be discerned.

There can, however, be problems if a life-cycle analysis of leisure is not supplemented by other explanations and perspectives. Ethnicity, social class, and employment status can all have as much or more effect on women's leisure as life-cycle stages (Deem, 1986). There are also some enduring constraints on women's leisure which operate at all stages of life. The extent to which women's leisure is shaped by dominant ideas about femininity, patterns of male power over women in public and private life, the patriarchal assumptions embedded in capitalist societies, ideologies about sexuality and the sexual division of labour, may actually outweigh the impact of the life cycle. However, in another sense these factors are a crucial part of the social construction of women's life cycle. In a different society or in a different historical era, the 'taken for grantedness' of our dominant life-cycle patterns would be questioned.

There are, then, some good reasons for using a life-cycle approach as one organising principle round which to analyse data about women's leisure. But the life-cycle approach cannot stand alone in the study of female leisure, nor should it be expected to do so.

NOTE

1.   Tina Everett, Physiotherapy Department, Milton Keynes General Hospital, Eaglestone, Milton Keynes, is currently looking at the effects of pregnancy on active sports participation.

9 Married Women at Midlife: Past Experience and Present Change

Susan Yeandle

INTRODUCTION

The working lives of married women in their middle years before statutory retirement age and after children enter secondary education, have not received a great deal of attention in the literature on women's labour. Yet this is a period when many changes typically occur in women's domestic and family lives, and when their decisions about working life are of particular interest.

This chapter reports some of the findings of an exploratory synchronic study of forty-two married women aged 38–60 years living in a town in South Wales.[1] Using a life-history approach, the study has investigated the determinants and consequences of the 'economic activity' of women in later working life, looking at household histories, the labour-market histories of women and their husbands, the domestic organisation of the household, and women's relationships with their kin, neighbours and friends. The women studied were grouped into three age/life-stage cohorts, as shown in table 9.1.

Any study of how individuals experience life events or stages in the life course must be located in the context of those individual, family and historical experiences which have shaped their previous lives. This chapter therefore draws together data on women's patterns of employment before, at and beyond midlife, looking at their accounts

Table 9.1 Characteristics of cohorts

	Pre-retirement cohort n = 14	Intermediate cohort n = 14	Late parental cohort n = 14
Woman's age	56–60	45–51	38–42
Date of birth	1925–1929	1934–1940	1943–1947
Age of youngest child	18 +	13 +	11 +

117

of withdrawals from and re-entries to the paid labour force and at the domestic labour and services which have been prominent features of all their lives. The latter part of the chapter then discusses changes and events which typically occur at midlife, and to which respondents drew attention in explanation of their own particular labour-market histories.

To study women's experiences at a particular stage in the life course is to investigate the *timing* of specific events in individuals' lives. Here, Hareven's distinction between different kinds of time is helpful (Hareven, 1982). Attention has to be paid to *individual* time (how old and in what state of health was a given woman when a given event occurred?), to *family time* (what stage in the cycle of family life had she reached?), and to *historical time* (what economic, social and political conditions pertained in the world beyond herself and her kin?). The comparison of the age/life-stage cohorts studied in South Wales permits investigation of the part that history plays in individuals' lives. Thus, for example, to be twenty and single at the outset of the Second World War, thirty and a young mother in the early 1950s, and forty-five with children 'off one's hands' in the relatively advantageous economic and employment circumstances of the mid-1960s, was to live through a specific set of personal, family and historical events, which shaped the individual's experience in particular ways. To be forty, fifty and sixty-five years old at those same historical points was quite another matter. The significance of one's place in history is recognised in popular discourse – thus we speak of being 'born too late', 'out of our time', and speculate about 'where we would be today' if only we had been born ten years earlier or later. The historical moment, then, influences the life course of each individual, although not in straightforward or predictable ways. As Elder (1982) has observed:

> Most occasions of social change defy a simple account of life effects by giving rise to contradictory or varied consequences, both continuous and discontinuous in the life span. (p. 76)

The changes in life activities on which respondents focused in explaining how their employment careers had been shaped, revealed a major shift from one stage of the life course to another. This Midlife Transition involves both gradual changes (the biological ageing process; the maturity of children; moving from being a younger member of one's family, neighbourhood or society to being one of its older generation) and specific events which mark the passage from one status or position to another at given points in time.

It is possible to observe the role which a variety of these changes played in structuring respondents' lives through their effect upon women's labour histories. The most important changes were: the maturity of children and their departure from the parental home; the physical decline and death of elderly parents and other kin of that generation; the acquisition of the role of grandparent; the approach of retirement from paid work (for women and their spouses); and changes in neighbourhood or community social relations. The nature and impact of the first two of these changes are explored here: both involve the weakening, irrevocable modification or loss of important inter-generational relationships which play a crucial role in structuring the individual's progress through the life course.

PATTERNS OF EMPLOYMENT BEFORE THE MIDLIFE TRANSITION: A COMPARISON OF THE THREE COHORTS

The past employment patterns and experience of the three cohorts studied must be viewed in the historical context of conditions in the labour market.[2] The gap of two decades between the 'pre-retirement' cohort and the 'late parental' cohort means that there are significant historical changes to be taken into account. These include the structure of opportunities for employment, statutory requirements about minimum ages for leaving full-time schooling, and managerial practices such as the tendency to require or expect women to resign employment on marriage.[3]

The 'pre-retirement' women first entered the labour force during the Second World War. Women in the 'intermediate' cohort began their working lives in the early 1950s, while the 'late parental' group was leaving school in the early 1960s. Thus, for example, the special conditions pertaining to a wartime economy (conscription, bomb damage, etc.) offer some explanation for the job-changing and other disruption in the early working histories of some women in the 'pre-retirement' cohort. Nevertheless, what all three cohorts had in common at the outset of their working lives was the relative ease with which they could obtain employment. Almost all respondents moved directly from full-time education into paid work, although the average age at which they did so was highest for the 'late parental' cohort and lowest for the 'pre-retirement' cohort.

Analysis of the detailed data on employment shows that all respondents had been in full-time employment prior to marriage and child-rearing. After marriage (often in association with a first pregnancy), all had withdrawn from the paid labour force, mostly temporarily rather than permanently, although this was not always a conscious decision. However, combining paid employment (whether full- or part-time) with the care of young children was characteristic only of the 'late parental' cohort, while the 'pre-retirement' group contained a few women who had kept child-rearing and paid employment completely separate. This kind of difference between the cohorts reflects the culturally based social changes which have occurred since 1945 and to which the sharply increased participation rates of married women are normally attributed (Yeandle, 1984, p. 19).

The period spent in employment prior to child-bearing was shortest in the case of the 'intermediate' cohort. This can be explained be reference to two factors. The first concerns historical developments, in particular the trend towards remaining in school or other full-time education until later ages. Comparison of the cohorts along this dimension reveals that over time, and under the influence of legislation (particularly the 1944 Education Act), the age of leaving school or college gradually increased. Thus the 'pre-retirement' cohort ceased full-time education at an average age of 14.0 years, the 'intermediate' cohort did so at 15.0 years, and the 'late parental' cohort at 16.0 years.

The second factor shaping the differences between the cohorts is demographic. Average age at marriage and at first child-bearing fell steadily between the early 1940s and the late 1960s (Office of Population Censuses and Surveys, 1978, p. 10), and this was reflected in the study. Since women in all three cohorts tended to enter paid employment on leaving full-time education, and in most cases to remain in employment until pregnant with their first child, the 'intermediate' cohort contained women with least experience of paid employment while childless.

While almost all the women returned to paid employment after leaving the labour market to bear children, the length of time outside of the labour force was longest in the case of the 'pre-retirement' cohort and shortest in the case of the 'late parental' cohort. Most women returned to part-time employment (30 or fewer hours of paid work per week), and some returned intermittently between the births of children.

Once child-bearing ends, patterns of employment for women are no longer shaped or affected by their fertility. None of the women studied had given birth to a child for over a decade, and all considered their families complete. This is important, since in a society where the care of infants and young children is normatively assigned to mothers, pregnancy/child-bearing is a frequent (although by no means the only) reason given by *younger* women for leaving paid jobs. However, once child-bearing was over, the women's patterns of employment were shaped by their own preferences and needs, by conditions in the local labour market, and by other demands upon their domestic, unpaid labour.

PATTERNS OF EMPLOYMENT AT AND BEYOND MIDLIFE

Although patterns of employment were similar in most important respects for all three cohorts during the pre-parental years and while young children were being raised, there were clear differences between the cohorts from the point at which the youngest child reached school age onwards, as shown in Table 9.2.

Table 9.2 'Snapshot' showing employment status for each cohort by family stage

Age of youngest child	Pre-retirement cohort n = 14		Intermediate cohort n = 14		Late parental cohort n = 14	
	In a job	Not in a job	In a job	Not in a job	In a job	Not in a job
5 years	2	12	7	7	9	5
11 years	3	9	11	3	10	4*

*Includes one woman who was registered as unemployed.

The reasons women gave for their return to paid employment help to explain these differences. Labour-market requirements for women's labour (demand factors) and women's own motivations (supply factors) had both had their part to play. Thus women might recall that they returned to paid work when approached by a former employer or by a local shopkeeper who required part-time labour, or 'to help somebody out' when another worker left or fell ill. Often the same informants would also comment that such opportunities arose at times when they were in particular financial need, when arrangements for children's supervision could be made (with the help perhaps of neighbours, or, more often, kin), or when they were finding being at home all day without small children to care for either lonely, depressing or simply unrewarding.

It is helpful here to focus more closely on what happens to women at 'midlife', and to select some crude 'markers' to define its onset and conclusion. The start is taken as either when the youngest child enters secondary education (a point in *family time*), or when they themselves attain forty-five years (a point in *individual time*) – whichever is the *earlier*. Its end comes when women consciously 'retire' from or become too ill to continue in paid work, or when they reach age sixty (statutory retirement age) – whichever is the *later*.

The 'pre-retirement' and 'intermediate' cohorts had reached the Midlife Transition so defined, and the majority of women in the former had been economically active during some or all of this phase. These who were no longer in employment when interviewed had all withdrawn from the labour market at age fifty or later, for reasons to do with their family responsibilities or their own health. None had been 'pushed out' at this stage by redundancy or unemployment. Those who were still in jobs when interviewed all hoped to keep them until they reached retirement age. Their commitment to employment may have been reinforced in some cases by husbands being in low-paid, insecure and sometimes part-time jobs following redundancy from more secure and better-rewarded jobs in the past. However, it was also striking that women in this cohort who were no longer working often had sick, redundant or early-retired husbands who would not (in all likelihood) ever be economically active again.

Women in the 'intermediate' cohort had all returned to paid employment *prior* to reaching midlife. Continuity of employment for this group had been disrupted by both health and domestic responsibilities, although in many cases breaks in employment had been only temporary. An example from this group may serve to illustrate the complexity of the factors which determine when and how women participate in paid employment during this midlife period.

Mrs Freeman[4] was first married when she was eighteen, and had four children during the eleven years before she left and subsequently divorced her husband. She then brought her family up alone, with some parental support, until she remarried aged forty-two.

During her first marriage, Mrs Freeman worked part-time as a ledger clerk when the needs of her children, and her health, permitted and when not helping her husband with farm work. While a single parent, she worked full-time for six years before leaving to take a part-time post enabling her to have more time for her children and her elderly parents. On remarrying, she gave up her job, explaining:

> I'd got to a pitch in my life where I thought, well, I've worked all my life. I'm going to get married now, and I'm not going to damn well work again!

Soon after this second marriage, her mother became seriously ill, and it fell to Mrs Freeman to look after her:

> I had to be down there about six in the morning, and she had to [be fed] every two hours. She had to be bathed and dressed – I'd be down there all day ... The children ... and my husband would come there [to eat]. I'd come home at half past eight [pm]. [That lasted] about six months.

Her mother made a brief recovery, and although daily visits still had to be made, Mrs Freeman was able to reduce her support in the last year of her mother's life. But she still did not get the 'rest' she had looked forward to. Her husband's overtime was stopped, and she explained:

> My husband's wages were very poor – so it was a case of going back to work again. I got a job washing dishes, four evenings a week, half past five till twelve. This was before my daughter left home. She was an unmarried mum with a baby. Then she went back to work, and I had the baby to look after ... Then, when my parents died [very close together], I went full-time in waitressing then, doing five evenings and six mornings. I just went to work full-time ... It isn't that I couldn't cope, but *everything* died for me at that time ... I just threw myself into work. [Not only had she the shock of her parents' deaths, but her new marriage was not working out either.] I did that up until last year. [Then] my hands went. I've got arthritis, they've found out now ... I thought I'd go back to office work, but I kept being told I'm too old, why don't I retire ...

Mrs Freeman subsequently spent a year claiming Unemployment Benefit and applying for office jobs, without success. Now, at forty-six and with no further entitlement to Benefit, she has given up hope both of finding employment and of making her marriage work.

Throughout her adult life a variety of factors have interacted both to 'push' her into employment (financial need, the stress of domestic upsets, her satisfaction in her ofice job), and to 'pull' her out of it (her pregnancies, a miscarriage, caring responsibilities for her children, parents and grandchild, her own ill-health, the lack of job vacancies, prejudice about her age and her own idealistic view of what a second marriage might have to offer). While not typical in a general sense, her case is especially interesting because at midlife it contains almost all the elements referred to by respondents, and because it illustrates well the way in which individual time, family/life-stage time and historical time interrelate and pattern individual experience.

A few women explained that they had left paid jobs in midlife in order to care for sick or elderly kin. It was striking, however, that even at midlife, decisions about paid employment and about caring responsibilities were only rarely *directly* related to one another. This was in marked contrast to the way in which earlier decisions to leave paid jobs had been directly related to childcare. The differences between the two main forms of 'caring' are significant here.

Caring for sick, elderly or infirm kin can in some respects be likened to looking after children. The tasks involved may be the same: preparing food, bathing, laundering clothes, providing a safe and clean living environment, supervising activities and accompanying on outings. Yet there are important differences between the two types of caring, not least the way in which the caring relationship begins, develops and ends.

Caring for children starts (in most cases) with pregnancy and its climax, childbirth, and is followed by several months in which the mother gradually recovers from her exertions, and by several years in which the infant is totally dependent upon her (or a substitute) for its needs. During the two decades which ensue, the child's dependence gradually reduces until, in most cases, it no longer needs to be cared for.

Caring for the sick or elderly, by contrast, often commences in small acts of support such as fetching shopping or help with housework, and gradually increases and becomes a heavy burden of responsibilities as the person's health and strength decline. It may end abruptly, when the carer can no longer cope, or when hospital treatment or death intervene.

These contrasting profiles of the 'caring career' to some extent explain the indirect relationship between paid employment and caring for the old or sick. In some cases, a specific event, such as a mother's fall down stairs, prompted an informant to resign from employment and to devote her energies to caring activities. But frequently women had undertaken to care for ailing kin (often on a daily basis, even when outside their own household) while remaining in paid work, or had accepted such responsibilities at a time when they were already outside the paid labour force.

Sometimes the needs of an elderly or sick relative gradually increase and can be 'predicted'. Indeed, some respondents quite explicitly incorporated such predictions into their future plans. Mrs Leonard (aged forty) explained how she foresaw her life once her children had grown up:

> I can see what it'll be . . . I mean, my [widower] father is getting older, and *now* I go over once a week, all day, to clean . . . and he comes here every day for a meal . . . [and] I pop in and out . . . So I can see it getting *more* so . . . And my mother-in-law – at the moment I don't have to do anything for her . . . but, she's not well. I can see what my future's going to be. I'm going to have to look after her . . . It's something you've got to take, isn't it? I could take a part-time job, but . . . I can see it – I'll have the responsibility of my parents . . . it happened with *my* mother, [she] always had my grandmother and my father's mother . . . I don't feel sorry for myself, it's just a thing I can see happening. I wouldn't want it any other way . . . A part-time job would be very nice, but I won't do it.

Thus women may allocate their labour to caring activities or to paid employment on the basis of anticipated future demand for their services, as well as in response to urgent and specific needs or to arrangements negotiated with others. Whether or not women confront decisions about caring while in or out of paid employment is likely to be significant in determining their response. Thus where the tasks of caring for kin are accepted (willingly or under sufferance) by women of working age while they are *outside* the labour market for other reasons (such as child-rearing), this may prevent or at least postpone returns to paid jobs which they might otherwise have been keen to obtain.

THE MATURING AND DEPARTURE OF CHILDREN

All the women in the 'pre-retirement' and 'intermediate' cohorts had experienced the departure from home of at least one of their children. When children left home, the pattern of the women's life activities was altered in a number of important ways. Thus women described both the subjective experience of 'losing' their children, and identified changes which they believed this 'loss' had brought to the way in which they organised their time and efforts.

A minority of the children who had left home had moved away from Wales altogether, and about two-thirds were still living in the same town as their parents. The majority of these departed children were or had been married, and more than half now had children of their own. Thus most respondents in these two cohorts had at least one grandchild.

The dispersal of some of their children and grandchildren restricted visiting and mutual help. Those whose grandchildren lived away from South Wales mostly saw them only three or four times a year, either by making weekend visits themselves, or by having their children and grandchildren to stay at holiday times. By contrast, those whose grandchildren lived relatively near mostly saw them several times per week, or in some cases daily, and two women had (illegitimate) grandchildren living in their households. Most of these respondents played some part in caring for their grandchildren, on either a regular or occasional basis, and some also played a substantial part in supporting them financially.

The experience of those who were able to have regular contact with their grandchildren demonstrates the role which the latter can play in drawing together parents and their adult children. Ties between the two generations of adults often become quite weak as the younger ones start work, leave home, marry and establish an independent network of social contacts. Yet in favourable circumstances the birth of grandchildren can reverse this process, and ties, especially between the adult women concerned, can become much stronger.

For some women, the period when their children moved away from home had been one of unwelcome changes, and women who had not returned to paid employment before this occurred seemed to find it especially difficult. As Mrs Perkins explained:

[I felt] terribly depressed [when he left] – I really missed him. I think for a boy you do such a lot ... Many times I used to sit in here, and I could see all the [neighbours'] doors closed, and everybody was out at work. Well, I don't think I ever want to go through that again, it was a dreadful time in my life.

Eventually, after several months of misery, she decided to take the chance of returning to her occupation of twenty years before, and began work as a shop assistant. This helped her, especially while her son and daughter-in-law were living on the opposite side of town. Later, when they moved with their daughter near to her home, she found she could become involved with her granddaughter, and when she subsequently gave up her job because of anxiety and stress at work, she felt differently:

> I'm on the spot if [my daughter-in-law] wants me – I was up there all day yesterday... [I] met [my granddaughter] from school ... then they come down here on Sunday... I'm free, I can go and help her ... *That's* why I don't miss working.

Mrs Daniels had returned to full-time employment while her only daughter was in secondary education, but had been forced to give her job up through poor health. She explained:

> [When my daughter went away] I think I came home and I cried *all* day. I was terrible. It was dreadful, absolutely dreadful... I knew, when she went, she'd never come back [to live], I just took it for granted. Of course, it wasn't long after that my mother died, and that we found [my husband's] cataract. Then he found that he couldn't do his work... Everything's changed. I mean, she went, and I had my husband home.

Other women who had missed their children a great deal when they left home and had been glad of their jobs at that time, later found that being in employment limited their contact with their grandchildren. Mrs Randall worked a split shift, six days a week, working a few hours each morning and late afternoon. She commented:

> I'd rather give the job up... If I didn't have the job ... perhaps at the weekend I'd keep them up here. Your grandchildren make you want to do things – I just haven't got the time to do it. I'd like to take the children swimming and that... The years are just flying by.

Mrs Randall's remarks show a recognition that her grandchildren might enable her to regain or replace some of the contact and activities which she missed so much when her son first married and went away from home. Her comments have an almost symbolic significance:

> It was a terrible thing, him leaving. Every day – after he'd left – I'd
> [still] be making his bed – I just couldn't get out of the habit . . . The
> only thing that could really stop me doing that – I gave his bed away,
> and I gave the quilt to my daughter-in-law. And that quilt now is on my
> grandson's bed.

The departure of children, then, could 'push' women into paid
employment, or at least be a time when, if other demands were not
also made on them, paid work took on a greater significance. Later,
when grandchildren were born, or when other events intervened,
participation in employment could once again become problematic or
exert pressure on women and cause them to reconsider what priority
they should accord it.

THE DECLINE AND DEATH OF OLDER KIN

So far, we have noted that, at midlife, parents are typically
confronted with the growing independence and autonomy of their
offspring, which is a normative expectation in our society. Their
children increasingly form their own relationships, from which they
as parents are frequently excluded, and make decisions about their
own futures which, both formally and informally, remove them from
parental care and control. While parent–child relationships continue,
in most cases, to have great significance until, and indeed after, they
are ended by death, the maturing of offspring marks the end, as one
respondent put it, of 'a phase in your life'. Grandchildren can bring a
renewed significance to such attenuated relationships and stimulate
more frequent interaction, but only where permitted by other factors,
especially proximity of residence and employment circumstances.

Very commonly, parents at midlife are also experiencing changes
in their relationships with their own parents. Indeed, the years of
mature adulthood involve the continual attrition and loss of relationships with kin of the ascending generation.[5] The birth of a descending
generation, geographical mobility, and the declining health and death
of older kin all tend to render contact with more distant relatives such
as the cousins and siblings of one's parents increasingly infrequent.
Most significantly, however, between the ages of about forty and
sixty years, many people face their own parents' failing health and
strength, and ultimately their death. For women in particular this
may bring much closer relationships again, as they become involved
in the care or support of their parents and parents-in-law, and in

some cases this new role of carer for the elderly may take over from or erode existing roles such as those of employee or mother.

The responsibility of caring for kin in the ascending generation frequently falls on women in midlife. The details of the tasks which women carers perform, unpaid, for their sick and elderly relatives do not need cataloguing here.[6] However, data from the study indicate that such caring can reshape the carer's field of activities and relationships, so that when such duties finally end (often through death) she is unable simply to 'pick up the pieces' of the life she had previously led. Jobs which were resigned while women cared for relatives could not afterwards be regained, nor could other relationships be retrieved.

Mrs Marshall had given up her job to look after her frail and confused mother who required almost constant attention. Her husband had recently retired, but as she explained, this did not really alter her situation:

> I don't go anywhere. My husband would stay in if I wanted to go out – but I've no interest to go anywhere. I just don't want to bother. You stay in so long you just don't *want* to go out.

The restructuring of activities and relationships which the needs of an elderly relative require seems likely to be an irreversible process. Caring may be expected of some women until they are well past statutory retirement age, while even if they feel free to return to paid work before this, obtaining a job in one's fifties is unlikely to be easy.

The death of one's parents occurs at a specific point in chronological time and marks an important shift. When it takes place during midlife, it may render individuals especially conscious of the process or transition which they are experiencing, as they cross the borderline separating one period of family time from another. A parent's death denotes the end of a whole set of relationships, and in this lies much of its social significance, for the bereaved child, though perhaps middle-aged, now faces the future as an orphan. Evidence from the study certainly belies any suggestion that an aged parent is not deeply mourned after death. Respondents spoke of the experience as being 'like losing a part of your own body' and as transforming them:

> You're inclined to think of time on that scale, like BC and AD ... I mean [before mother died] life was completely different ... *I* was

completely different, mentally – I was just a girl with two children, but I'm not any *more*. I'm older in my head sometimes than my mother-in-law.

Respondents also noted that their parents, mothers in particular, had been the focus of interaction between themselves and their siblings and families, and that contact with siblings tended to decline once the mothers were gone.

SUMMARY AND OVERVIEW

I want in conclusion to return to the part that history plays in people's lives. This is not to suggest a crude determinism; for, as I have tried to show, it is the interplay of individual, family and historical events – all of which have both intended and unintended consequences – which shapes the trajectory of the life course. Historical evidence for this has been offered by Hareven,[7] who observes of the New England community she studied:

> Decisions were not made exclusively on the basis of individual preferences; they depended rather on the choices and needs of the family as a collective unit, and on available institutional supports. (981, p. 167)

I have pointed to historical developments which influenced the early labour-market histories of the women studied, and have attempted to uncover some of their impact by comparison of the cohorts. Changes in patterns of education, child-bearing and employment opportunities, combined with shifts in the normative expectations about the role of married women, account for some of the differences revealed.

Two changes which typically occur at a given point in the life course, and which play an important role in structuring women's experiences at that point – in midlife – have been highlighted here: the maturity and departure of children and the decline and death of older kin. These changes affect intergenerational relationships in a number of ways, and, in so doing, restructure activities, such as paid employment and friendships, which appear only indirectly concerned. The way they are managed or coped with has important implications for how individuals will experience old age. In attempting to understand how such changes, and the events and experiences which precede them, may influence women's passage through midlife, the chapter has sought to indicate some ways in which study of the life course may yield new insights and paint a more complex, but less fragmented, picture of women's lives.

NOTES

The research for this paper was conducted at University College, Swansea, and funded by a grant to Professor C. C. Harris from the Economic and Social Research Council. I would like to thank Professor Harris for his advice, encouragement and many helpful suggestions throughout the project; Griselda Leaver, who conducted some of the interviews and is assisting with the data analysis; and all those informants who gave so generously of their time.

1. The sample was drawn from GPs' age/sex registers. Women born in selected years were chosen at random and screened for family and occupational circumstances. Only married or cohabiting women with children in appropriate age-groups, and with husbands in, or formerly in, manual occupations, were then selected for interview. The study contained both employed and non-employed women living in two localities – a traditional, 'tight-knit' working-class area, and a post-1945 housing estate.

    Data were collected using semi-structured, tape-recorded interviews with both spouses, and a diary was kept by the wife. The first interview was with the wife (alone if possible), and the second was either joint or with the husband alone, or with each spouse in turn (as was convenient to respondents). Interviews typically lasted between one and a half to two hours.

2. Cf. Tilly and Scott (1978), who offer historical evidence from different periods concerning patterns of women's employment over the life cycle.

3. The latter practice became illegal under the Sex Discrimination Act (1975). Coussins (1976) reports several cases brought to industrial tribunals under the Act; some respondents in the present study reported dismissal on marriage as a common practice in their youth.

4. Names used are not real names.

5. This point is discussed in more detail in a paper prepared for the ESRC Research on Ageing Workshop, September 1986 (Yeandle and Leaver, 1986).

6. See, for example, Finch and Groves (1983); Briggs and Oliver (1985).

7. Hareven (1982) suggests that the pattern of life transitions is now 'more orderly and compressed' (p. 167). While this may be so, relative to the late nineteenth century, increased longevity, rising rates of divorce and re-marriage, and the rapid economic and social change of the current period, indicate scope for more variable arrangements and responses.

Part III

The Displacement of the Structural to the Personal

10 Women's Three Working Lives and Trade-Union Participation[1]

Sheila Cunnison

INTRODUCTION

Over the past twenty years, as the old male-dominated heavy industries have declined, so women's employment in the service sector has increased. Their membership in the trade unions has grown even faster; but their participation, always very low, has changed little. Unions, which subscribe to democratic values, are somewhat embarrassed by this (Fryer *et al.*, 1974; 1978; Harrison, 1969). Considerable effort has been made to encourage women to participate. Union literature and education programmes have been designed specially for women. Women's advisory committees have been set up and a modicum of positive discrimination has been introduced. Yet, as paid officials and lay officers, men continue to dominate at local and at national level.

I argue here that the lesser participation of women must be understood in terms of the different positions which they hold, as compared with men, in the two major systems by which our society is organised: the system of production which organises the creation of goods and services with wage labour, and that of reproduction, which organises the maintenance and renewal of the labour force itself with unpaid labour. I suggest further that women's active involvement in unions varies with the cycle of procreation and marriage through which they move in the course of a working life. Their working lives tend to conform to a pattern of three fairly distinct phases and it is during the third phase that they are most likely to become active trade unionists. But increasingly, and in certain 'professional' jobs, activity can be expected during the first phase.

I begin by discussing how women's position in the two systems constrains their will and ability to participate in the union movement. But my main focus is on the way that men within the unions draw on the powerful ideology surrounding women's life cycle to maintain their position of male dominance. I show how men select and stress the second phase of women's life cycle – woman as dependent wife and mother of small children – fixing this phase into a stereotype which is then applied to all working women. I note briefly some of the challenges made by women to male control at a local level and comment on current changes in the position of women in the unions.

The subject of women's involvement in trade-union organisation is complex. It straddles the disparate institutions of family and paid work; it deals with atypical behaviour. And it covers an area marked by change: broad changes in industrial structure, change in the position of women in the labour market and family structure; changes under the influence of the feminist movement; and reactive changes on the part of the unions to the expanded service sector and the influx of women workers. Since 1980 there has been the crisis of increasing unemployment, the threat to the public services and the government attacks on the trade unions themselves. These factors may have raised women's consciousness and engendered in them a new readiness to question capitalist, male-dominated ideology and to participate more actively in the union movement.

The arguments I set out about the relevance of women's life cycle to their position in the union movement are exemplified by data referring to relationships at a local level, in a particular context and at a particular time. Observations were made at workplaces and union branches in an industrial city. Interviews were carried out with women activists and with men (paid officials, lay officers and activists.[2] Data were collected mainly from two groups: manual public and health service workers; and school teachers. Space allows me to consider only the former. The main unions referred to are NUPE (National Union of Public Employees), GMWU (General and Municipal Workers Union), and COHSE (Confederation of Health Service Workers). These data are of special relevance to an understanding of the position of women in trade unions: the service sector is the main growth area in the economy, particularly for women; the public service unions have been becoming increasingly 'feminised' and have a growing financial interest in their female membership. The timing is significant. Fieldwork coincided with the Winter of Discontent (1979), the year when public sector strikes contributed to the defeat of the Labour government and the beginning of Thatcherite attacks upon the unions which, by 1986, had emasculated the traditional male union strongholds, notably the miners, thus underlining the tendency of the unions to pay greater attention to women.

WOMEN'S THREE WORKING LIVES

As a result of their different position in relation to production and reproduction, women have interests, objectives and priorities in paid work which differ both in emphasis and, to some extent, in content from those of men (Young, 1984). The trade-union movement, since its inception a male-dominated institution, has developed goals, strategies, priorities and procedures relating to men's working lives, largely ignoring, until recently, the specific needs and objectives of women.

However, it is necessary to consider not only how women's and men's labour is structured by the family and the capitalist organisation of production, but also how their lives are ideologically incorporated into these institutions: to think in terms of culture as well as structure. We live in a society with an over-arching capitalist culture, encompassing values both of competitive striving, relating mainly to paid employment and to men, and of non-judgmental acceptance relating mainly to the family and to women. The competing ideologies within this culture are selected and used by people to interpret their lives, to explain and justify their experience.

The family is an arena of unpaid work performed by women, as a social duty, in service of the physically dependent and able-bodied men. Ideologically it is ruled by values of care, nurture and romance. However, most women of working age are also involved, if intermittently, with paid employment, many in client-oriented services, especially in caring work. Men's working lives, in contrast, focus largely on the single dimension of paid work. Their main role in the family, providing financial support, relates directly to paid employment. However, most families find a man's wages insufficient; hence, most women, in addition to unpaid housework, take paid employment.

Women in full-time employment earn on average only two-thirds of what men earn, barely enough to support themselves, let alone dependants. In part-time work they must inevitably be partially dependent upon men. Consequently women generally think of men, as men do of themselves, as family breadwinners. This has had far-reaching effects on gender segregation within the labour market, on the notion of a family wage for men and of dependency for women.

Trade unions are reactive institutions which have grown up in an industrialised society to defend men's jobs and their interests as members of the working class. Women came into trade unionism later than men. They were deliberately excluded by the first men's craft unions (Cockburn, 1983; Taylor, 1983). In the 1870s women began to organise their own unions, under the Women's Trade Union League. At the turn of the century semi-skilled and unskilled women began to join with men in general and industrial unions. But it was not until the 1950s and 1960s, as health and local government workers became organised, that women began to join unions in large numbers (Bain, 1970).

The first of women's working lives lasts from school till marriage. In it young women in paid jobs appear to be preoccupied with an idealised future as married women and mothers and with practical saving towards that goal (Pollert, 1981). Their attitudes differ from those of young men. They tend to ignore future employment prospects while men look ahead and calculate the effects of present actions on future possibilities. This first working life is experienced by women within the dominant male-framed ideology which identifies them primarily as wives and mothers, the 'romantic family mode'.

The second life which begins after settling down with a partner and the birth of children is dominated by childcare and housework. The ideological framework remains firmly domestic, but shifts from the 'romantic family' mode into the 'caring' or 'nurturing' mode. Most women leave full-time employment, returning usually to part-time work when the children go to school (Hakim, 1979). During this phase domestic demands are heaviest; the need for money is greatest, but women's participation in employment is lowest, hence they are at their most dependent. This is a major paradox in women's second working life (Cunnison, 1983).

Women's third working life begins when children leave home or are considered to be adult. Their second lives may have shattered romantic illusions about motherhood, housework and life on a single wage. Their third lives gives them time to take stock – of themselves and their position in life. Though most still work part-time, many now have a greater interest in work itself. More find time to become active in their union.

Not all women conform to this pattern: some remain single, some childless, some become single parents. In these cases and when divorce and widowhood are not followed by remarriage, a stronger work identity and a raised union consciousness may result (Cunnison, 1980; 1983; 1986; Elliot, 1984).

It is noteworthy that the majority of the women activists interviewed in this study were primary rather than secondary earners within their families (mainly due to sickness or the low wages of their spouses), and, of the secondary earners, the majority had at some time, through divorce or widowhood, been the primary earners.

Fractured Identities and Conflicting Priorities

The meaning or sense of identity which attaches to women's working lives is fractured and contradictory. It is located in three basic areas: in the family, and in their own and their husbands' paid employment (Cunnison, 1983; Porter, 1978). A married women often has two employment identities: a direct one of her own and a vicarious one deriving from her man. Because men are the major source of income, her vicarious employment identity is often more closely linked to the family identity than is her own employment identity. Her three identities are not alternatives, but exist in uneasy cohabitation.

Her family identity is perhaps the strongest, most firmly endorsed by society, pervading the work situation (Pollert, 1981), exemplified by sayings such as 'women's place is in the home'. It predominates in the first working life. Her vicarious employment identity comes into play in the second. Only in the third is the direct identity of paid employee likely to predominate. At any time, however, in the event of industrial dispute, the direct identity of paid worker may suddenly overwhelm the others. But the strength and persistence of the family identity, particularly in its romantic aspect, must not be underestimated. Women of any age, as my data have shown, may throw up employment or union careers for love and marriage.

Men find their main identity in their own work, not that of their wives. In spite of unemployment, men's working lives are far more often marked by continuity than are women's and they often develop a strong job identity.

Union Participation and Women's Three Lives

Women's unpaid domestic labour imposes material constraints on their participation in unions; the fracture of their identities creates ideological constraints (cf. Charles, 1983). Both kinds of constraints are likely to be lessened in their third working lives.

Throughout their working lives women have a more tenuous relationship with employment than men. In their first working life some young women do see the relevance of unions, but they tend to encounter difficulties not faced by men. For instance, young women expecting to marry and leave work may be reluctant to use union educational facilities, feeling they may never be able to repay the union in any way. Older women, too, often still regard themselves as temporary (Pollert, 1981), and their impending 'retirement' may deflect them from involvement in the union. Union officials realise the fragility which this brings to women's links with the movement, yet many seem to criticise or despair rather than to give support.

In their second working lives, demands on women are heaviest and there is little time for union activity. Many regard it as yet a third job to add to those they already have. Moreover, union meetings tend to be held at times (evenings) and in places (pubs) inconvenient or unacceptable to many women.

In the third phase more women do become more active: the proportion of women shop stewards over forty reflects this (Coote and Kellner, 1980; Horton, 1986; Martin and Roberts, 1984; Stageman, 1980). Among two health service branches I found that over 90 per cent of the women stewards, but only 30 per cent of the men, were over forty.[3] All the branch officers except one were men over 50. Older women activists report getting more satisfaction from union work than from housework, but they still find themselves inhibited both by domestic demands and by lack of experience. Men do not suffer from such difficulties.

It may seem 'natural' therefore that men should be in control, that they become stewards, officers and officials by default. But this is not the whole story. Men have used their past dominance within the union to further their own interests: this is clearly reflected in the gross inequity between women's and men's pay levels. The exclusion of women from 'men's' jobs and the use of male definitions of skill in context of collective bargaining have contributed importantly to this differential. Maintenance of male pay levels goes hand-in-hand with maintenance of male control. Women may not have come into the unions with the same enthusiasm as men. But, until recently, they have been systematically, though not necessarily always consciously, subordinated by men. A major process in this subordination has been the use of phase two of women's life cycle to typify the working

life of all women. The ease with which men have been able to fix this
stereotype is in part a consequence of women's fractured and shifting
identity.

UNION MEN, UNEQUAL PAY AND THE FAMILY WAGE

The assumption that this stereotype is a reflection of reality acts as an
unwritten justification for men's pursuit of the family wage (Land,
1980). I look now at male attitudes to women's pay, at the
dependency inherent in the second working life and at the
consequences on women's participation in the unions.

Attitudes to Women's Pay

Unions are supposed to be sex-blind. They exist to protect and
improve the pay and conditions of their members. In the UK,
women comprise over 90 per cent of low-paid workers, yet few of the
paid officials contacted in 1978 were working specially to improve
women's pay. Of eleven paid officials three volunteered that they
were against equal pay: they believed men to be better workers, so
that equal pay would lose women jobs. Three were against positive
discrimination, regarding women as 'privileged' already, because,
for example, they could take time off unpaid to look after sick
children. A fourth thought the abolition, in his union, of reserved
seats for women (as a result of the Sex Discrimination Act he
claimed) to be fair. The official from NUPE, which, since 1975, had
applied positive discrimination, was an exception.

   The branch secretaries were even less interested in women's pay
than the paid officials. Only one out of eleven showed concern. An
unemployed husband of a sheltered-housing warden, he had experienced life on a woman's wage. The views of the majority are
represented in the following quotations:

> Basically women are not for equal pay. They look at their wage
> differently from a man. They depend on a man. Women who are low-
> paid are mostly married women and so that out of all women said to be
> low-paid, only 3 per cent [a figure he had taken from the newspapers]
> are actually on low wages.

and:

> A man sees himself as low-paid if he earns less than the average wage.
> A man discounts his wife's wage in this. But a woman will count a
> man's.

The officer who said this claimed that at a branch meeting several
years earlier the women had actually voted against equal pay.

Shifting and fractured identities lead women to hold contradictory
views about equal pay, often lending support to men's claim for a
higher wage. Two dinner ladies were discussing equal pay. One said,
'I think that if men and women do the same job, they should be paid
the same.' She paused, then continued, 'But, if you think about it, a
man should get more because he's got a wife and family to keep.
When you married him, your husband agreed to look after you,
didn't he? You expect that, don't you?' 'But do you? Nowadays?'
asked her friend.

The conflation between a 'man's' wage and masculinity also leads
women to support higher wages for men. Women and men both feel
that women should not earn more than their husbands. Women who
do earn more often hide the fact. A woman with a disabled husband
put her earnings straight into the bank: they lived off his pension. 'I
like to live off his money. He has to feel that he is supporting us. If he
didn't he'd feel, how shall I put it, less of a man.'

Economic Dependency, Family Wage and Breadwinner

Implicit in these views is an image of women in their second working
life, an image consonant with the stereotypical view articulated by
several men that 'woman's place is in the home'. This was partly a
personal proscription: 'My wife has never gone out to work. It would
have hurt my pride and I am a proud man.' It was also a rule, ideally,
for all women. The men assumed that most women saw things the
way they did. 'The working class is very conservative and moral about
the performance of home duties,' as one explained it. But the men
recognised that not all women agreed. They disapproved strongly of
those who did not, expressing particular dislike of any connection
with the Women's Movement which one described as 'a threat to
family life'.

The union men recognised that not all women were dependent, but
included 'she who works for herself, she who supplements a wage for
necessities, she who goes out to work for luxuries'. Nevertheless the
image to which they continually returned was the latter: 'she who
works for luxuries', 'for bingo', 'for stockings', 'for cars' or 'to go on

foreign holidays'. They rarely drew attention to women's contribution to family income. The idea of women working for extras or pin-money assorted better with their strategies for keeping up their own earnings.

The men resented women spending money on themselves, 'on pleasuring, on fags and on booze'. Women's earnings, men seemed to think, should be devoted to the family. They conveniently forgot that even low-paid men customarily retain pocket money for their exclusive personal use (Pahl, 1983; Whitehead, 1984).

Dependency, Control and the Consequences for Women's Union Involvement

There is a conflict between the image of dependent, home-oriented women and the fact of women wanting to establish themselves, their views, and their rights within union organisation. Dependency implies control, and the men appeared to want to control women, to tell them what to do rather than allow them independence of expression within the union.

Men's need to control women was seen in the way they talked about them: 'Women are used to being dominated by men. They rely on them. They like them to lead.' Or, in response to my request to contact women shop stewards, 'Our ladies don't like to talk. They are very hesitant in coming forward. You have to lead them. But,' he added, 'they wouldn't like me to say that.' Or a shop steward announcing a strike: 'I don't expect you will stay away unless your husbands make you; but if you do you will have the full support of the union.'

According to the men, women's economic dependency meant that they lacked serious commitment to work. Their opinions, therefore, were not to be taken seriously. They were also considered to be 'lax' and not to 'pull their weight' in the union. 'They've got no idea. They don't understand how things are done.' All these things justified to men their habit of ignoring women's views.

Women are thus deemed incompetent, irrelevant and hence ineligible for union activity. Three local women reported that men had deliberately prevented them from becoming shop stewards, claiming, falsely, that union rules prohibited this. One of these women was trying to break men's control over wage negotiations in a mainly female factory; another, a cleaner, was challenging male caretakers' control over her job. In one branch the men nearly persuaded their secretary that women could be excluded from the Annual General Meeting. A full-time official disabused him.

More than one union official expressed dismay at holding meetings with large numbers of women. 'Have you ever been to a mass meeting of 700 women?' one asked me. 'It's terrible. By hell they take some getting through to. I had to take seven votes one meeting. I'd just get counted and someone would say, "I didn't hear what you said", and I'd have to start again.' Women's difficulty in following union procedure troubled the men; but they also feared that women might act against male interests. Underlying this was a fear of women who act outside the stereotypical role assigned to them, the dependent and home-oriented wife and mother.

Officials, paid as well as unpaid, expressed uneasiness about women in positions of power or authority. One complained about women officials: 'You can't let your hair down with women. With men you can joke, swear and bugger around and it doesn't affect your professional relationship, but not with women.' Another claimed to be 'frightened' by the aggression and bad language of two women stewards. He believed women should stay 'feminine' even if they entered the public sphere which was properly men's space. His difficulties with these women stewards, he confided to me, lay in their femininity and not in his masculinity: he could, he explained, 'drop his trousers with the best of them'. Again there is the conflation of sexuality, this time with union roles. A branch officer expressed his fear that the new dominance of women would lead to impotence among men.

PHASE TWO OF THE LIFE CYCLE AND THE 1979 STRIKE

I have shown how the stereotype of women's second working life influences men's attitudes, justifies their control over women and in some instances excludes women from union participation. This stereotype can also be used to mobilise women in industrial action in support of men's levels of pay rather than their own. This happened in the 1979 (Winter of Discontent) strike by public service workers against the government-imposed 5 per cent pay limit (Cunnison, 1983).

The strike was national, but action varied over the country. Locally, it was limited to health workers. Four unions were involved; NUPE and COHSE were the most important locally.

Women were crucial to the strike: they constituted the mass of the workforce and they staffed two of the three hospital departments (the laundry and central sterile supply) whose operation was essential to maintenance of the service. Yet the strike was run by men and for men. Only two of the twenty-four-strong strike committee were women. They were aware that they were engaged in a strike for men: 'We are fighting for the male staff, for men who are trying to raise a family. It is hard to start up a home now.' The speaker saw most women as working for 'pin money', but she worried about older women who might suddenly have to support themselves. Three female colleagues had recently been widowed. She asked the married women to think about this. She herself was supporting a sick husband and several children.

The union case, argued in public and private, revolved around the family wage. Men spoke about difficulties in raising families and in paying rent and mortgage. I heard only one woman on a public platform put the case for low-paid women.

Many women thought hospital workers should not strike. In one hospital where the majority objected, a union meeting was held. The women claimed satisfaction with their £40 a week; their husbands worked; more pay would mean more tax. To persuade them to strike, the union leaders asked the women; first, to put themselves in the place of a man in the hospital service with a family to support and, second, to imagine themselves married to hospital workers. Would they be so satisfied then? The women considered and then agreed to strike. They were, said one of the men, 'very unselfish'.

To resolve the dispute a comparability study on health workers' pay was set up. An interim award of one pound a week was made to full-time workers. Part-time workers (that is, women) were to receive nothing. At a meeting held to consider this proposal a ward housekeeper suddenly became aware that this settlement discriminated against women. She spoke in protest. Women had carried the strike, women were the lowest paid, but women were to get nothing. Applause followed, but no further support. Incensed, she wrote to the General Secretary. The letter she received in reply did not comment on the discrimination claim.

CHALLENGING MALE CONTROL

Women could and did challenge male control, in workplace and in branch, but their struggles were protracted and often failed. For example, the part-time women mentioned earlier took between one and three years to become shop stewards. Women in the branches outnumbered men, but numbers were not enough. Women activists, coming late to an interest in unionism, often lacked both experience and confidence in themselves and ordinary women members often lacked trust in them. Structural factors were important. The interests of women and men might be in direct conflict: for example, low-paid women would benefit more from a flat-rate, and higher-paid men from a percentage, increase. If women forced through a flat-rate increase, men stood to lose materially. In one instance, men faced with just this prospect used their experience and knowledge of union rules and procedures to outwit their challengers and hoodwink the female membership as a whole.

Union policy and the attitudes of local officials also played a part. Their consciousness raised by the Winter of Discontent, some of the women attempted to leave their old branches and set up new ones specifically for their own jobs (cleaning and catering). Those who belonged to the GMWU failed. They got agreement but, they felt, not the wholehearted support of their officials. Those who belonged to NUPE were strongly supported by their local officials and succeeded. Structural factors played a role: in the GMWU branch cleaners were organised with caretakers who had a material interest in cleaners' jobs, and the caretakers ran the branch; the old NUPE branch had a much larger spread of jobs and the male officers had no material interest in the work of the women.

CHANGE WITHIN THE UNIONS

It seems that women in the trade-union movement are undergoing a fairly profound change in consciousness – namely, beginning to think of themselves as workers who deserve a just reward for their labour. They are also becoming more aware of the material contributions made to society in the form of unpaid housework and caring work. This change in consciousness must be set in context of a movement in society towards equality with men, a movement fuelled by the feminist movement and formally expressed in legislation on equal pay, sex discrimination and abortion. Nothing like equality has yet been achieved. The gains already made are not irreversible; women are now coming under threat from government policies, expenditure cuts, privatisation and community care policies.

Nevertheless things are stirring. Within the unions this is apparent from the increased contributions by women at national conferences. For example, two days spent at the 1979 NUPE Conference showed participation by women to be minimal: twenty-eight men but only two women proposed motions. During two days at the 1985 Conference five women proposed motions compared with twenty-three men. Only six women spoke from floor in 1979, thirty-six spoke in 1985; the younger women were the more articulate.

The question arises, How far can women change within a society whose basic structure and culture appear to be more or less static? Their working lives appear to be changing very little. Despite the increase in single-parent families, in divorce and remarriage, and in the number of women primary earners, there is no evidence of basic change in respect of responsibilities for housework or for the care of children, the old and the sick. There is no evidence of a shift away from the values of romantic love, family life, home-centred leisure and all the cultural paraphernalia which support the stereotype of the dependent wife and mother.

I have argued in this chapter that men tend to perceive and relate to working women in terms of this stereotype which is drawn from the second of their working lives. The stereotype is used to bolster men's claims for higher earnings (the family wage), to control women and smother views which conflict with men's interests. Evidence in support of this argument has been produced from a study of relations, at local level, between women and men in unions catering for manual public service workers. Men not only feel that the differential between the earnings and those of women is under threat. They also resent the inclusion on the union agenda of items such as childcare, abortion, reproductive health at work, close to the interests of working women but outside traditional union concerns.

In order to make their voices heard, women have to struggle against rank-and-file men and male shop stewards. Latterly, the union movement has begun to support them in this struggle, realising it is against their interests to alienate a large and increasingly vocal section of their membership.[4] Support is strongest at national level. NUPE is one example of a growing number of unions taking this line. With an early programme of positive discrimination it is in the forefront of unions encouraging women's participation.[5] In 1979 the fifth largest in the country, it has also changed from being a predominantly male to a 66 per cent female union. It has changed also from being a union predominantly of labourers to one of carers.

It is the only really large union within which women form a majority. It is thus by definition a union of low-paid workers, a large percentage of whom work part-time. Ever since the Low Pay Report of 1967 publicised the extent of low pay and its association with women's work, NUPE has waged a campaign against low pay, a campaign in which the unfair treatment of women has increasingly been recognised.[6]

NUPE has also recognised that the growth and, more particularly, the power of the union – in the sense of the ability to carry its members into industrial action – depends, in the words of one official, on 'creating conditions where women can identify with the union', on developing 'a whole new philosophy', a way of thinking which no longer reflects 'the opinions of the full-time man'. This means having women in positions of authority and influence, as full-time officials and as shop stewards with a brief to go out and organise. But the question remains, how far change can go within the present structures of society.

NOTES

1. My thanks to the SSRC who financed the research and to Tanya Baker for contributions throughout its preparation.
2. The workplaces were a school kitchen and a comprehensive school; activists interviewed were shop stewards from health (10), local government (8), factories (7).
3. At the NUPE health branch an average of approximately 1 in 180 women and 1 in 28 men attended meetings, over a 22-month period.
4. 1986–7 has brought new directions in union thinking which, if implemented, must involve women workers more. Edmonds of GMBATU (General, Municipal, Boilermakers and Allied Trades Union), Chairman of the TUC, has stressed the importance to the union movement of women, the community, the unemployed and popular culture (*Guardian*, 26 May 1986); the TGWU (Transport and General Workers Union) is leading a campaign to recruit part-time temporary workers (*New Statesman*, 16 January 1987).
5. In 1975, NUPE reserved six seats for women on the national executive committee. In 1985 more women on the Executive occupied non-reserved than reserved seats. There are eleven women out of twenty-six members.
6. NUPE was the first union (1985) to frame a minimum wage in terms of an hourly rather than a weekly rate.

11 Transitions: Changing Work, Leisure and Health Experiences among Mothers with Young Children
Erica Wimbush

THE TRANSITIONS OF MOTHERHOOD

Accepting long-term responsibility for the care and welfare of a child within the household is one of the definitions of parenthood and one which has repercussions for the lifestyle of parents. Gender marks a fundamental divide in the experience of parenthood and its encumbent transitions for men and women into their roles as mothers and fathers. While sex determines the physiological roles played, gender defines the uneven division of responsibilities for childcare and distribution of resources within families, both between the parents and between the generations.

As a consequence of the social allocation of unpaid caring responsibilities to women in the sexual division of labour, becoming a parent marks a point in the life cycle where gender inequalities become more deep-rooted, or perhaps only more transparent. Becoming a mother is a point in a woman's life cycle which marks major transitions. As well as adjusting to a general change in lifestyle, becoming a parent, for women, also often means adjusting to changes in employment opportunities, social status and identity, workload, social networks and access to personal resources (for example, money, clothing, food). The extent of the changes will differ between women, as will the way in which they are understood and coped with. Most important, the meanings, values and circumstances of motherhood vary with social class and ethnic background. But within these parameters, age and marital status also affect the experience of having children to look after.

The coincidence of parental responsibility for childcare with the woman's part in childbirth has brought a tendency to 'naturalise' the social transitions that women experience in becoming a mother. Having to make sacrifices and stay at home more, are viewed as 'natural' aspects of this part of women's lives. This naturalisation of changes obscures the material and ideological forces which shape them and make gender the central relation structuring the experience of parenthood and 'family life'.

In this chapter I will argue that, for women, the transitions around motherhood are also characterised by the diminution of personal time and space available. Women's recreational participation is often dropped or becomes increasingly intermittent as domestic responsibilities increase and their leisure becomes co-opted by the family. Their 'choice' and control over personal time become limited both ideologically and materially.

While the socially isolated and stressful working conditions that many mothers experience have been shown to have ill consequences for the mental health of women in families, there has been little consideration given to the health implications of their lack of time for themselves and their restricted access to social opportunities outside the home and family. In this chapter I will argue that having time for yourself and, in particular, getting out of the house and meeting other adults, also plays an important role in the health and well-being of mothers with young children.

THE STUDY

The material used in this chapter is drawn from a two-year research study of mothers with pre-school children living in Edinburgh (Wimbush, 1986a). The aim of the study was to evaluate the importance and meanings that mothers attach to their leisure opportunities in daily life and the ways in which these feature in their general health and well-being. As well as seeking to identify the constraints upon leisure for mothers, the aim was to assess the various resources and support systems that contribute to making accessible leisure and social opportunities outside the home. The multiple transitions that women experienced in becoming mothers emerged as an important theme during the research process.

In researching leisure in the lives of women in terms that are meaningful to the women themselves, the way in which leisure is conceptualised and the methodology adopted to research it underwent critical review. The dichotomous conceptualisation of leisure as separate from, and opposite to, paid work was clearly inadequate in relation to women, among others, for whom full-time employment outside the home is not the norm and for whom the relations between paid employment, unpaid work and non-work are shifting and where the boundaries are becoming blurred. Thus, we were concerned to explore the times and spaces that women found or carved out for themselves within their working lives as well as those areas of leisure that were distinctly separate from their work. The aim of the research was not merely to describe activities in women's daily lives that were recreational, but to identify the processes which shape these opportunities and define leisure options as well as women's scope for autonomy.

The study comprised two surveys of mothers with children under five years old. The Phase I survey involved in-depth interviews with seventy women. In these interviews we explored the outlets that mothers had in their daily lives for things that they regarded as important to their well-being. For the purposes of quota sampling, respondents were selected from different household circumstances (one- and two-parent), class backgrounds (working class and middle class) and areas of the city (suburban and city centre). Twenty-one of these mothers were employed.

The Phase 2 survey was questionnaire-based and involved interviews with 115 mothers who participated regularly in some form of non-employment activity outside the home and family for their own interest or enjoyment. Among this sample, leisure included not only the mainstream forms of recreation and sport, but also forms of voluntary work, community and political activities, adult education classes and informal discussion groups.

TRANSITIONS IN WORK

The early years of motherhood are a stage in women's lives characterised by major transitions in their employment profiles. The majority of women withdraw from the labour force just before their first baby is born and when they return it is often on a part-time basis. According to a national survey of women's employment in 1980, only 27 per cent of women with pre-school-age children were employed, compared with 84 per cent of those without children and 52 per cent of those with children under sixteen years. Among working mothers with pre-school children, there were three times as many with part-time jobs as full-time jobs. Downward occupational mobility was also strongly associated with returning to part-time work after childbirth (Martin and Roberts, 1984).

So, as well as moving out of the labour market, albeit temporarily, becoming a mother is also characterised by a change in status within the work force. The employment of married women has grown in the post-war period and is an expansion geared to providing a cheap and flexible source of labour in response to changing market demands (Beechey, 1978; Coyle, 1984). For the most part these jobs are confined to low-paid and unskilled work and to a narrow range of occupations and industries. But for women with families, these jobs are taken on in addition to, rather than instead of, unpaid domestic and caring work within the home. Working mothers thus take on a dual work role.

On the domestic front, the transition to motherhood marks a dramatic increase in workload. Being a mother entails more than taking primary responsibility for the care and welfare of children. Mothers also take on the major responsibilities for family health, and caring roles often extend to include her partner and other dependent family members. The housekeeping duties of housework, home-making and the management of time, territory and resources within the home are also incorporated in mothers' domestic workload. As several feminist writers have observed, it is very difficult to differentiate the housewife role from that of child-rearing (De-lamont, 1980; Oakley, 1974). Ideologically, the roles are merged. Accordingly, Seiter (1986) has argued that the stereotype of the good mother is a distortion, because:

> it defines the practice of mothering in terms of characteristics which are not essential to the care of children but which are essential to a social order in which women serve men, care for their material needs . . . as well as their emotional ones. Many features of the good mother stereotype (such as, chastity, self-sacrifice, cleanliness, obedience) are in fact characteristics of the good wife in traditional marriage, where the wife has very little social power. (Seiter, 1986, p. 67)

The ideological implications of being a 'good mother' and putting 'family' welfare first have important repercussions for the changing nature of leisure for women in motherhood, as well as for the wider gender inequalities in the allocation of resources within the house-hold.

CHANGING EXPERIENCES OF RECREATION AND LEISURE

There is consensus within the sociology of leisure that 'women experience inequalities in gaining access to leisure "space" and activities' (Deem, 1982, p. 27) although considerable variation is found between social classes. From the few studies of women's leisure that exist, it can be ascertained that those with responsibility for young children are among those for whom recreational participation is most constrained (Deem, 1982; Green, Hebron and Woodward, 1986).

The division of leisure within households between parents reflects the divisions of labour between them. As with employment, fathers more often maintain their outside recreations and social life, whereas mothers have to reconcile any personal interests or outside activities with domestic responsibilities. Where outside activities were retained by mothers our study showed that it was more often in the form of a part-time job. Having a job could more easily be justified in terms of its contribution to family welfare, and thus childcare could be delegated legitimately. Personal recreations independent of the home and children were more difficult for mothers to justify or to fit in with timetables; for the most part these had been jettisoned. Their social lives had also diminished – they went out less and stayed at home more.

The main reasons given for these changes in access to personal time and outside activities were having responsibilities for children and the shortage of 'spare' cash for personal use as household resources became stretched. The expectations of others, and themselves, about what they could and could not do as mothers also constrained their leisure options. These material and ideological limitations meant that the women's experience of leisure in motherhood had become complexly interwoven with their working lives and the everyday texture of family life.

As such, mothers defined in recreational terms times or situations that were not necessarily free from commitment nor ones that implied 'not working'. For the Phase 1 mothers, more than half of all the opportunities described as recreational in some way were either related to work settings (for example, having a laugh with workmates) or mixed with domestic servicing work and childcare (for example, reading the kids a story, family outings).

Most of the mothers, however, found some time or space for

themselves in their daily lives that was unrelated to work/family obligations. When interpreted as 'time for yourself', personal leisure was assessed by the mothers in Phase 1 as one of the most important elements for their well-being, although it was something often in short supply and available only intermittently. Two-fifths of the mothers interviewed had not experienced any time to themselves over the few weeks prior to the interview.

Having time for yourself was widely associated with 'family-free' moments. When children were asleep, out at nursery or preoccupied, mothers felt that they had more autonomy, or choice, over what they could do since they were less likely to be disturbed by the demands of children. Some mothers fiercely guarded these moments as valuable opportunities to relax, put their feet up, read a book or watch television. Others would make use of the time to catch up with domestic chores in relative peace. For nearly half of the married mothers, 'time for yourself' was also associated with their husbands being out, whether at work, our for recreation or taking the children out. Indeed, married mothers found that they would welcome their husbands being out: his absence enhanced her opportunities for leisure.

The presence of the family, particularly in the context of the home, defined the limits of personal leisure for mothers. Thus, within the home leisure was largely enjoyed alone. This was often a considered choice made by mothers whose working day is characterised by constant activity and the noise and demands of young children and housework. With the most commonly cited ill-health symptom being tiredness and lack of energy, any opportunities for peace and quiet and relaxation were highly valued.

Outside of the home, personal leisure was most commonly defined in terms of being able to get out of the house, have a break away from the kids and have contact and companionship with other adults. These meanings derive from their contrast with the solitary nature of the working day for most mothers where children provided their main company. Like most workers, they wanted a break from their workplace and its contingent routines, demands, pressures and worries. Having children and becoming more housebound increased the importance attached to outside involvements and social contacts. For example, this mother who lived alone in a small flat with her child described the changed significance of outings away from home:

> The thing that hits you first – as someone else pointed out, another girl
> who has a baby – your trip to the corner shop becomes a highlight. It's

a big event. Before I thought nothing of going to a shop. And if somebody says 'hello' to you, you note it. A small thing becomes a big thing because you're living in a small isolated world where you're no longer going to work each day, you're no longer taking these things for granted. When I go out I usually have a good time whereas before I'd sit and be bored. You appreciate going out. Sitting on a bus on my own is great! These things must seem ridiculous.

Evenings out with friends were highly valued but only irregularly enjoyed. In daily life, regular outlets included the contacts made through employment, via children's activities or through their own recreations (Phase 2 sample). Of the forty-eight Phase 2 mothers who were continuing pre-motherhood recreations, two-thirds said that their reasons for participation had changed since having children. For these mainly middle-class women, the emphasis was now on their need for an involvement, interest and identity separate from their home and family.

AUTONOMY, CONTROL AND CHOICE OVER PERSONAL TIME

The stereotype of the housewife/mother is often portrayed as a 'powerful' and 'autonomous' figure who, as 'mistress of the household', exercises control over its timetable, space and resources as well as over its members. But women's control over, and responsibility for, domestic order is equivocal in its consequences (Martin, 1984). Female domestic control contains the paradox that it is often at the cost of the woman's own personal time, space and resources.

In the study reported here, for example, for married women in households with low incomes, and particularly where the woman had no wage of her own, an important component in making ends meet was being able to exert control over the husband's personal spending. Thus, this married working-class respondent spoke of her efforts to curb her husband's recreational spending and his 'right' to go out when he wanted:

He can be quite selfish. If we've got no money and he wants to go out with his pals and that, he'll make a big fuss. He's worse than the bairns. He wants to go out at weekends and we've got no money... I watch the money.

For this control to be effective, the woman is obliged to curtail her own spending and leisure. Graham (1984) also referred to the way in which mothers sacrificed their own consumption in order to fulfil their role as carers within the family:

> As the carer, she acts as a buffer, protecting the welfare of her family by absorbing shortages herself. By cutting back on her own consumption, she is able to release additional resources for her husband and children. By reducing her needs for food and leisure, for example, a mother can provide a better diet and more attention for her children. (Graham, 1984, p. 62)

The social priority attached to male needs in the distribution of resources within families is underpinned by the principle of 'self-sacrifice'. This lies at the core of the ideology of the 'good mother'. Inequalities in the distribution of resources are thus often instigated by the mother and regarded as a matter of 'choice'.

The pervasive image of the 'good mother' who devotes her personal time, energy and resources to attending to the needs and welfare of her children, husband and home, was a strong force in shaping respondents' priorities and their (lack of) entitlement to personal leisure. Where mothers prioritised their own needs for personal time and space and adjusted household timetables and resources to facilitate this, they emphasised the need for 'self-motivation' in order to make the effort to secure and organise them. The need for self-motivation was at a premium not only because mothers were often tired, but also because they faced resistance from others in the family. Motivation was often fuelled by the importance to their sense of well-being which they attached to having some personal leisure, as this working-class mother explained:

> My husband gets annoyed about me being involved in these things. He thinks I've got enough to do with the family and should stay in more. He gets annoyed at answering phone calls for me about my groups and moans a lot about my activities. My brother too, he gets really annoyed if he rings and I'm out – he thinks I should be content with the house and family like his wife is. But I stick to it because I know that without it I would be very unhappy.

Although there were exceptions, self-motivation was an attribute associated with the educational/occupational background of the middle-class women and their greater concern to maintain individual identity. Lone mothers also expressed a greater sense of self-orientation in their management of time and money compared with their married counterparts.

The significance of male partners in delimiting the timetables and norms which mothers were obliged to adopt was indicated by a number of differences in the experiences of mothers in one- and two-parent households. For example, lone mothers had a much more 'relaxed' attitude to getting housework done (or not). Married women more often felt obliged to be constantly 'on the go', and felt guilty about relaxing unless this was combined with doing something productive, such as knitting, sewing or ironing. The following quotes from two married mothers illustrate this:

> When [the husband's] here, he's the sort of person that I feel I shouldn't be sitting down. I should be ironing, making a cup of tea, doing the washing, doing [the child's] hair – so I keep busy.

> It's purely the idea of sitting and relaxing watching television – knitting's just another dimension. It means I'm not sitting doing absolutely nothing. I feel quite justified in sitting down if I'm knitting. So if anyone comes in and asks 'What are you doing?', 'Oh, I'm knitting'.

In contrast with the single mothers, the forms of home-based leisure that the married mothers described were more frequently allied to their work. In comparison with their married lives, separated mothers who were now living alone with their children were apt to regard their present circumstances, however poor, as entailing greater independence with regard to their social lives and greater control over their finances.

Caring roles are defined as a family obligation for which mothers are primarily responsible. For mothers, any personal time away from the home and family is dependent on the availability of alternative childcare. Married mothers in particular are expected to be able to cope on their own or with the occasional back-up support of other family members, primarily their husbands and mothers. Thus, who babysitters are, when and how often they are used, were not decisions left to the mothers' own choice. Babysitter options were therefore circumscribed by a range of other considerations – most important, the availability and proximity of husbands and mothers (in-law). They provided the mainstay of support as regular babysitters to facilitate the mothers' outside activities, whether employment or recreation. However, husbands and mothers (in-law) were also the main source of resistance or disapproval experienced by the recreationally active mothers.

In addition to not wanting to 'palm off' their responsibilities on others outside of their own families, the mothers did not wish to feel obliged to them and so were reluctant to ask them to babysit. If the favour could not be reciprocated (which was often the case), this would place them in an invidious position and could mean that they were more accountable to the babysitter in some way (for example, having to justify their absence from home). This could compromise the woman's autonomy. Rather than expose themselves to the accountability or reciprocity associated with 'feeling obliged', many mothers 'chose' to minimise their requests for babysitters.

Due to these informal social controls, the minority of mothers with independent recreational lives were liable to feel guilty. Their guilt was not only fuelled by other people's attitudes about how mothers should behave, but also by popular beliefs or 'myths' which label such women as 'selfish', 'neglectful', 'irresponsible', 'immoral', etc. For example, Dixey and Talbot (1982) gave an account of the myths of family neglect and squandering the housekeeping money that surround women bingo-players. Ideas about 'maternal deprivation' are still apparent in relation to the social and recreational activities of mothers, even if images of 'latchkey children' are being gradually eroded in relation to working mothers.

Control over personal time is not only limited for mothers through the ideology of the 'good mother'. The material and political realities of resource distribution also limit women's control and autonomy as carers of children.

Publicly provided childcare for under-fives was, in general, highly valued and in great demand by mothers, but of limited availability. Times when children were attending nursery school offered mothers some personal time in the day, but this time was more often used for doing household chores. Where creches were provided alongside recreational activities and classes, the take-up of these services was mediated by cost and location as well as the 'acceptability' of the service provided.

Money and transport are important facilitators of recreational participation but are resources to which women in families have limited access. Of the seventy mothers interviewed in Phase 1, twenty-nine had household incomes at or below poverty level (140 per cent Supplementary Benefit level) and nearly two-thirds of these were one-parent families. The majority of these mothers either did not drive or did not have access to a car. Lack of money and restricted mobility (walking and buses were the main forms of travel) were major constraints on recreational and social activities that were not free, low-cost or local. Since having children, reduced finances were regarded by mothers from all groups as an important reason for their recreational and social patterns having changed. It is therefore significant that the Phase 2 sample of recreationally active mothers showed much higher levels of household and personal income as well as a higher level of personal access to a car. Less than half walked or used buses as the regular mode of travel to their recreations.

So, for the majority of mothers with young children, their everyday recreational outlets were free, cheap and within the local area, such as informal visiting to/by nearby friends and family, and combined with domestic roles (for example, shopping, tupperware parties) and children's and family activities (for example, going swimming with the kids, family outings). However, the geography of current provision for recreational and social amenities is increasingly moving towards centralised services in the forms of shopping centres, leisure centres, sports centres, etc., which are accessible primarily to those with cars. This trend away from dispersed local provisions has particular implications for children and their carers, who are heavily dependent on quick and easy access to facilities in their neighbour-hoods. Public transport systems are also designed primarily for journeys to and within city centres rather than geared towards the local journeys that mothers make to shops, schools, nurseries, etc. A common complaint from mothers with young children who travel by bus is about the physical difficulty of manoeuvering on and off buses with children and buggies, a situation made worse without the services of bus conductors. This was seen as another factor influencing the 'choice' of mothers to walk to most places.

Women's mobility after dark is also restricted by their fear of sexual harassment or violence (Green, Hebron, Woodward, 1985). Parents' constant concern for the safety of their daughters in public places (Rapoport and Rapoport, 1975) also indicates some of the real factors that limit the choice that women have in recreational and social life.

IMPLICATIONS FOR WOMEN'S HEALTH

The sexual division of labour within the job market and the family underpin many of the sociological explanations of the health inequalities between men and women in families. The overall conclusion from all the studies carried out to assess general health and well-being is that women in families have poorer psychological health than men. For example, recent surveys of mothers have reported the widespread experience of tiredness, loneliness and depression among those who care for young children (Richman, 1976; Graham and McKee, 1980). As the primary carers, mothers are known to be vulnerable to mental strain, a common side-effect of caring (Bayley, 1973; Equal Opportunities Commission, 1982).

Factors seen as contributing to the higher levels of ill-health symptoms among housewives/mothers have included their social isolation, the lack of alternative sources of gratification outside the family, and the low-status, unskilled and monotonous nature of housework (Grove and Tudor, 1973). A lack of supportive relationships brought about through social isolation is another factor identified as important in the aetiology of depression (Brown and Harris, 1978). The role of mothers in the health care of others also impinges on their own health, by limiting both their access to material resources necessary for health (Graham, 1984) and their ability to take time off when ill themselves. For example, in this study few mothers expected the time and care which they gave to others when ill to be reciprocated. Lone mothers in particular felt obliged to remain healthy since they had less immediate access to support, unless they lived with their own parents.

But the health of mothers is not only penalised by their inability to take 'time off' when ill. As the carers, their general health and well-being is also influenced by the quality and quantity of personal time and space available for their own leisure. For example, Sharpe suggested the significance of personal leisure for the health of mothers, when she wrote:

> Caring has many rewards but it can also be overwhelming and intermittently depressing as their [children's] constant demands leave women no time to themselves, no time to think, no time to give expression to their own individuality. (Sharpe, 1976)

Some understanding of the relationship between the access of mothers to personal leisure and their general health can be gained from the research reported here by examining the health scores of the two samples. The Phase 1 sample of seventy mothers showed a generally low level of recreational participation outside the home and family, whereas the Phase 2 sample comprised mothers who managed to keep up regular participation in outside recreations of their own. The analysis of the data on health collected is limited, however, by the relatively small samples of the two surveys and the variations in the sample structure and survey seasons.

A symptom-based health questionnaire was used in both surveys. This lists eighteen symptoms and respondents were asked to report whether, in the last few weeks, they had been bothered by any of them. They then assigned a score to each symptom according to intensity using a 4-point scale (0 = not at all; 1 = a little; 2 = quite a lot; 3 = a great deal). The sum of the scores for each symptom provided each respondent with an overall health score. The lower the health score, the fewer the symptoms and therefore the better the health.

Comparing the health scores for the two samples, a striking feature was the much higher level of health scores (i.e. poorer health) shown for the Phase 1 sample of mothers. The average health score for this sample was 10.6, in contrast with the Phase 2 sample who altogether had a low average health score of 4.6. This difference in the overall level of health scores for the two samples of mothers could be indicative of ill-health reducing the likelihood of regular recreational participation, so that only mothers in good health would have been included in the Phase 2 survey. It could also indicate that regular recreational participation outside the home and away from the family is beneficial for the health of mothers with young children.

However, the health benefits appeared to be less for those with more extensive responsibilities or commitments, whether in their job (i.e. mothers with full-time jobs), or at home (i.e. mothers with more than two pre-school children), or in their outside recreations (i.e. mothers who spent more than seven hours a week on these activities).

These findings lend support to those of Arber, Gilbert and Dale (1985) who recently examined the relationship between paid employment and women's health, using data from the 1975 and 1976 General Household Survey. They concluded that, for mothers under 40 who work full-time, there was evidence to suggest the detrimental health effects, or strain, of occupying multiple roles. The mothers under 40 who had part-time jobs, however, showed better health but similar levels of illness as non-employed mothers.

In our Edinburgh study, role strain was manifest mainly in the problems that the Phase 2 recreationally active mothers encountered in coping with the often complicated arrangements involved in organising their outside-home activities with domestic commitments. Difficulties were centred primarily around the arduous task of making babysitter arrangements. But role strain was also apparent in the mothers' frequent need to reconcile conflicts between the demands of children, the employment hours and commitments of husbands, as well as themselves, and other social and recreational commitments. Although partners provided the main source of regular childcare to facilitate the woman's outside recreations, the responsibility for making the arrangements and preparations before-hand remained in the mothers' hands.

Among the recreationally active mothers, the benefits of outside participation were seen most clearly for the one-third of the sample who stated that they found 'no problems' in maintaining these outside activities. None of these mothers had full-time jobs and nearly half attended activities where childcare was provided. The implications for health of such absence of problems or strains were indicated in the lower symptom levels (average health score 2.4) among this sub-group.

CONCLUSIONS

In this chapter, I have looked at three broad areas of transition that are associated with the experience of becoming a mother. There are powerful material and ideological factors which shape the transitions that mothers experience in work, leisure and health, and circumscribe the options available. I have sought to highlight both the similarities and the variations in women's experiences of motherhood and their scope for autonomy and control over time and space for their own leisure.

Just as the 'liberating' effects of the expanded employment opportunities for women have brought greater benefits and continuities for middle-class mothers, social class and employment status also play an important part in women's access to, and attitudes towards, independent leisure.

Employment provided the major arena in which the women had established, and some maintained, regular independent roles, contacts and identities outside domesticity and motherhood. Personal leisure away from the home and family was less often a feature in the lives of mothers. Yet, having 'time for yourself' was regarded by mothers in both surveys as an important aspect of their well-being and was facilitated by the absence of children and male partners. For the majority of the mothers interviewed, leisure had become assimilated within the complex pattern of childcare, domestic tasks and paid work. Their own jobs and own leisure had to be fitted around the timetables and demands of children, husbands and home. For those mothers who managed to maintain regular outside recreations, the potential health benefits of these additional roles were mediated by 'role strain' among those with extensive commitments.

12 The Resumption of Employment after Childbirth: a Turning-Point within a Life-Course Perspective

Julia Brannen

This chapter is about the resumption of employment following childbirth and its implications for the lives of women in Britain who follow this currently deviant course of action. My aim is to locate the decision to resume employment after childbirth in the context of the careers or trajectories which constitute a woman's life course. By drawing upon a life-course perspective (Hareven, 1978; Elder, 1975, 1978a, 1978b) I hope to illuminate the question whether such an employment decision signifies a new departure in women's lives.

A LIFE-COURSE PERSPECTIVE

A life-course perspective is to be distinguished from the notion of family life cycle in which 'family' is commonly used as a shorthand for household and 'cycle' is given a number of stages. The emphasis of the family life-cycle approach tends, moreover, to be on the stages of *parenthood* and pays little regard to the many other roles which actors play and the way these change and affect the household over time. By contrast the notion of life course is more individual in its emphasis and, as Morgan (1985) puts it, 'more appreciative of difference and variation and ... concerned with linking historical time with individual biography as with tracing individual progressions through particular typified stages' (Morgan, 1985, p. 178).

Elder (1978a) develops the notion of life course beyond a single path to encompass multiple interdependent pathways, an approach which he also suggests is most pertinent to the study of complex societies. He notes that the theoretical language of sociology has little to offer in temporal formulations beyond the concept of career. Careers refer to sequences of activities on particular roles, and each career line is equivalent to an individual life history in each role domain. Entry into particular careers is marked by transitions. As Morgan remarks, the key-word 'transition' has much more 'dynamic and purposive connotations' than the earlier 'stage of the family life cycle' (1985, p. 178). Though transitions 'happen' to individuals, individuals also construct them. At the same time they are shaped and influenced by wider historical, ideological and structural forces. In effect the notions of career and transition allow for both sides of dialectical social processes.

A transition tends to be associated either with an addition of a particular career (for example, getting married), or with the loss of a career, as in retirement. Often there are both losses and gains involved. Moreover, transitions do not always occur singly. Elder (1978a) addresses himself to the phenomenon of concurrent and overlapping transitions.

In this chapter I am concerned with a group of women who had recently undergone the major transition of becoming a mother for the first time. This event marks the beginning of their reproductive careers. Unlike the majority of women in Britain who reach this transition point, motherhood does not terminate their employment careers except for a few months of maternity leave. The resumption of their employment careers, therefore, cannot be seen as a transition in the same sense as becoming a mother. It is not a gain but a continuation. However, these women resume paid work under a new set of conditions. Though in the employment world a woman may be treated no differently on her return to work, none the less the new responsibilities of motherhood may have some effects on several aspects of her life – for example, her employment orientations and behaviour, and her marriage. Likewise her continuing employment career may have some effects upon her life as a mother, wife and consumer.

The application of a life-course perspective to this group and in general has several advantages. First, it facilitates the dissection and portrayal of contingent career lines which women and other household members have to synchronise and manage. In households where both parents are employed full-time, issues to do with time-scheduling and resource management are likely to be central. The differentiated careers in the life course imply differentiated social worlds which compete for women's scarce resources – time, energy, affection. Women develop strategies in order to manage these finite resources and the inherent strains and stresses. Second, a life-course perspective provides a historical emphasis which may be particularly helpful in showing us the interplay between home and work and between public and private spheres (Morgan, 1985, p. 179). Third, the temporal concerns of the life-course perspective are particularly relevant to longitudinal research.

THE EMPLOYMENT OF MOTHERS OF YOUNG CHILDREN IN BRITAIN

Since the war there has been little increase in the proportion of mothers of young children in employment in Britain. In 1982, 21 per cent of women with a child under two were employed, a very low figure compared with the USA and many other European countries (Moss, 1986). But some changes are taking place in the British pattern. Women are increasingly returning to work *between* births and are returning *earlier* after each birth (Martin and Roberts, 1984). None the less the situation has not changed dramatically since the introduction of legislation in 1975 giving women the right to reinstatement in their jobs and a maximum period of maternity leave (largely unpaid) of 29 weeks. The conditions of eligibility are of course stringent (two years with the same employer prior to childbirth). This, together with the very limited childcare facilities for young children and the requirement that women resume their jobs on a full-time basis, has contributed to a situation whereby only about 5 per cent of women in Britain giving birth return under the statutory provisions (Daniel, 1980). These, then, are the formal conditions under which women in the study resumed work after childbirth.

THE STUDY

The chapter draws upon some interim findings of an empirical study of the experiences of two groups of women: 188 women who, following childbirth, intended to resume their full-time jobs, and 60 women who intended to stay at home with their children. The study is longitudinal and follows the women and their children from four to five months after the birth until the children are three years old. The women and children were seen at four separate age points of the children. Of the women resuming employment, 97 per cent were covered by the maternity rights legislation. In addition to expressing a firm intention to return full-time for at least six months, and to the job held before childbirth, these women were selected according to a number of other criteria. They included: having a first child; being born in Britain; being in a two-parent household at the start of the study; and intending to have the baby cared for by a child-minder, relative or nursery.

Because we attempted to balance high- and low-status groups, women's occupations were not randomly selected and did not exactly replicate the distribution in the general population of women in the labour market six months after childbirth (see Daniel, 1980). Manual workers were greatly under-represented. For much of the analysis we have divided women into two groups: those in high-status jobs (Registrar General Social Classes I and II) and those in low-status jobs (Social Class III non-manual and below). Almost a quarter of the women were teachers, with a further third split between nursing, medical and social service occupations (13 per cent) and 'other intermediate non-manual occupations' (for example, librarians). Of the remainder, 36 per cent worked in clerical or sales jobs and only 11 per cent in skilled or semi-skilled manual work.

The consequences of resuming employment after childbirth for women's subsequent employment careers was a central empirical question which the study sought to address. A concern with the significance of *continuity* for women's employment therefore became a key issue. There is a growing body of evidence documenting the psychological, social and material losses women incur when they leave employment to have children. For example, on the material side, motherhood asks a high price of women over their lifetimes: a 40 per cent chance of downward occupational mobility (Martin and Roberts, 1984), and lost earnings which, largely because most women return to part-time work, on average amount to *twice* as many years as are sacrificed in labour market membership (Joshi, 1985).

Looked at in these terms, continuity of employment around childbirth *appears*, on the surface at least, to herald a major change in women's employment careers if not in other spheres. But how long these women will remain in full-time employment is open to question. Although the time span of the research is only three years and the project is incomplete, there are some indications of the patterns and meanings of women's involvement following their return to work after the birth of their first child.

WOMEN'S CAREERS

The life course of women comprises several careers, including production (paid and unpaid work and caring), consumption and reproduction. These careers not only interact one with another, they also intersect with the careers of other people, especially partners in the household. Careers must therefore be examined in relation to one another in order to elucidate their influence on women's decisions to resume work after childbirth. These decisions and careers also continue to shape women's experiences after their return to work and influence whether or not they remain in the labour market.

The decision to resume work occurs in the context of a major social transition in women's lives – the occasion of becoming a mother. Going back to work at this point contravenes the normative British assumption that motherhood automatically entails withdrawal from the labour market. Nor surprisingly, around the time of the birth, women portrayed their decisions to return as individualistic and uncertain. None the less these decisions are made in the biographical and temporal context of their other careers (not only motherhood) and those of the fathers of their children.

I now focus on women's employment careers and show how, over the course of the return to work, they are influenced by other careers – women's careers as mothers, the consumption careers of the household, and the careers of fathers – thereby suggesting some of the ways in which structural factors mediate individuals' lives. In reality all these careers overlap and interrelate. None the less the attempt to tease them out analytically may enable us to see some of the ways in which individuals negotiate and construct pathways through their lives. It may also provide a means of integrating the actions of individuals in the household (traditionally depicted and studied under the rubric of 'family life' (Bernardes, 1986)) with other areas of social experience and, in this instance, employment.

EMPLOYMENT CAREERS

Because of its longitudinal design this study has been able to cover key phases in women's employment careers around childbirth. First we explored (in this case retrospectively) women's employment behaviour and orientations *prior* to pregnancy. Next we examined women's employment intentions and reasons given for resuming work *in* pregnancy and during the maternity leave period. Finally we examined women's employment behaviour and orientations some months *after* their return to work.

Before the Return

Women in high-status jobs had given birth at an older age than women in low-status jobs (on average aged 30 years rather than 26). (Moreover our main study group did not appear to differ in age from the smaller group of women not returning to work.) However, because of their greater opportunities for further education and training, women in high-status jobs had spent similar lengths of time in the labour market (on average between nine and ten years) as those in low-status jobs.

There was more of a trend in the main study group for those in high-status jobs to be married to men in low-status jobs (in this case, manual workers) (15 per cent of marriages) than for the converse situation – that is, for women in low-status jobs to be married to husbands in high-status jobs (8 per cent). However, the majority of couples were not 'cross-class' families (McCrae, 1986) but were married to or living with partners on the same side of the occupational divide.

Whilst on maternity leave, women were questioned about their motives for deciding to remain in the labour market. Women very much saw the decision as theirs alone. Even where they felt heavily constrained to return they talked about working as women's 'choice'. By contrast, women who gave up work at childbirth did not see their actions as constituting decisions at all. They simply took it for granted that this was the normal and acceptable thing to do. Financial and housing reasons for resuming work predominated, but with women in low-status jobs more likely to give these as main reasons (73 per cent versus 44 per cent). None the less, taking all the factors mentioned by women, around two-thirds of both groups mentioned material considerations (72 per cent in the low-status group and 63 per cent in the high-status group). In fact the average net household income of dual-earner households was 44 per cent more when the woman returned to full-time employment.

In attempting to make sense of the material factors which impinge on women's decisions to continue in their occupational careers, we have considered the meanings they attributed to their own and their husbands' jobs and earnings. On the whole women put the major emphasis on the *consumption* career of the household and in particular on the importance of adequate housing on the arrival of children – the characteristically British desire for a house and garden of one's own. Eighty-six per cent of the couples were buying their homes and two-thirds of the women said that their earnings contributed towards housing costs. However, despite this fact, they appear to have viewed their earnings as a short- rather than long-term commitment even though they had already, in many cases, been contributing for some years. They regarded their continuing to work as fulfilling immediate or middle-term goals – often as meeting particular items of expenditure – housing improvements for example, or as a means of 'helping out' in current financial crises (often related to being on maternity leave without pay), or as stopgaps until their partners were able to earn more. As a careers officer said:

> In the short term finances are the most important reason. But I think even if we had the money I would like to go back. But then again if we had the money in the bank I might not be thinking about going back to work and having all these other justifications.

Although in some cases husbands emerged as having been highly instrumental in influencing their wives' decisions to return to work, women never gave this as a specific reason. Moreover, almost no one mentioned the risks of leaving the labour market during the economic recession and hence the difficulty of re-entry at a later date. No women referred to long-term gains in their earnings and promotion opportunities either to themselves as individuals or to the household. Few appeared to project their employment careers into the future in the way that men in 'careerist' types of occupations appear to do (Brown, 1986). No one mentioned the possibility of divorce or separation which might require women to become economically independent.

Women in high-status jobs were more likely to give expressive factors as their *main* reasons for resuming work (42 per cent versus 18 per cent). They talked about satisfaction derived from the nature of their employment and from their occupational identities. But a significant proportion emphasised their employment in the context of a negative experience of being at home on maternity leave. Some of the women in low-status jobs made similar points. A bank clerk explains:

The chance of buying the house gave me the idea of going back to work. But I've found since then that I do need the stimulation . . . I just didn't know what it would be like to be at home all day with the baby.

It is thus possible to see the ways in which aspects of other careers, both those of the women themselves and of their partners, influence their decisions to resume their employment careers. One concerns the household as a unit of consumption. The priority given to the short-term economic needs of the household at the transitional point of 'becoming a family' commonly legitimated women's return to work. Men's employment careers were also implicated. Even though women's attachment to the labour market in behavioural terms had been equivalent to their partners (before the return to work), women still tended to regard their partners' employment as salient to the household.

Women's decisions also took cognisance of their careers as mothers and normative constructions of full-time motherhood. Before the return to work over two-thirds of women felt anxiety and concern about 'leaving' their babies. 'At the moment I could easily cry about it. But I know it's because I don't want to leave her. I feel worse the nearer it gets'. This sort of anxiety had been fostered not only by the dominant ideology that mothers should be with their children, but also by the actual experience of having established the main relationship with their child, usually a very intense and exclusive one, in the first six months. A likely consequene of being the sole caregiver of a young baby is that women feel the separation to be a considerable wrench and especially so since they see themselves as the most important person in the child's life. Women therefore bore the emotional scars of this powerful ideology even if they did not explicitly subscribe to the belief. However, although the majority (73 per cent) felt considerable loss or guilt initially when they first left their children with the carers (and it was almost always mothers who took their children to carers), the majority 'got over' these feelings very quickly, which was a great and welcome surprise to them. None the less, despite their anxieties about leaving their children and a general lack of support for their decisions to return, either from society at large or from their own social networks, women had not idealised their experience of being at home on maternity leave. Women resuming work had significantly higher negative feelings about the experience of being full-time housewives than those who were not returning to work (55 per cent expressed high or moderate negative feelings in the returner group compared with 28 per cent in the non-returner group). Many said that they were only able to bear it because they knew it was 'temporary':

> I didn't really enjoy it. Although I didn't mind it so much because I *knew* I was going back to work. I knew it wasn't going to be forever. If it had stretched out for years into the future I think it would have been awful.

After the Return

We re-interviewed women about five months after their return to work when their children were ten to eleven months old. At this point 85 per cent had returned full-time with the remaining 15 per cent split between those who had given up and those who had gone part-time. Reasons for not returning full-time ranged from job-related difficulties, difficulties connected with children's carers, to health problems of the women and children. Women returned on average five months after the birth, that is two months before the end of statutory maternity leave, and largely because they couldn't manage any longer without pay.

Women's employment careers and their experiences of returning to the labour market are strongly affected not only by their other careers and those of partners but also by employers, bosses and work organisation. By and large almost all the returners received their statutory rights and were reinstated in roughly the same jobs held prior to pregnancy. When women returned to work, few obtained any concessions that made it easier to combine employment and motherhood, though this depended to some extent on the status and organisational context of their jobs. Opportunities to job-share, for example, were very rare, and likewise the chance to ease oneself gradually back into the job by working shorter or flexible hours at the start. But, on the whole, women appeared to have very low expectations of their employers and work colleagues concerning their response to their new status as working parents. More often than not the climate of the workplace appeared to be marked by indifference. Where work colleagues were understanding they were portrayed as paying 'lip service' to women's status rather than proffering practical assistance. In this context it is not surprising that women interpreted and reported the slightest positive comment as supportive and considerate. In some instances women experienced negative undercurrents concerning their performance at work which were no doubt based on the stereotype of working mothers as 'unreliable'. This led to many women feeling the need to constantly prove themselves and reinforced their belief that working mothers should not be treated as a 'special case'.[1]

After the return, women were again asked about the meaning and importance of paid work with respect to elucidating its relationship to other careers. Asked to estimate the relative importance of their jobs in relation to those of their partners, half said their jobs were less important and half said their jobs were equally or more important. Most women who gave priority to their partners' jobs implicitly referred to the needs of the household. Moreover, when asked why, women declared that the reasons were obvious – 'He earns more', or will do in the long run. Sometimes, however, they referred to the stereotypic view of men needing to be breadwinners. 'Men need to work more than women do.'

Those who rated their own jobs equally or more highly than their husbands' sometimes had difficulty in expressing a reason. Those who earned more than their husbands rarely mentioned this as a factor. Instead, women dwelt on the personal and expressive aspects of their work – the 'independence' and sense of purpose it gave them.

The most striking feature of women's definitions of their economic contribution to the household is the extent to which they played it down (Brannen and Moss, 1987). In the same way that women had described continuing in work as their decision or as women's 'choice', so too did they suggest, once back at work, that they might opt out of employment either from choice or necessity in the future. Thus even so rare a group of women as ours took for granted that the arrival of children might, sooner or later, entail a period of withdrawal from the labour market and the supercession of the dictates of their partners' employment careers and their own careers as full-time mothers. On this last point, before their return over half the women had said they wanted to work part-time and 17 per cent to give up altogether. Some women envisaged the birth of a second child as a critical change-point while a few regarded their children starting school as a time for giving up.

Once back at work women varied in their ambitions as to seeking promotion. Ambitions are likely to be affected by women's attachment to the motherhood career but also by the nature of their jobs and the opportunities open to them. In some cases ambitions were clearly affected by motherhood, whilst other women, especially those working in the public sector, were frequently disenchanted by low morale in the workplace. Some women talked about imposing a temporary break on their ambitions, described characteristically as 'treading water for a time'. This would provide them with a breathing space while they became skilled at managing the demands of babies, jobs and homes. Others saw the effect of the break as more permanent. Yet others said they had no wish to step onto the next rung of the career ladder which was frequently seen as involving more work and responsibility but at the expense of the satisfaction intrinsic to their main work tasks.

Just as many women saw their employment careers as less central to their households than those of their husbands if it came to the 'crunch' and one partner had to give up work, so too, in some cases, did they tend to view their earnings as marginal. Asked about the ways in which their earnings were important to their households, most said their money was vital and necessary to the provision of the household's basic needs. However, a significant proportion played down the real impact of their earnings, suggesting that they went on 'luxuries' and 'extras'. 'It's probably more like an extra – clothes and holidays and things over and above the basic weekly life.' Even in the face of the fact that, in response to specific questions, *all* the women said that some of their earnings contributed towards basic household expenditure, a quarter simultaneously maintained this contradictory stance – a rationale which might subsequently prove useful if they later decided to withdraw from work or lessen their working hours.

Women's attachment to the labour market shortly after their return to work is further elucidated if we consider the consumption career of the household and more especially ways in which the costs of the dual-earner lifestyle were met, *childcare* constituting one of the major expenses. Despite the fact that *both* parents were in full-time employment, childcare was seen as mainly women's financial responsibility, in the same way that the children were seen as the responsibility of mothers. A third of women were jointly responsible (because they shared joint bank accounts with their husbands) and a half solely responsible for meeting this cost which, on average, accounted for 24 per cent of women's earnings. In practice, since women collected the children from the carers women also took on the responsibility for actually handing over the money. But the great majority 'classed' childcare as coming out of their earnings. Moreover, women considered the financial aspects of the childcare issue in terms of whether or not it was 'worth their while' working:

Half of my money gets paid out on childcare and the cleaner. [Interviewer: 'Why?'] I think it's to do with the fact that I work that their cost is down to me. Because we've got a joint account, in theory it doesn't matter. But I class it as coming out of my money. [Interviewer: 'What about your husband?'] Yes, I suppose he does. Because he talks about 'As long as we're not spending more than half your salary it's probably worth it'.

Women engaged in a mental accounting procedure whereby they calculated how much they as workers could afford to pay for childcare, a responsibility which was a taken-for-granted feature of combining employment and motherhood careers. Childcare costs therefore constituted a charge on women's earnings rather than on household income, which had the effect, in real and definitional terms, of reducing the value of women's contribution to the household. Any implicit comparisons that were made about the relative value of the two incomes coming into the household were based on deducting the costs of mothers' employment but not fathers'.

Similarly some of the other costs of the dual-earner lifestyle were frequently met by women. Private transport was more common in the dual-earner than in the single-earner households and cars were often used by the women to take the children to the carers. The cost of a second car was often met by women. Moreover, in combining their careers as mothers and workers, women simply assumed that the child's routine had to be fitted around their working days and not those of the fathers. Three-quarters of the women were responsible for transporting their children to and from daycare.

The ability of dual-earner households to buy in extra goods and services could not solve all their problems. Indeed they often created new ones since their management required additional time, effort and responsibility. Not surprisingly, since women already bore the major brunt of responsibility for children and the housework, many preferred to do a lot of the tasks themselves (Brannen and Moss, in press). They made the childcare arrangements and liaised with the carers. More often than not they took time off when the children were ill or needed to go to the doctor. Some fathers were highly constrained by their work hours, especially those in manual occupations who had to clock in and out at set times and lost money if they were not there, whilst others, mostly in high-status occupations, made their jobs the excuse for not being able to pick up their children or to have time off. Moreover the legitimation of the fathers' excuses was reinforced by women's strong sense of responsibility for their children and their decisions to resume work.

IN CONCLUSION

Women in Britain are structurally and ideologically constrained to withdraw from the labour market when they give birth. These constraints are emphasised in the accounts of the 'deviant' few who resume full-time employment after childbirth. On the whole the women studied their careers as mothers and workers not by shedding or sharing tasks. Rather, they coped with both old and new responsibilities, juggling them simultaneously.

Women justified their decisions to stay in the labour market less in terms of the demands of their own careers as workers and more in terms of the consumption careers of the household. At the transition point of 'starting a family', priorities centred around the household unit and especially the immediate 'family' needs for a 'house of one's own'. Moreover, in the context of hostile attitudes towards the employment of mothers of young children, housing and finances were considered to be a socially acceptable legitimation for the separation of mother and child. Long-term and careerist views of future employment were remarkable by their absence. When women talked about the importance of their work – and most did – they dwelt on the day-to-day satisfactions of the job and being 'out at work' or 'out of the house'. Women's short-lived experience of being a full-time housewife whilst on maternity leave was one career which served to reinforce women's commitment to their employment careers.

Partners' employment careers – in particular their ability to 'provide' for the family – also shaped women's careers as mothers and workers. Although it was characteristically women married to men in manual jobs who held the traditional view of a man needing to be the breadwinner, many others prioritised their husbands' jobs because of their better earning prospects. Additionally most women felt that their own labour-market attachment might, at some point in the future if not in the present, become tenuous and conflict with their maternal responsibilities. For they were in no doubt that the overall and day-to-day responsibility for children rested with them. The persistence of the ideology and practice of women's responsibility for childcare and domestic work was also evident in the way they defined the costs of the dual-earner style – financial as well as practical and emotional – as largely falling to them, which in turn had the effect of marginalising their financial contribution to the household.

Our understanding of women's employment careers and their decisions to remain in the labour market after childbirth is enhanced by examining the additional careers which constitute the life course – motherhood, consumption and housework – though they also need to be studied in the context of the labour market and the workplace. The impact of partners' careers has also been touched upon. Not surprisingly, women appear to have taken for granted the fact that men's employment careers take precedence over their careers as fathers and houseworkers. All these careers meet at the same point when couples become parents for the first time. In so far as each careers is regarded as a full-time occupation they are likely to compete and conflict with one another. The traditional British solution after childbirth has been for women to leave their jobs and to become full-time housewives, and for men to invest the greater part of themselves in employment. When women combine mother-hood with full-time employment the old patterns of childcare and domestic responsibility are still in evidence and result in management and coping problems *for women* – typified in classical sociology as 'a conflict of roles'.

NOTES

The research project on which this chapter is based is funded by the Department of Health and Social Security. The project is being undertaken by a team of researchers at the Thomas Coram Research Unit. I am therefore indebted to the work and ideas of my colleagues.

1. I should like to pay particular thanks to Heidi Mirza for her work on the analysis of women's experiences in the workplace on their return to work.

13 Interrupted Lives: A Study of Women Returners

Elizabeth Bird and Jackie West

INTRODUCTION

This chapter looks at the life histories of approximately 100 women all of whom attended special courses for women seeking a return to paid employment during the period 1982 to 1984. Many recent studies have looked at women's life cycles and work histories. These include two large-scale surveys (Dex, 1984; Elias and Main, 1982) and two smaller regional studies (Chaney, 1981; Yeandle, 1984). Three of these studies have concentrated on classifying work histories and relating them to other factors. In contrast, our study, based in Bristol, looks at the specific problems that women have faced in actually trying to get back into paid employment.

The chapter first examines the evidence of surveys into women's working lives, noting how this national data contrasts with or confirms the patterns of work and non-work followed by the women in the Bristol study. The main part of the chapter focuses on how the experience of these women shows that marriage may be as significant as childbearing in determining 'career' paths, that divorce and separation have significant even spectacular impacts on women's relationship to the labour market, and that the question of whether women have or *do not have* children affects their employment.

EVIDENCE OF OTHER STUDIES

Prior to these studies it was assumed that women's working life cycles were characterised by full-time work on leaving school, a period out of the labour market while having children, then a 'return to work' upon completion of childbearing, usually part-time. Where labour-market activity is, however, tightly defined so as to include any participation including casual or part-time work, it has been found that this pattern is actually the exception rather than the rule. For example, the Women and Employment survey (WES) found that only a third of women with children conformed to this bi-modal pattern. It was more common for women to work *between* having their children, though such work was usually part-time or shift work so as to fit in with the demands of childcare (Dex, 1984, p. 15). Chaney (1981) and Yeandle (1984) found similar patterns, and the post-war period has undoubtedly seen a decline in this bi-modal pattern (Dex, 1984, p. 37). The women in our study, however, do appear to have followed the more traditional pattern, as we might expect, because they all were attending a course for women 'seeking a return to work'.

Since many studies of women's participation in the workforce assume that women will be different from men *because* they have children, they inevitably focus on domestic circumstances rather than wider economic forces. However the WES data show that childbearing and rearing do not adequately account for all variations in women's working patterns. Although time spent out of employment may be accounted for by domestic circumstances, to a considerable extent and in both the initial and final workphase, job-changing itself is work-related (Dex, 1984, pp. 22–3, 66). Dex (1984, pp. 24–6) also quantifies the negative effects of recession both on job prospects on leaving school and generally. Increased levels of unemployment, especially in women's labour markets, have countered the established trend of women returning to work earlier.

Economic forces also clearly constrain where and what kind of work women do. The influence of women's experience in the labour market is shown in WES data on the occupational profiles of women with children, that is those who are most likely to be affected by domestic rather than economic circumstances. Two groups of women, those who fitted the bi-modal pattern of first completing their family and then returning to work, and those who never returned to work (within the time-scale of the survey), were more likely to be clerical workers (37 per cent) than those who worked between having some or all of their children (25 per cent). Over half of this latter group were in semi-skilled or shop work (Dex, 1984, p. 43, table 22).

This pattern is reinforced by associations between women's patterns of returning and the socio-economic position of their husbands (Dex, 1984, p. 44). Those who worked between childbirths had higher proportions of skilled and semi-skilled, and fewer non-manual, husbands. This is a reflection of the economic and social circumstances of households rather than the domestic influence of husbands or marriage as such, and is supported by Yeandle's (1984) much smaller and regionally specific study. Her 'family completers' were mostly married and living with their first husbands who were in white-collar occupations and whose fairly high earnings enabled their wives to remain out of paid employment. By contrast, the women who returned to work between births, moving frequently in and out of the labour market, were mostly married to men in poorly paid or insecure occupations or to men who were just starting their careers (Yeandle, 1984, pp. 61–3). The women in the Bristol study, most of whom are 'completers', fit the former pattern of being supported by husbands in employment, many of them also falling into the clerical category.

For most women, however, economic and domestic factors are inextricably interrelated. Marriage itself plays an important part and this has often been understated by large-scale surveys. Certainly, and in contrast to what is believed to have been the case in the past, women do not now give up employment on marriage. Only a tiny minority of women in the WES sample left work on marriage, and half of this group was over 50 at the time of the interview. But changing jobs in the initial work phase was due in 10 per cent of cases to husbands' job move or moving for other reasons, and was often coincidntal with marriage (Dex, 1984, p. 23). This 'marriage effect' is particularly striking amongst the women in our study, as we shall explore later.

In the WES survey, moves on marriage in effect ended the initial work phase for some women. Dex (1984, pp. 42–3) found that those who left work for these 'marital' reasons were also more likely to return to work only after their family was completed, compared with those whose initial work phase ended with pregnancy. Marriage breakdown, and also the death of a child, often prompts an earlier return to work or increases women's participation from part-time to full-time. This appears to be both for economic reasons and to boost confidence and self-esteem (Dex, 1984, p. 39; Yeandle, 1984, p. 72). This is certainly confirmed by the experience of women in our study. We can also confirm Yeandle's (1984, pp. 82–6) and Chaney's (1981, *passim*) conclusions that there is no single one-dimensional effect of family crises. For some women they increase their attachment to work; for others, especially if accompanied by poor mental or physical health, they result in discontinuous employment and problems in finding and retaining jobs.

Perhaps the most striking of all conclusions reached by these studies is the extent, often dramatic, of downward occupational mobility on women's return to employment. The WES survey shows that the least occupational change is experienced by women who work for the longest continuous period, and are in higher-paid and higher-status occupations (Dex, 1984, pp. 46–8), and there is some suggestion that frequent moves in and out of employment can be associated with a small increase in skill levels (Chaney, 1981, p. 23). But all this is dwarfed by the huge scale on which women shift into semi-skilled distribution and service work as domestics and shop assistants. This work is typically part-time (especially so for those who have completed their families) (Dex, 1984, pp. 48–9). Yeandle's returners, in particular those who had returned relatively quickly to work, were predominantly in agricultural, domestic or catering work. Even family 'completers' who had been in clerical jobs now found themselves in sales, factory or other low-grade manual work. Most of Chaney's sample also mirrored the national picture and were working as domestics, cleaners or in food preparation. Elias and Main found part-time work was especially associated with downgrading for women returners. Amongst women employed part-time in 'other personal service' work, one in five had had a full-time job at higher status ten years earlier. Of part-time women workers with teaching qualifications, 4 per cent were in such service work, as were 8 per cent of part-timers with nursing qualifications, and 16 per cent of women part-timers with clerical or commercial qualifications (Elias and Main, 1982, pp. 82–3).

The nature and size of these occupational shifts are so substantial that they can only reflect the changing economic structure, in particular the decline in manufacture. But as Dex observes:

> a natural break in women's working activity over childbirth is coinciding with or being used to shift the women's workforce out of non-manual and skilled work into part-time semi-skilled work. (Dex, 1984, p. 48)

For women in non-manual work, especially professionals (including nurses), full-time work again becomes widespread as women grow older; in contrast, women employed as shop assistants, semi- and unskilled workers are as likely to be in part-time work during their final work phase as when they first returned. These sectors of employment rely almost totally on part-time women workers.

The decline in manufacturing industry and the growth of the public sector and the service sectors has influenced the kinds of work which working-class women are able to find. Chaney's study of Sunderland showed how working-class married women had to find work which fitted in with domestic commitments. Allied to their own lack of qualifications, this resulted in a heavy reliance on social networks for finding work which typically was poorly paid, part-time, and usually in food preparation or domestic work. The shift into unskilled service work and out of manufacturing industry for these women in the North East of England, particularly demonstrates the interconnections between the domestic situation of married unskilled women, and the national economy.

These recent studies have shifted ideas about women returners. In terms of policy there is also an assumption that professionally qualified women are returning to work quickly, thereby avoiding breaks in employment and consequent downward mobility, provided they can organise childcare and/or participate in part-time work. Retainer schemes such as those advocated by the Manpower Services Commission are seen as the most effective way of 'managing the career break' (MSC, 1981; Cooper, 1982; Povall and Hastings, 1983). Women also find they are obliged to take poorly paid part-time work because of childcare responsibilities (Freeman, 1982; Joshi, 1984). Policies to avoid this kind of downward mobility range from the provision of more and cheaper childcare, unionisation of part-time workers to raise wages and conditions in this sector, and general policies to regenerate the manufacturing sector of the economy. Thus childbearing rather than marriage is seen as the cause of breaks in employment and consequent downward mobility.

Our study of Bristol women returners leads us to question some of these assumptions, and suggests that additional policies and strategies may be needed to solve the kinds of problems faced by the women in our study.

THE BRISTOL STUDY

The 97 women in this study all attended courses designed for women who were either 'currently unemployed or redundant or actively seeking a return to work'.[1] A total of six courses were run during the period surveyed from 1982 to 1984, and data available included an initial application form (giving details of age, marital status, ages and numbers of children, qualifications held, and outline employment history); a detailed curriculum vitae for each woman (prepared as part of the course); and information on employment outcomes gathered six months after the end of the course. In addition, as part of writing this paper, a follow-up questionnaire was sent to all 97 participants in September 1985; this was returned by 42 women and many sent detailed letters. One of the authors of the research reported in this chapter was Course Director and acted as counsellor to the students; therefore a significant amount of the information given here comes from personal contact.

The sample is obviously not a representative one. As we would expect, it is composed predominantly of women aged 30 to 50; three-quarters have children under 16; most had not worked since having their children. One-quarter had no formal educational qualifications (this was particularly marked amongst the older women, with four out of the five aged over 50 having none). As compared with the general population, such women are still grossly under-represented, but this is not surprising given that choosing to join a course will imply a positive valuing of education. One-quarter were graduates or equivalent. This again is not surprising given that the course was run by the university. The proportion of divorced or separated women – one in four – is higher than for the general population, perhaps reflecting a higher motivation to work among such women, or to seek a course to help them back to work.

Excluding those who had only ever held temporary jobs, all previous occupations (based on the last employment prior to the course) were non-manual, but women's work in the white-collar category includes unskilled routine clerical work. Over one-quarter of our sample, and most of the women who had no educational qualifications, had done this sort of work before marriage. A further 10 per cent had been to secretarial college and worked as secretaries. Many of these women also had O-levels. The one-quarter of the group in 'professions' were almost exclusively in teaching and nursing. A further one-sixth had been in retail/services, mainly shop work but also including hairdressing and catering.

It is obvious from the occupational classifications that the range of jobs done by the women in this study is very different from those in the Yeandle or Chaney studies. The absence of women in manual occupations is not surprising given the low rates of participation in adult education by people in manual occupations. On the other hand, women's work *is* very concentrated into a few categories. The very high proportion of women in the broader category of office work (nearly 50 per cent) shows how clearly office work is women's work, as are teaching and nursing.

RETURNING TO WORK

The majority of the women in the Bristol study could be classified as family 'completers' in that they had finished having children before seeking a return to work. Several had worked prior to enrolling for the course, but the majority were seeking work for the first time after long periods out of the labour market, in some cases over twenty years. Thus here the 'bi-modal pattern' clearly predominated.

Our analysis revealed no association between level of educational qualification and the speed of return to the labour market. However, divorce, changes in marital status, and ages of children were equally significant in leading women to seek a return.[2] This finding relates to the second set of questions on the relative importance of domestic circumstances and economic factors. To examine this we need to follow the women back into the labour market.

Discussion so far has suggested that all the women studied did in fact return to work. Although our data is incomplete, 70 per cent either found work or re-training within six months of leaving the course, rising to 73 per cent after three years. Of these successful women, fourteen were on training courses and fifty-five in employment, most of which was part-time work. These figures for placements are very high in comparison with other courses for women returners, and some of the possible reasons for this are explored later.

Distressingly, a number of women who had achieved their aims within six months of leaving the course, found their successes to be short-lived:

> Soon after the course had ended I took a job as a sales representative, which enabled me to see most of England and Wales. A lot of driving but also a challenge which I am happy to say I was able to meet. One of the targets of the firm was five new accounts every three months. I obtained thirty-eight in six months. Unfortunately I was made redundant as the firm ran into financial problems. So, end of sales career.

> I changed direction completely (my reason for attending the course was because I wanted to), and took a job as a Rep... The change

proved to be most enjoyable and I achieved very good results. However, I left a couple of months ago to take a job which involved Admin/Secretarial and selling and ended up £300 down because the company went bust!

I was lucky enough to get a job before the course actually finished – working as a nurse/counsellor at a home for adolescent girls. I worked there – very happily – until the home closed down, and was then transferred to a 1 200 pupil school as a school nurse. I tolerated it for six weeks and then had to hand in my notice – I was expected to do far too much for my number of hours and I felt that I was not doing my job efficiently, and, in short, I was unhappy.

The effects of the recession can be clearly seen here. Another effect which became more marked as the courses proceeded was the increase in the number of women who decided to set up their own business or become self-employed; some of them were receiving the Enterprise Allowance.

However, even those women who had subsequently lost their jobs were not entirely defeated. Nearly all the women had used the course to formulate plans and to take steps to reorganise their lives so as to meet their own objectives, in most cases designed to fit in with their family responsibilities. For many this inevitably means part-time work, but the course had enabled women who had previously been trapped in the cycle of very low-paid, casual work to break out of it, either by re-training or by seeking and finding work which could lead to full-time employment.

The success of the women in finding work is of course related to the local economy. In Bristol, local manpower studies have identified a labour-market shortage of mature women with office skills; part-time office work is also well established and many companies have operated flexi-time schemes for several years, especially in offices. Moreover, during the period of this study there was an expansion in white-collar ofice work due to the relocation of many previously London-based insurance and financial companies. When the courses first started, women wishing to return to office work were disadvantaged because of their lack of knowledge of the new technology, but Bristol is well endowed with colleges and training agencies and between October 1982 and October 1985 at least sixteen agencies initiated training and updating in ofice skills. The majority of the women in the study either took up opportunities for re-training or benefited from the local economy by taking up part-time employment in office work. Despite public sector spending cuts, employment in the health services has also been relatively buoyant. However, in education, government cutbacks have coincided with an existing over-supply of qualified personnel. Indeed, the women who were least successful in gaining employment were those who had qualified as teachers. Their experiences need to be discussed in detail.

Twenty-five of the women had higher-education qualifications. It is believed that such women return to work earlier and are less likely to suffer downward mobility than the less qualified. However, although fifteen of our twenty-five had previously been teachers, none of them has been able to return to schoolteaching, other than on a supply or casual basis. Avon does not employ part-time teachers and there are few full-time vacancies. Two of the women live in Somerset where there are also no vacancies. One is teaching part-time for the WEA, the other works voluntarily for the Citizens Advice Bureau. Three have taken courses to extend their teaching qualifications and are hoping eventually to re-enter the profession. One, not wishing to return to primary teaching, has taken a TOPS course in typing and a training course for adult education tutors, and hopes to teach commercial subjects to adult students in Wiltshire. Three are still doing supply and casual work. (See also Trown and Needham, 1980.)

The remaining ten women with higher qualifications were no more successful. Five decided to try and gain *teaching* qualifications in order to find work which was congruent with their educational level (three were taking a diploma in adult education). Only one of the ten non-teaching graduates found a job which she enjoys – editing a magazine for a group of estate agents – and of all the women with higher qualifications only one has a job which uses her qualifications, and she had previously been a university lecturer and had worked almost continuously when her children were young. As many of these women are married to professional men whose careers have been unbroken, they are, not surprisingly, resentful of their interrupted lives.

The inability of teachers to return to teaching lies in the local economy, not their domestic circumstances. From our study, well-qualified women were the *most* disadvantaged in the local labour market. Women with secretarial or clerical skills easily found full- or part-time work at this level, and in this sense they had the least-interrupted lives and were the least downwardly mobile.

By contrast, many of the least-qualified women had taken jobs prior to coming on the course that were typical of the downward pattern. These included working in pubs, shops, agricultural work, and occasionally cleaning or domestic work. However, the decision to join the course marked a determination not to return to such work, and for the most part the course helped them to break that pattern. Reasons for undertaking such work in the past were not always financial: often they were linked to low self-esteem, or to the fact that such work was easy to get, secured by a neighbour or friend, and thus involved little effort and no risk of rejection. As with other surveys, such jobs were accepted because they fitted in with responsibilities for young children, and here women saw the growing independence of their children as freeing them to seek more fulfilling work.

THE MARRIAGE TRAP

It is a reflection of the restricted work opportunities for women returners that we view the avoidance of downward mobility as an achievement. There was very little acknowledgement among any of the women that they might be upwardly mobile by their own efforts rather than through marriage. The current view about the 'career' paths of qualified women is that *children* interrupt their upward climb, and schemes for professional women involve either retainers, or part-time work to accommodate childcare responsibilities. (Cooper, 1982; Povall and Hastings, 1983). But retainer schemes do nothing to alter the idea that it is women who have the domestic commitments. Evidence from the women here suggests that marriage may be at least as significant as having children, and that, even where there are no children, women are not necessarily able to pursue their upward careers in the single-minded way certain occupational structures demand. For many women in our study, husbands not children were the problem.

This emerges very clearly from the curricula vitae prepared as part of the course. At first, following the model of CVs produced by and for men, we tended to confine what was considered appropriate to paid-employment details. But in many cases there were shifts in working patterns which showed that women had moved from well-paid career-orientated work into temporary or less secure jobs, often less skilled, or below the level of their qualifications, and poorly paid. In some cases a 'good' job had been followed by no job at all. For the professional CV reader this kind of movement suggests incompetence, mental instability or misconduct, and the gap of 'nothing' suggests incarceration. None of these explanations fitted these women; all that had happened to them was that they had married, or, in some cases, expected to marry. If the women were not to be assumed to be criminals or lunatics their CV had to include details of their domestic circumstances, even though some women bitterly resented this.

Marriage or anticipated marriage can thus cause either a break in employment or a change to a lower-status job. What is also rarely discussed is that the decision to have or not to have children may not be so easy to plan. There were several cases of plans which did not quite work out as anticipated. Where women had to move because of their husband's job this was often seen as an appropriate moment to begin a family. However, sometimes children did not appear to order, and women found themselves unable to look for a new post because they were hoping to conceive but uncertain as to how long this would take. In the circumstances they either did not work, producing a gap in the CV, or took temporary posts at a lower salary. Some women who had stayed in work after marriage and then found it difficult to conceive, were advised by their doctors either to give up work, to step down to a less demanding post, or to work part-time. If they still failed to conceive, then adoption inevitably meant leaving work in order to be seen as a suitable parent.

Twenty-eight of the women studied were either divorced, widowed or separated at the time of starting the course. The effects of divorce or separation on women with dependent children are well researched. For many women in receipt of supplementary benefit there is little point in seeking paid or official employment, since they cannot earn enough in a full-time job to pay for childcare, or in a part-time job to leave them better off than they would be on supplementary benefit. Most of the single parents in our study were not in receipt of benefit as they received maintenance from their ex-husbands. They could, therefore, earn money without being penalised, although a significant increase in earnings could have resulted in their husbands returning to court to vary the maintenance. Such women were often anxious to find either work or training which would lead to a fairly well-paid job before their children were sixteen. At this point, or at the end of the children's full-time education, the house would be sold and their maintenance would end, leaving them facing poverty.

One of the most distressed and distressing groups of women were those whose marriage had ended relatively late in their lives. Some had been married for over twenty years, their children had left home, they had rarely worked in anything other than low-paid part-time jobs, and they were now faced with trying to find employment in their late forties or fifties. Divorced and separated women are those who are most urgently in need of employment, but social security and divorce settlements discourage them from seeking anything other than well-paid work, and here their age, their lack of training, and lack of confidence due to their experience of divorce, generally make it very hard for them to get such work.

Although it can be argued that those (sixty-seven) women who were still married were better off than the divorced or separated women, marriage had in some ways disadvantaged many of them in their attempts to find work. Some had had to move with their husbands, and give up 'good' jobs. Others had problems which stemmed from the actual marriage relationship. There were some women whose marriages were so unsatisfactory that they had already decided to separate before the course started. They were, therefore, seeking work in order to leave a marriage. Some women had openly obstructive husbands. One was so convinced that his wife would sleep with another man at the (all-female) residential weekend that she had to abandon the course. Another appeared at the course venue looking for his wife who had left him during the week because of his violence towards her. Another had stopped his wife working in the local garage, which she quite enjoyed, because he felt it unsuitable following his recent promotion.

Open and admitted obstruction of this kind was rare. Much more common was the attitude of many husbands that they had no objection to their wife getting a job as long as it did not affect them in any way – in other words, as long as they did not have to cook, clean, pick up children, or stay at home if the children were ill. During the course we explored how women might persuade their husbands to do more, and while some of them thought they might do more about the house, particularly in response to the fact that their wife was now earning money, the one thing that nearly everyone agreed their husbands would never do was to stay at home if the children were ill. Of course that was not true of all the married women, and on the whole the more qualified the women were the more their husbands were prepared to help. Such women also *expected* their husbands to share in the housework, once they were back at work, while women with few qualifications did not expect their husbands to change their ways. Although information about husbands' occupations was not collected, we have the impression that many of the 'unqualified' women were married to men who had done relatively well in their careers, leaving their wives to look after the home and children, but also 'providing' for them so that they did not feel they had to work out of economic necessity.

CONCLUSION

Our study raises several theoretical and methodological issues that need further comment. First, women's work histories have typically been surveyed either by sample interview/questionnaires carried out at one point in a woman's life, or by use of data collected in longitudinal studies. Women on our course found it very hard to recall exactly when they had been in or out of work, the type of work they had done, and how much they had been paid. They often overlooked work which had been casual or part-time. Moreover, their skills and competence had often been predominantly gained through work that does not count as such – the work of being a wife and mother, and voluntary work. Thus surveys which attempt to quantify the contribution of women's paid employment to the economy or the resources available in the form of women's skills, will grossly underestimate these if only formal employment and education/training are included.

Second, women's life (as distinct from work) histories present a number of contrasts to those of men. While men may increasingly be involved in 'helping' to bring up their children, the impact on their lives in no way compares with the impact on women's. This is even more the case with marriage. Nearly all the women in our study had been married, and their marital situation crucially influenced their movements in and out of work. This is an under-explored area, though it does not imply that marriage constitutes a career. Nor is 'marriage' necessarily the appropriate term, as many women were actually neither married nor single but somewhere between the two states. Whether this state was likely to change was again a crucial factor in determining the extent to which women had any real control over their future lives. Women's lives may be said to be dominated by two events – marriage and childbearing – but they do not and cannot ever bring these events under their control. This fact has an enormous effect on life cycles and the extent to which they are directed by individuals. If we contrast the effects of gender and class then we see that the attempt to control and predict the future, a strategy associated with the acquisition of educational or other marketable qualifications in some men's life cycles, cannot have the same result for women. Thus even those women who had followed an upwardly mobile route were ultimately frustrated by the effects of marriage and children.

Third, the most striking evidence from our study is the inability of the 'qualified' women to re-enter careers. Whatever may be the policy issues in relation to maximising national resources, it is clear that the impact of such unemployment on women's lives can be devastating.

Finally, the current argument over the extent to which new jobs have been created by the Thatcher government has often produced statements that, to the extent that such jobs are part-time and done by married women, they are not 'real' jobs. This debate raises conflicts for feminists. Where women's jobs are low-paid and highly exploitative then no one would wish to defend them. There should not, however, have to be a choice between lousy jobs which fit in with childcare, and staying at home and suffering the consequent loss of self-esteem, along with what was for many women the worst indignity, financial dependency. Most important of all, our experience shows that women returners need a boost in confidence and a positive self-image in order to challenge both the domestic division of labour and exploitation in the workplace.

NOTES

Thanks to Susan Yeandle for her comments on this paper.

1. The courses were run by Bristol University Department of Extra-Mural Studies, and sponsored by the Manpower Services Commission.
2. Details of the quantitative data, omitted here due to lack of space, are given in the version presented at the Loughborough Conference.

14 'Liberators', 'Companions', 'Intruders' and 'Cuckoos in the Nest': A Sociology of Caring Relationships over the Life Cycle

Dennis Marsden and Sheila Abrams

This chapter describes a small study of thirty-eight married daughters caring for their elderly mothers who live with them. We have devised a typology of caring relationships involving different degrees and balances of tending and emotional support, and we have explored whether current relationships can be explained in terms of socialisation, altruism or reciprocity over the life cycle.[1] It has been argued that the government's policies of so-called 'community care' have been cost-cutting measures which load the burdens of care onto a small number of informal carers, usually female kin (Walker, 1982; Finch and Groves, 1983), so we ask whether the physical, financial or psychological burdens of caring for disabled people can cause the breakdown of caring relationships.

The elderly are increasing in numbers and dependency and are heavy users of health and social services (Moroney, 1976; Rossiter and Wicks, 1983). It looks as though the commonest caring situation for the elderly is going to be the care of lone elderly women by their daughters living in the same dwelling.[2] We anticipated that this situation might represent high costs[3] for the carers because married daughters are unlikely to receive official support.[4] Moreover, the mother–daughter relationship has been of some interest to sociologists who have argued for its persistent strength in industrial society on account of women's shared caring role (Willmott and Young, 1960; Young and Willmott, 1957).[5] Our study population comprised all but two of the available households from a number of doctors' practices

192

in one northern and one southern city, where the mothers were seventy-five or over, living with married daughters. Three-quarters (28) of the mothers were in their eighties, with a majority (23) of daughters in their fifties; and while 14 of the mothers were rated 'very severely incapacitated' and 15 'severely incapacitated', about a quarter (9) of the mothers proved still quite active.[6]

WHAT IS CARE? TENDING AND LOVING: THE POLICY ISSUES

Care is used with two interwoven but separable meanings: emotional support, and tending or the provision of physical services and attendance (Parker, 1982). Official community-care policy seems blandly to assume that informal tending will be naturally more loving, but critics argue that, even if this proves true, carers should not be exploited. Adequate support should be provided by the state, so that carers would not be compelled to care for dependants whom they hate or reject.

The current re-thinking of the origins of dependency is long overdue (Townsend, 1981; Phillipson, 1983).[7] Some of the needs for care which entail the highest stress have their origins not in biological ageing, but in what has recently been identified as the 'structured dependency' of the elderly, particularly women; that is the way capitalism, industrialism and patriarchy, expressed in policy neglect or malfunction, force elderly people into dependency.

The motivations underlying care have also come under scrutiny, particularly from feminists who argue that women's identity is socially constructed to make caring integral to being female. Some, however, see this as too passive a view of women and ask whether women themselves find caring natural or whether they resist its burdens (Ungerson, 1983a). The assumption that altruism lies at the roots of caring looks very different when we recognise that women rather than men are constructed to be altruistic. An alternative view is that caring might be seen as reciprocity in evenly balanced relationships, governed by short- or long-term calculations of opportunities and rewards as against disadvantages and costs (Abrams, 1986). Thus we might ask whether carers now tend their dependants because in better times those dependants once tended the carers or helped in some other way.

We set out to contribute to this debate by asking how women feel about caring. The discovery of hostility would challenge the bland official assumption of a genetic or socially induced disposition to care, and we hoped to be able to see whether more loving feelings were associated with an exchange of tending.

SOME HYPOTHETICAL MODELS OF CARING RELATIONSHIPS

From a conventionally gender-stereotyped perspective there should be evidence, over the life cycle, of a reciprocal switching of caring tasks and roles between the mother and her daughter (Table 14.1).

Table 14.1   Hypothetical switches in caring roles between mother and daughter over the life cycle

Stage in the life cycle	Tending and emotional content	Relationship
Daughter as dependent child	Mother loves and tends daughter	Mother as carer
Daughter becomes independent	Mutual emotional support between mother and daughter	Companion
Daughter has dependent child	Mother shares childcare with daughter	Ally, joint carer
Daughter works, with dependent child	Mother cares for children	Liberator, substitute carer
Daughter's children independent	Mutual emotional support	Companion
Mother becomes dependent	Daughter loves and tends mother	Daughter as carer, mother as 'Child'?

If the mother becomes incapacitated early in life, she may become prematurely a substitute 'child' (or whatever sort of relationship develops), needing tending and thus restricting the daughter's ability to work. And if there are dependent children in the household, the disabled mother may constitute an extra or double burden (even 'quadruple' if the daughter works and her husband is unco-operative and demands services!). For demographic reasons it turns out to be comparatively rare for an elderly mother to live in her daughter's household for reasons of incapacity when there are still dependent children at home. Thus, although almost half of our households contained three generations, most contained independent children, if any, and there remained only seven with teenagers or young children in them.[8]

If we allow that in tending relationships there may be mixed feelings or merely a sense of duty, possibly rejection or even hatred, the typology can be expanded as shown in Table 14.2.

Table 14.2 Hypothetical caring relationships between mother and daughter, tending and emotional content from the daughter's viewpoint

Tending	*Emotion*		
	Love	*Mixed feelings, duty*	*Hate/rejection*
Daughter tends mother	Loved dependent 'Child'?	Patient	Burden Cuckoo in the nest
Little tending needed	Companion	Boarder	Intruder
Mother provides tending	Ally		Competitor
Mother tends daughter or daughter's family	Ally, Liberator, Carer		Usurper

We may then find situations where the mother's 'childlike' dependency assumes the intrusive aspect of the 'Cuckoo in the nest' (always remembering that the term tries to encapsulate an abrasive relationship which may be forced upon the mother more than the daughter). Alternatively, a disliked mother who needs little tending may be seen as an 'Intruder', a mother who offers unwanted services may be seen as a 'Competitor' or 'Usurper' of the daughter's role, and a mother cared for out of duty, neutrally, may appear as a 'Boarder' if she needs no tending, or like a 'Patient' if she is dependent.

We may consider briefly the impact of caring on the marital relationship in two types of marriage described in the literature as conjugal (more often middle-class or 'respectable') and as segregated (more often working-class) (Bott, 1957). In role-segregated marriages the husband would be less involved with and might avoid the mother. In conjugal or companionate marriage with a positive view of care it might be suggested that ideally the dependent 'Child' might go to make up a sort of 'Nuclear Family', or alternatively the active

'Companion' may become part of a *Menage à Trois*. However, in conjugal marriages one or both spouses may reject the caring role.

Clearly we have reached the point where any further complexity in these typologies would threaten our main purpose, which is to try to make explicit some of the major relationships that may exist, and then to identify whether such relationships are present in our sample. While incidence will vary, it is hoped that such a typology may be generalised usefully to other areas.

CARING HISTORIES OVER THE LIFE CYCLE: LIVING TOGETHER AND CARING

We also had the more ambitious goal of trying to see whether current situations were linked with past relationships. In our study we had caught some households at different stages of a common caring history, but we also discovered that not all caring histories followed the same pathway. Mothers and daughters may have had caring relationships, whether or not actually living together, for only part of their lives, and families may live together without caring taking place.

The average age at which the mothers had started living with their daughters was seventy-six; for 16 mothers co-residence had begun 'earlier', and for 22 'later' than that.[9] The 'late' arrivers had been with their daughters on average only three years when we saw them, and altogether about half (20) had been there less than five years. In contrast, only 3 of the 'early' arrivers had been there less than ten years, during which time there had been more changes in the family and their incapacity level.

About two-thirds (25) had begun to live with their daughters at least partly because of illness or incapacity, but for the remainder these were not the immediate causes of living together. Nor was widowhood of itself a major cause, a majority (23) having been widows for twenty years before living with their daughters, and the remainder sometimes needing only tending or emotional support or being substantially self-sufficient when they came.

The mothers who had gone to live with their daughters earlier than the average were less likely to be incapacitated and hence were more able themselves to provide care. On the other hand, most (17 out of 22) 'late' arrivers were already incapacitated on arrival.

Thus the onset of care could come as the daughter's response to the increasing incapacity of a mother already in the household, who may herself have provided care at some time in the past, or alternatively as a sudden crisis bringing the incapacitated and hitherto distant mother precipitately together with her daughter. In a third of the families, the mother's incapacity had developed only slowly and the daughter had usually begun caring for her mother in a separate household, sometimes at a distance with great inconvenience. Broadly speaking, there were three main pathways or histories of care which branched and occasionally recombined as households moved to a different balance of need or tending, as indicated in Figure 14.1.

The largest group of mothers (the central pathway, 21 cases) began the current phase of the relationship needing only emotional support. Some (7) indeed subsequently became more active and helped their daughters with childcare or domestic chores, occasionally enabling them to go out to work (moving to the lefthand pathway). Others, however, provided little help, and 11 became more disabled (moving to the righthand path). The next largest group, initially, began with severe disabilities (9, the righthand path) and continued to need tending. A smaller group (8, the lefthand path) had not initial needs, although some were later to become incapacitated.

Over one-third of these households had lived together, sometimes for many years, in relationships of mutual tending or without the mother needing help; 5 mothers were still looking after the daughter, her husband or the grandchildren, whilst 7 others now needed or exchanged few services. Over two-thirds (26) of the mothers now had severe needs for tending, according to their daughters. In about one-third (9) of these instances the relatively sudden onset of tending had been the beginning of the current caring relationship, whereas there were rather more (17) instances where the mothers' current severe needs had developed only after living together. In six of these families the mothers had at some points provided substantial services, whether or not living with the daughter at the time.

LOVE, DUTY AND HATE: THE DAUGHTERS' EMOTIONAL RESPONSE TO THE MOTHERS' TENDING NEEDS

The clearest tendency was for longer-term relationships with active mothers who could sometimes exchange services to be viewed by the daughter as comparatively harmonious.[10] Among relationships

Figure 14.1 Pathways of the development of 38 mothers' need for care, and their daughters' emotional responses

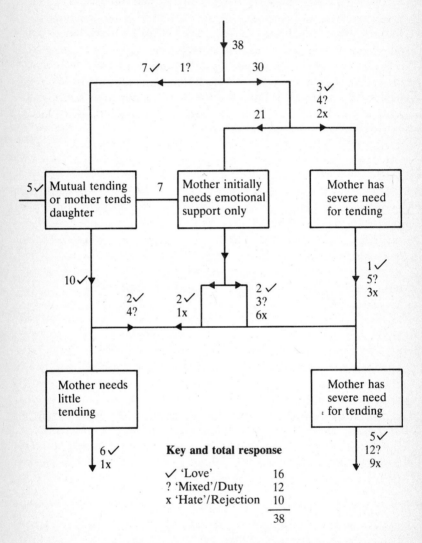

Note: The figure includes close relationships before co-residence (in separate households). Need for care based on daughter's description of tasks needing to be performed. (See note 10 of this chapter.)

where the mother initially needed emotional support we found difficulty in classifying earlier emotions, but there seemed to be two cases where daughters had always felt unwilling to live with their mothers and give the support they needed. Such an early rejection of the mothers' needs was more marked where severe needs for tending had developed suddenly and late in life.

Rejection appears to have increased with the development of disability and the continuation of caring, only one active mother being rejected compared with a majority of those with severe needs. Among this last group, over one-third (10) of the daughters were actively considering alternative means of care for their mothers. *We must conclude that only a handful of these disabled mothers (5 out of 26) were receiving tending which was predominantly loving and matched the ideal of community care.*

In terms of our earlier typologies (Tables 14.1 and 14.2), eleven of the less disabled mothers could be described as 'Companions', of whom three were also 'Liberators' and two 'Carers'. However, another less disabled mother (an eighty-one year old whose daughter had a baby) was rejected as an 'Intruder'. Eleven dependent mothers fell into the role which we tentatively called 'Child'. Another was treated by her ex-nurse daughter much like a 'Patient' – the only way she felt she could cope. No fewer than fourteen were viewed with a hostility which made the description 'Cuckoo in the nest' seem comparatively mild. In fact, even among the more harmonious relationships there could be a fair degree of strain, with 'Companions' sometimes viewed as 'Intruders' or as 'Usurpers' (four cases), and one, who lived in substantially separate accommodation, virtually as a rather tedious 'Boarder'.

The eleven companionate caring relationships had elements of the *Menage à Trois*, albeit with the accompanying tensions of a threesome. Also there proved to be eleven situations roughly approximating to the 'Nuclear Family', but in the remainder of the families husbands joined the daughters in their rejection of the 'Cuckoo in the nest'.

There appeared to be a marked social class difference in the emotional tone of these caring relationships, with middle-class daughters more prone to reject their mothers, despite the mothers' lower level of incapacity.[11] Thus almost half (9 out of 21) of the middle-class mothers were still reasonably active (average score for the group was 10.5), whereas scarcely any (3 out of 17) of the working-class mothers were not severely incapacitated (average score

14). (See note 6 of this chapter for information about the incapacity scale used.) Even the incapacitated middle-class mothers were more often 'severely' (10 out of 15) rather than 'very severely' (5 out of 14) incapacitated. However, while most of the 'loved' middle-class mothers were still active (8 out of 9), over half the 'loved' working-clas mothers (4 out of 7) were incapacitated. Almost all (9 out of 10) of the remaining working-class daughters had at least mixed feelings or a strong sense of duty towards their mothers. Yet a majority of the remaining middle-class daughters (9 out of 12) expressed feelings of rejection or hatred, and the only active mother who was rejected was middle class. All the ten who rejected their mothers, including only one working-class daughter, were actively considering a range of alternative care.

We may be seeing here greater middle-class articulacy, curbed by fewer inhibitions about revealing family discord to a middle-class interviewer and with more confidence that ways to escape family stress can and must be found. However, this finding warns us that we cannot simply equate stress with the burdens of tending and financial costs, which we now summarise.

THE PHYSICAL AND FINANCIAL BURDENS OF TENDING

Almost all (24) of the 'severely' or 'very severely' incapacitated mothers were housebound and receiving help with the large majority of basic activities. In contrast, the active mothers needed help with only the heaviest shopping and housework; all but one could be left for whole days or longer, whereas few (5) of the incapacitated could be left as much as four hours, and nine could not be left at all.

Virtually all care was provided by the daughters, and the little help from husbands (for example, with repairs, shopping or collecting pensions) did not breach traditional roles or even entail being with the mother. Even if we include other informal carers, in twenty families with severely or very severely incapacitated mothers, daughters remained responsible for the great bulk of continuous predictable care, official help being minimal. The relatively more confused mothers seemed unacceptable at or unprepared to go to Day Centres; two-thirds (8) of the incontinent mothers and a third (5) of the mothers with nervous trouble did not receive Respite Care, sometimes because the mothers themselves refused it.

Almost half (16) of the daughters perceived themselves to be restricted in their work opportunities by caring. Of the daughters who worked at all, most (13 out of 18), and no fewer than seven out of eight of the full-time workers, were middle class. Half of the workers had mothers who were incapacitated, indicating the career commitment of middle-class daughters and the need to pay for costly housing moves. Up to ten households appeared to qualify for Attendance Allowance but were not receiving it. On the whole (in 12 out of 15 cases), Attendance Allowances were paid to the lowest income households. This made a substantial contribution towards evening the balance of financial transactions and making relationships more comfortable, although heating costs remained a problem in nine families. Only in eight households did daughters consider they were helping their mothers financially, almost all in the higher income groups.

Some quite striking social class differences had emerged as the relatives began to live together. In all but two households, the mother had moved house to live with her daughter. With the exception of one family which obtained a fresh council house, all the working-class families stayed in the same house, half of which were council houses, in the majority of cases (14 out of 16) with no structural alterations. However, a substantial minority (9 out of 21) of the middle-class families moved straight away or soon after the mother's arrival, and a further seven built extra accommodation. As a result, while only a minority (5) of mothers in working-class families had separate accommodation suited to their needs, almost all (19) of the mothers in middle-class families had suitable accommodation, in two instances a substantially separate flat. In some ways the six daughters who complained of the increased expense of their mortgages (all of them middle-class) were suffering problems of relative affluence – over-investment in a rising housing market – rather than poverty, with the better-off families in larger houses most prone to confess to financial difficulties.

Considerable caution should be exercised in interpreting this evidence of relatively small financial difficulties; because daughters tended to ignore the opportunity costs of restrictions on work, the finances of three-generation households were difficult to work out, and in any case daughters were reluctant to admit that the mother was an expense or was subsidising them. Perhaps the visible costs of care did not seem so great because the mothers, apart from requiring heat, did not do much or consume much; life proceeded at a slow pace with few outings or social occasions.

THE MOTIVATION TO CARE: ATTACHMENT, DUTY AND RECIPROCITY

Rather than speaking of a decision to care, for daughters who did not want to care there would have been serious problems of conscience and perceived public disapproval had they *not* cared. In about a third of the families the mother had 'chosen' the daughter to look after her. In about a quarter (10) the daughter was in any case the only child, and several others were like only children because of age gaps. About three-quarters (27) wished there was someone with whom they could share the responsibility, which caused friction in almost a third (12) of the families. About two-thirds (25) said there had been some advantages when the mother initially came to live, but a third stressed mainly disadvantages.

Almost all agreed that caring for their mothers was a natural thing to do; all but two would do the same for their husbands and indeed most (23) felt they would do the same for a less close relative. Some spoke of a family tradition but only a few (8) would agree that caring was something a *son* should do. Moreover, only half felt that their children would care for them in turn, expressing ambivalence over whether they should. Very few of the daughters (5) would say they had not been emotionally close to their mothers in early childhood or in early marriage and child-rearing. However, a few specifically mentioned loss of contact in adolescence, for example through boarding-school or working away, as leading to later coolness. All but five daughters felt that their mothers had done their share of caring in their lifetime, some stressing unusual early sacrifices, and indeed a majority (20) of the mothers had earlier cared for another ailing person, including their own mothers or husbands.

There were thus often reservoirs of caring feelings to be tapped by the mothers, which tended to overlay any current reciprocity in relationships. While the current phase of living together had sometimes contained a calculation of mutual benefit (emotional support and security in exchange for childcare), almost invariably there seem to have been warm feelings between mother and daughter *before* the offer of sharing a dwelling was made. Only one household afforded an example of a relationship – reluctantly formed as a consequence of housing problems – which worked well while the daughter and her husband both went out to work and the mother cleaned and cooked, but which had soured with the cessation of work and the mother's increasing disability. We must stress, however, that the foregoing relatively cosy picture of motivations is from families who have mostly come to live together voluntarily.

LIVING TOGETHER AND STAYING TOGETHER: SOCIAL CLASS DIFFERENCES

In the accommodation changes when relatives began to live together, we seemed to be encountering situations similar to those in the early community-studies literature (Young and Willmott, 1957; Willmott and Young, 1960). There were middle-class, geographically mobile families where the widowed mother had been encouraged to move early, in the hope of postponing decline but also from a positive desire for her companionship, reinforced by the sometimes large benefits of childcare, domestic services, improved accommodation and even cash which she might bring. Middle-class families had greater choice both to buy adequate accommodation or to build it, and to live together with less intimacy because the mother could have separate accommodation. Such a move would, however, entail a greater upheaval for the mother because of the severing of the mother's local social relationships. There came a tension between becoming a *Menage à Trois* or encouraging the more active and socially confident middle-class mother to make new relationships of her own.

In contrast, working-class families might live together only 'later' or in circumstances of more severe incapacity, partly because accommodation was more cramped with less privacy, but also because living closer meant that care in separate households remained feasible and there was less need of a move. (Such a suggestion implies that the working-class dependants who are cared for at a distance will also be more disabled than their middle-class counterparts.) Correspondingly, a move over a shorter distance should involve less social upheaval in relationships, although the disruption caused by any disability will be more drastic.

We should hardly expect a complete social class polarisation. Because mothers and daughters were often relatively old, working-class families had sometimes moved, and, conversely, some middle-class families had stayed close because the locations of our study afforded pleasant environments and good jobs. It seems confirmation of the above picture, therefore, that, of the active mothers, most (9 out of 12), including four out of five of the carers, were middle-class and all but two had arrived 'early'. We showed earlier how the middle-class mother had considerably lower incapacity levels. Yet despite this and the larger, better-suited accommodation of the middle class, there was something about these middle-class daughters' relationships with the more heavily disabled mothers which made sharing a household less tolerable to them than for working-class daughters.

DAUGHTERS AS MOTHERS, MOTHERS AS CHILDREN? THE DECAY OF ATTACHMENT

As we have seen, a substantial minority of daughters did reject their mothers. We attempted to explore what went wrong, with the suggestion of an inversion of roles, with the elderly mother becoming more like a 'child', the daughter more like her mother. All but five daughters agreed that they still felt like their mothers' daughters. On the other hand, almost half (18) said they now felt, at least at times, like mothers to their own mothers, usually where the mothers were disabled and also where two still-active mothers were very old. However, almost half (16) of the daughters also felt that their (mainly disabled) mothers were not the mothers they had known earlier. To say 'I treat her just like a child really', expressed a view of the mother as fractious and irrational rather than endearing, and daughters openly complained that their mothers were now garrulous, boring, aggressive, confused, miserable and sullen, lacking in sparkle or any interest in life. A few were said to lack interest in people, television or radio, and food.

Indeed, in over half the households with severely incapacitated mothers, it was the breakdown in *personal* interaction and reciprocity which the daughters found most distressing, burdensome and hard to take. Some said the heavier chores of tending would have been considerably eased and would have brought some satisfaction had their mothers been able to respond in the old way or if they had appeared to enjoy and appreciate being cared for. Several daughters of very disabled mothers nevertheless derived great satisfaction from caring because the mothers remained overtly happy, or expressed gratitude for the care they received, and did not undermine the relationship by aggressive, critical or too gloomy behaviour.

The daughters who were most articulate about changes in their mothers' personalities and who responded most adversely were predominantly middle-class, in those families where there had been greater upheavals consequent upon moving from a distance, and where new relationships depended more upon the mother's ability to fit into the household or to make new friends. Some mothers led lives of social isolation, possibly improperly treated by an array of drug controls, akin to a sort of institutionalisation within the 'community'. There had been a decay of the daughters' sense of attachment, duty and willingness to care; these were the daughters who most actively planned to end the caring relationship.

Further, in almost half the marriages (17) the husbands were reported as being to some extent hostile to the mother, such hostility emerging as mother-in-law avoidance (13), loss of temper (8) or direct expressions of jealousy (5). In these circumstances almost half the daughters felt under an obligation to their husbands, and almost as many (13) felt guiltily torn between their mothers and their husbands and sometimes the children too. Such guilt may explain why daughters who usually felt they could ask their husbands to help with care did not in fact do so. In situations where the mother was a 'Companion' in a *Menage à Trois*, daughters were apt to say their marital relationship was closer or unaltered, whereas among the middle-class daughters who rejected their mothers three expressed mixed feelings about their marriage and four said it had deteriorated and their mothers were the cause. Similarly, the four families who described arguments about the children were middle-class, which reinforces the impression that caring was seen as more intrusive in middle-class relationships.

CONCLUSION

This chapter has described some of the findings of a small study of the costs of care to informal carers. We have not been able to present the very detailed qualitative evidence which underlies our typology of relationships, nor much of the data on the actual physical and financial burdens of care. Our hypothesis of an idealised life cycle of reciprocal care proved (as in exchange theory generally) too simple-minded for modern industrial society, although it has served the purpose of highlighting the way in which some of the elderly mothers who are now dependent had often earlier, and even to an advanced age, provided valuable care themselves.

Unhappily, at least in our small but real populations of carers, the ideal of loving care which seems to underlie official 'community care' policies was found only infrequently, and then at considerable cost to the carers. On the whole the women carers did not acquiesce in the burdens of care. Tending, even in our restricted range of relationships, was not usually a positive decision but rather a product of circumstances, often imposed upon, and resented by, a large proportion of carers of the more disabled. Our findings have suggested that there may be distinct class differences in the patterns of social upheaval consequent upon caring, with the middle class using their greater purchasing power to foster an exchange of services with mothers who are still fit, but subjected to greater psychological strains because of their desire for privacy if the mother becomes disabled and unable to communicate.

In far too many of the relationships, which we have described as the 'Cuckoo in the nest', the situations seemed to be forced upon carers and dependants for lack of an adequate alternative. On grounds of social justice, even the carers in more harmonious situations should receive much greater official support. Society's neglect to provide adequate supportive and alternative services is reinforcing and perpetuating the 'structured dependency' of the elderly and the subordination of women.

NOTES

1. The origins of our study lie in the work on 'the sociology of good behaviour', neighbouring and caring which was initiated at Durham by the late Professor Philip Abrams, and which has been carried out by the Rowntree Research Unit, variously funded by the Rowntree Trust, the DHSS and the ESRC (see Abrams, 1986).
2. Although Levin *et al.*'s (1984) excellent study shows that caring situations are surprisingly varied, other common carers being spouses.
3. For other studies of the costs of care, see Nissell and Bonnerjea (1984), Equal Opportunities Commission (1980; 1981) and Wenger (1984). Research on carers was reviewed by Parker (1985).
4. Parker (1985, p. 70, table 4.2) shows that 59 per cent of disabled people living with married children and 73 with unmarried dependent children received no help. See also Levin *et al.* (1984) for a detailed discussion of the impact of help on relationships.
5. Townsend's (1963) postscript to *The Family Life of Old People* argues that the early studies paid insufficient attention to conflict.
6. Moroney (1976) suggests that over age 75 incapacity begins to increase more rapidly. Townsend's (1979) mammoth national study (from which we take our incapacity scale) shows a considerable increase (27.9 per cent to 42.3 per cent) between 70–74-year-olds and 75–79-year-olds, in those scoring more than 7 on the scale. The

incapacity scale is described in Townsend, pp. 638–92, and table A71, p. 1048. People are scored 0, 1 or 2, according to whether they can do something easily, with difficulty, or not at all, the activities being such things as shopping, washing, and cooking. There are nine questions giving a maximum score of 18, with 'severe incapacity' starting at 11 and 'very severe' at 14. We interviewed the daughters only, so these were their assessments of their mothers' conditions. Apart from physical incapacity the mothers sometimes suffered from a range of disabling conditions of sight, hearing, balance, incontinence, paralysis and 'nerves'; and while the active mothers were relatively free of trouble from these sources, the 'severely incapacitated' mothers on average suffered from two such troubling conditions, and the 'very severely incapacitated' on average from three. Trouble with nerves seemed to be evenly distributed over the whole group. We asked very elaborate questions about all sorts of daily activities, but we found that on the whole the very simple incapacity scale coincided quite well with the daughters' descriptions of their mothers' need for care. Only four mothers seemed to have actual levels of dependency and need for tending, according to their daughters, which moved them across the boundaries of the scale from relatively active to incapacitated or vice versa. It was this reclassification (giving 26 incapacitated mothers) which has been used later in the chapter.

7. If we really take on board the notion of structured dependency, then it becomes very difficult to measure incapacity objectively. Daughters' assessments contain moral judgements, or fluff over the issue of how care may rob the mother of her autonomy, through over-protection.

8. The point is best made by the extreme contrary instance of a very difficult situation of an 81-year-old woman whose 40-year-old daughter had a baby; that is, two unusually large generation gaps.

9. If we had included younger mothers, the age of living together would necessarily have come down, though there will be a lower limit set by the norms of kinship and available housing.

10. Classification of feelings was based on an extensive range of questions about how close the daughters had felt, changes in relationships, ease of communication, satisfaction in caring, guilt, perceptions of the mother's personality, friction in the household, and so on. 'Rejection' was based on the daughter stating a clear aim of ceasing to care; 'mixed feelings' included some evidence of affection or a strong sense of duty, with evidence of regret and strain; and 'loving' relationships included strain-free relationships, along with some where there was stress and friction but where the daughter made strong statements of affection for her mother and showed a desire to continue caring. Our broad summary classifications tend to *under*rate the degree of stress, hostility and rejection to be found in these relationships.

11. The ratio of working clas (manual) to middle class (non-manual and professional) proved remarkably similar to that in Levin *et al.*'s (1984) study, at 45 per cent to 55 per cent, or 17 to 21.

Bibliography

ABRAMS, M. (1959) *The Teenage Consumer* (London: Routledge & Kegan Paul).

ABRAMS, P. (1986) 'Altruism and Reciprocity as Source of Neighbouring and Neighbourhood Care', in M. Bulmer (ed.), *Neighbours: The Work of Philip Abrams* (Cambridge University Press).

ACKER, J. (1973) 'Women and Stratification: A Case of Intellectual Sexism', *American Journal of Sociology*, vol. 78, pp. 936–45.

ALBERONI, F. (1983) *Falling in Love* (New York: Random House).

ALLAN, G. (1985) *Family Life* (Oxford: Blackwell).

ALLATT, P. (1981) 'Stereotyping: Familism in the Law', in B. Fryer, A. Hunt, D. McBarnet and B. Moorhouse (eds), *Law, State and Society* (London: Croom Helm).

AMOS, V. and PARMAR, P. (1981) 'Resistances and Responses: The Experiences of Black Girls in Britain', in A. McRobbie and T. McCabe (eds), *Feminism for Girls: An Adventure Story* (London: Routledge & Kegan Paul).

ARBER, S., GILBERT, N. and DALE, A. (1985) 'Paid Employment and Women's Health: A Benefit or a Source of Role Strain?', *Sociology of Health and Illness*, vol. 7, pp. 375–400.

ARIES, P. (1962) *Centuries of Childhood* (New York: Vintage Books).

ASHTON, D. N. and FIELD, D. (1976) *Young Workers* (London: Routledge & Kegan Paul).

ATKINSON, J. (1971) *A Handbook for Interviewers* (London: HMSO).

BAIN, G. (1970) *The Growth of White Collar Unionism* (Oxford University Press).

BAKER, T. and CUNNISON, S. (1986) 'Trade Unions and Women's Three Working Lives' (Paper presented to the British Sociological Association Annual Conference, Loughborough).

BALLINGER, L. B. C. (1975) 'Psychosomatic Morbidity and the Menopause: Screening of General Population Sample', *British Medical Journal*, vol. 3, pp. 344–6.

BANKS, M., ULLAH, P. and WARR, P. (1984) 'Unemployment and Less Qualified Urban Young People', *Employment Gazette*, vol. 92, pp. 343–5.

BARKER, D. L. and ALLEN, S. (eds) (1976a) *Dependence and Exploitation in Work and Marriage* (London: Longman).

BARKER, D. L. and ALLEN, S. (eds) (1976b) *Sexual Divisions and Society: Process and Change* (London: Tavistock).

BARRETT, M. (1980) *Women's Oppression Today* (London: Verso).

BARRON, R. D. and NORRIS, G. H. (1976) 'Sexual Divisions and the Dual Labour Market', in Barker and Allen (1976a).

BATES, I., CLARKE, J., COHEN, P., FINN, D., MOORE, R. and WILLIS, P. (1984) *Schooling for the Dole? The New Vocationalism* (London: MacMillan).

BAYLEY, M. (1973) *Mental Handicap and Community Care* (London: Routledge & Kegan Paul).

BEECHEY, V. (1978) 'Some Notes on Female Wage Labour and Capitalist Production', *Capital and Class*, vol. 3, pp. 45–66.

BELL, C. and NEWBY, H. (1976) 'Husbands and Wives: The Dynamics of the Deferential Dialectic', in Barker and Allen (1976a).

BERNARD, J. (1973) *The Future of Marriage* (London: Souvenir Press).

BERNARD, J. (1975) *Women, Wives, Mothers: Values and Options* (Chicago: Aldine).

BERNARDES, J. (1986) 'Multidimensional Developmental Pathways: a Proposal to Facilitate the Conceptualisation of "Family Diversity"', *Sociological Review*, vol. 34, 590–610.

BEURET, K. and MAKINGS, L. (1986) 'Women, Class and Courtship in a Recession' (Paper presented to the British Sociological Association Annual Conference, Loughborough).

BEURET, K. and MAKINGS, L. (forthcoming) *Courting Change* (London: Polity Press).

BOTT, E. (1957) *Family and Social Network* (London: Tavistock).

BRAKE, M. (1984) *Comparative Youth Cultures: The Sociology of Youth Culture and Youth Subcultures in America, Britain and Canada* (London: Routledge & Kegan Paul).

BRANNEN, J. and MOSS, P. (1987) 'Dual Earner Households: Women's Financial Contributions after the Birth of the First Child', in J. Brannen and G. Wilson (eds), *Give and Take in Families: Studies in Resource Distribution* (London: George Allen & Unwin).

BRANNEN, J. and MOSS, P. (in press) 'Fathers in Dual Earner Households: Through Mothers' Eyes', in C. Lewis and M. O'Brien (eds), *Constraints of Fatherhood* (London: Sage).

BREEN, D. *The Birth of a First Child* (1975) (London: Tavistock).

BRIGGS, A. and OLIVER, J. (eds) (1985) *Caring: Experiences of Looking After Disabled Relatives* (London: Routledge & Kegan Paul).

BROWN, G. and HARRIS, T. (1978) *The Social Origins of Depression* (London: Tavistock).

BROWN, R. (1986) 'Occupational Identity and Career Change' (Paper presented to the British Sociological Association Annual Conference, Loughborough).

BROWN, W. (1985) *Young People and Leisure* (Milton Keynes: Milton Keynes Youth Council).

BUNGAY, G., VESSEY, M. and McPHERSON, K. (1977) 'Study of Symptoms in Middle Life with Special Reference to the Menopause', *British Medical Journal*, vol. 1, pp. 435–6.

BURGOYNE, J. and CLARKE, D. (1984) *Making a Go of It – A Study of Stepfamilies in Sheffield* (London: Routledge & Kegan Paul).

CAMPBELL, B. (1984) *Wigan Pier Revisited: Politics and Poverty in the 1980s* (London: Virago).

CARTER, M. P. (1962) *Home, School and Work* (Oxford: Pergamon Press).

CARTER, M. P. (1966) *Into Work* (Harmondsworth: Penguin).

CHANEY, J. (1981) *Social Networks and Job Information: The Situation of*

Women Who Return to Work (Manchester and London: Equal Opportunities Commission/Social Sciences Research Council).

CHARLES, N. (1983) 'Women and Trade Unions in the Workplace', *Feminist Review*, no. 15, pp. 3–22.

CHATEAU, P. DE and WIBERG, B. (1976) 'Long-term Effect on Mother–Infant Behaviour of Extra Contact During the First Hour Postpartum', *Medical Presentations. New Series*, no. 20 (Lund University, Sweden).

CHETWYND, S. J. (1975) 'Sex Differences in Stereotyping the Roles of Wife Mother', in P. Slater (ed.), *The Measurement of Interpersonal Space by Grid Technique: Vol. 1, Explorations of Intrapersonal Space* (London: John Wiley).

CLARKE, J. (1978) 'The Fan and the Game', in R. Ingham (ed.), *Football Hooliganism* (London: Interaction).

CLARKE, J. and CRITCHER, C. (1985) *The Devil Makes Work: Leisure in Capitalist Britain* (London: Macmillan).

CLOSE, P. and COLLINS, R. (eds) (1985) *Family and Economy in Modern Society* (London: Macmillan).

COCHRANE, R. and STOPES-ROE, M. (1981) 'Women, Marriage, Employment and Mental Health', *British Journal of Psychiatry*, vol. 139, pp. 373–81.

COCKBURN, C. (1983) *Brothers* (London: Pluto).

COCKRAM, L. and BELOFF, H. (1978) *Rehearsing to be Adults: The Personal Development and Needs of Adolescents: A Review of Research Considered in Relation to the Youth and Community Service* (Leicester: National Youth Bureau).

COHEN, P. (1986) *Rethinking the Youth Question*, London University Institute of Education, Post-16 Education Centre/Youth and Policy Pamphlet.

COLLINS, R. (1985) 'Horses for Courses: Ideology and the Division of Domestic Labour', in Close and Collins (1985).

CONGER, J. (1979) *Adolescence: A Generation Under Pressre* (London: Harper & Row).

COOPER, C. L. (ed.) (1982) *Practical Approaches to Women's Career Development* (Sheffield: Manpower Services Commission).

COOTE, A. and KELLNER, P. (1980) 'Hear this Brother: Women and Work and Union Power', *New Statesman Report* No. 1.

COUSSINS, J. (1976) *The Equality Report* (London: National Council for Civil Liberties).

COWRIE, C. and LEES, S. (1981) 'Slags or Drags', *Feminist Review*, no. 9, pp. 17–31.

COXON, A. P. M., DAVIES, P. M. and JONES, C. L. (1986) *Images of Social Stratification: Occupational Structures and Class* (London: Sage).

COXON, A. P. M. and JONES, C. L. (1978) *The Images of Occupational Prestige* (London: Macmillan).

COXON, A. P. M. and JONES, C. L. (1979) *Class and Hierarchy: The Social Meaning of Occupations* (London: Macmillan).

COXON, A. P. M. and JONES, C. L. (1980) *Measurement and Meanings: Techniques of Studying Occupational Cognition* (London: Macmillan).

COYLE, A. (1984) *Redundant Women* (London: Womens Press).

CROMPTON, R. and MANN, M. (1986) *Gender and Stratification* (London: Polity Press).

CUNNISON, S. (1980) *Trade Union Participation by Married Women in Relation to their Family Role*. Social Science Research Council Report (lodged at Boston Spa: British Library).

CUNNISON, S. (1983) 'Gender and Participation in Local Union Organization: A Case Study', in E. Gamarnikow, D. Morgan, J. Purvis and D. Taylorson (eds), *Gender, Class and Work* (London: Heinemann Educational Books).

CUNNISON, S. (1986) 'Care on the Cheap: Gender, Consent and Exploitation Among Sheltered Housing Wardens', in K. Purcell, S. Wood, A. Watson and S. Allen (eds), *The Changing Experience of Work* (London: Macmillan).

DALE, A. (1986) 'Life Cycle and Stratification: Some Evidence of the Influence of the Life Cycle on Three Dimensions of Stratification' (Paper presented to the British Sociological Association Annual Conference, Loughborough).

DALE, A., GILBERT, G. N. and ARBER, S. (1985) 'Integrating Women into Class Theory', *Sociology*, vol. 19, pp. 384–409.

DANIEL, W. W. (1980) *Maternity Rights: The Experience of Women* (London: Policy Studies Institute).

DAVIDOFF, L. (1976) 'The Rationalization of Housework', in Barker and Allen (1976a).

DAVIES, L. (1979) 'Deadlier than the Male? Girls' Conformity and Deviance in School', in L. Barton and S. Meighan (eds), *Schools, Pupils and Deviance* (London: Nafferton Books).

DEEM, R. (1982) 'Women, Leisure and Inequality', *Leisure Studies*, vol. 1, pp. 29–46.

DEEM, R. (1986) *All Work and No Play: The Sociology of Women and Leisure* (Milton Keynes: Open University Press).

DELAMONT, S. (1980) *The Sociology of Women* (London: Allen & Unwin).

DELANEY, J., LUPTON, M. J. and TOTH, E. (1977) *A Cultural History of Menstruation* (New York: Mentor Books).

DELPHY, C. (1981) 'Women in Stratification Studies', in H. Roberts (ed.), *Doing Feminist Research* (London: Routledge & Kegan Paul).

DELPHY, C. (1984) 'Continuities and Discontinuities in Marriage and Divorce', in D. Leonard (ed.), *Close to Home* (London: Hutchinson).

DEUTSCHER, I. (1959) *Married Life in the Middle Years: A study of the Middle Class Urban Postparental Couple*, Ph.D. Dissertation (University of Missouri).

DEX, S. (1984) *Women's Work Histories: An Analysis of the Women and Employment Study*, Research Paper No. 46 (London: Department of Employment).

DIXEY, R. and TALBOT, M. (1982) *Women, Leisure and Bingo* (Leeds: Trinity and All Saints College).

DORN, N. and SOUTH, N. (1983) 'Of Males and Markets: A Critical Review of "Youth Culture" Theory', Research Paper 1 (Middlesex

Polytechnic: Centre for Occupational and Community Research).

EDGELL, S. (1980) *Middle Class Couples* (London: Allen & Unwin).

ELDER, G. J. (1975) 'Age Differentiation and the Life Course', in A, Inkleser, J. Coleman and N. Smelser (eds), *Annual Review of Sociology* (California, USA: Annual Review Inc., Palo Alto).

ELDER, G. H. (1978a) 'Family History and the Life Course', in T. K. Hareven (ed.), *Transitions: The Family and the Life Course in Historical Perspective* (New York: Academic Press).

ELDER, G. H. (1978b) 'Approaches to Social Change and the Family', in J. Demos and S. S. Boocock (eds), *Turning Points: Historical and Sociological Essays on the Family* (Chicago: University of Chicago Press).

ELDER, G. H. (1982) 'Historical Experiences in Later Years', in T. K. Hareven and K. J. Adams (eds), *Ageing and Life Course Transitions: An Interdisciplinary Perspective* (London and New York: Tavistock).

ELIAS, P. and MAIN, B. (1982) *Women's Working Lives: Evidence from the National Training Survey* (Coventry: Institute for Employment Research, Warwick University).

ELLIOT, R. (1984) 'Trade Unions and the Radicalizing of Socialist Feminism', *Feminist Review*, no. 16, pp. 64–73.

ELSHTAIN, J. B. (1981) *Public Man, Private Woman* (Oxford: Martin Robertson).

EQUAL OPPORTUNITIES COMMISSION (1980) *The Experience of Caring for Elderly and Handicapped Dependents: Survey Report* (London: Equal Opportunities Commission).

EQUAL OPPORTUNITIES COMMISSION (1981) *Behind Closed Doors* (Manchester: Equal Opportunities Commission).

EQUAL OPPORTUNITIES COMMISSION (1982) *Caring for the Elderly and Handicapped: Community Care Policies and Women's Lives* (Manchester: Equal Opportunities Commission).

EQUAL OPPORTUNITIES COMMISSION (1985) *The Fact About Women is . . .* (Manchester: Statistics Unit, Equal Opportunities Commission).

ERIKSON, R. (1984) 'Social Class of Men, Women and Families', *Sociology*, vol. 18, pp. 500–14.

FAULKNER, F. (ed.) (1980) *Prevention in Childhood of Health Problems in Later Life* (Geneva: World Health Organisation).

FAWCETT, H. and PIACHAUD, D. (1984) 'The Unequal Struggle', *New Society*, vol. 70, p. 473.

FEATHERSTONE, M. and HEPWORTH, M. (1981) 'Ageing and Inequality: Consumer Culture and the New Middle Age' (unpublished paper presented to the British Sociological Association Annual Conference, Aberystwyth).

FEDERATION OF CLAIMANTS' UNIONS (1985) *Women and Social Security* (London).

FINCH, J. and GROVES, D. (eds) (1983) *A Labour of Love: Women, Work and Caring* (London: Routledge & Kegan Paul).

FOGELMAN, K. (ed.) (1983) *Growing Up in Great Britain: Papers from the National Child Development Study* (London: Macmillan).

FORD, C. S. and BEACH, F. A. (1951) *Patterns of Sexual Behaviour* (New York: Heuber).

FREEMAN, C. (1982) 'The "Understanding" Employer', in J. West (ed.), *Work, Women and the Labour Market* (London: Routledge & Kegan Paul).

FREUD, A. (1952) 'Adolescence', *Psychoanalytic Study of the Child*, vol. 13.

FRYER, B., FAIRCLOUGH, A. and MANSON, T. (1974) *Organization and Change in the National Union of Public Employees* (Department of Sociology, University of Warwick).

FRYER, B., FAIRCLOUGH, A. and MANSON, T. (1978) 'Facilities for Female Shop Stewards: The British Protection Act and Collective Agreements', *British Journal of Industrial Relations*, vol. 16, pp. 160–74.

FRYER, D. and PAYNE, R. (1983) 'Pro-activity as a Route into Understanding the Psychological Effects of Unemployment', Sheffield University Social and Applied Psychology Unit Paper.

GARDINER, J. (1975) 'Women's Domestic Labour', *New Left Review*, no. 89, pp. 47–58.

GILROY, P. (1981) 'You Can't Fool the Youths': Race and Class Formation in the 1980s', *Race and Class*, vol. 23, pp. 187–206.

GLAZER, B. G. and STRAUSS, A. L. (1971) *Status Passage* (London: Routledge & Kegan Paul).

GOFFMAN, E. (1961) *Asylums* (New York: Archer Books).

GOLDBERG, M. and HATCH, S. (eds) (1982) *A New Look at the Personal Social Services*, Discussion Paper No. 4 (London: Policy Studies Institute).

GOLDTHORPE, J. (1983) 'Women and Class Analysis', *Sociology*, vol. 17, pp. 465–88.

GOLDTHORPE, J. (1984) 'Women and Class Analysis: A Reply to the Replies', *Sociology*, vol. 18, pp. 491–9.

GOLDTHORPE, J. and HOPE, K. (1974) *The Social Grading of Occupations* (Oxford: Clarendon Press).

GRAHAM, H. (1984) *Women, Health and the Family* (Brighton: Wheatsheaf Books).

GRAHAM, H. (1985) 'Providers, Negotiators and Mediators: Women as the Hidden Carers', in E. Lewin and V. Olesen (eds), *Women, Health and Healing* (London: Tavistock).

GRAHAM, H. and MCKEE, L. (1980) *The First Months of Motherhood*, Research Monograph, 3 (London: Health Education Council).

GREEN, E., HEBRON, S. and WOODWARD, D. (1985) 'A Woman's Work', *Sport and Leisure*, July/August, pp. 36–9.

GREEN, E., HEBRON, S. and WOODWARD, D. (1986) *Leisure and Gender: A Study of Sheffield Women's Experiences*, Report to the Economic and Social Research Council/Sports Council Joint Panel on Leisure Research (London: Sports Council).

GREEN, E., HEBRON, S. and WOODWARD, D. (1987) 'Women, Leisure and Social Control', in J. Hanmer and M. Maynard (eds), *Women, Violence and Social Control* (London: Macmillan).

GREENLEAF, B. K. (1978) *Children Through the Ages* (New York: Harper & Row).

GRIFFIN, C. (1981) 'Cultures of Femininity: Romance Revisited', stencilled paper (Centre for Contemporary Cultural Studies, Birmingham University).

GRIFFIN, C. (1985a) 'Turning the Tables: Feminist Analysis of Youth Unemployment', *Youth and Policy*, no. 14, pp. 6–11.

GRIFFIN, C. (1985b) *Typical Girls? Young Women From School to the Job Market* (London: Routledge & Kegan Paul).

GRIFFIN, C. (1985c) 'Young Women's Experiences of Unemployment', (unpublished paper presented at Westhill Sociology of Education Conference).

GRIFFIN, C. (1986) 'It's Different for Girls: Problems With the Gang of Lads Model', *Social Studies Review*, vol. 2, pp. 21–7.

GRIFFIN, C., HOBSON, D., McINTOSH, S. and McCABE, T. (1982) 'Women and Leisure', in Hargreaves (1982).

GRIFFITHS, V. (1986) 'Adolescent Girls: Transition from Girlfriends to Boyfriends', (Paper presented to the British Sociological Association Annual Conference, Loughborough; revised version this volume).

GROVE, W. R. and TUDOR, F. (1973) 'Adult Sex Roles and Mental Illness', *American Journal of Sociology*, vol. 78, pp. 812–35.

GROVES, D. (1983) *Members and Survivors: Women's Welfare, Women's Rights* (London: Croom Helm).

GUISE, W. (1986) 'Child Care and Development Group', unpublished paper (Cambridge: Child Care and Development Group).

HAKIM, C. (1979) *Occupational Segregation*, Research Paper No. 9 (London: Department of Employment).

HAKIM, C. (1980) 'Some Aspects of Employment: Data for Policy Research', *Journal of Social Policy*, vol. 9, pp. 77–98.

HALL, G. S. (1904) *Adolescence, Its Psychology and its Relations to Physiology, Anthropology, Sociology, Sex, Crime, Religion and Education* (New York: Appleton).

HALL, M. H. and CARR-HILL, R. (1982) 'Impact of Sex Ratio on Onset and Management of Labour', *British Medical Journal*, Vol. 285, pp. 401–3.

HALL, S. and JEFFERSON, T. (eds) (1975) *Resistance through Rituals: Youth Subcultures in Post-War Britain* (London: Hutchinson).

HAMMERSLEY, M. and ATKINSON, P. (1983) *Ethnography: Principles in Practice* (London: Tavistock).

HAREVEN, T. K. (1978) 'Family Time and Historical Time', in A. F. Rossi, J. Kagan and T. Hareven (eds), *The Family* (New York: W. W. Norton).

HAREVEN, T. K. (1982) *Family Time and Industrial Time* (Cambridge and New York: Cambridge University Press).

HARGREAVES, J. (ed.) (1982) *Sport, Culture and Ideology* (London: Routledge & Kegan Paul).

HARRIS, C. C. (1969) *The Family* (London: George Allen & Unwin).

HARRISON, M. (1969) 'Participation of Women in Trade Union Activities: Some Research Findings and Comments', *Industrial Relations Journal*, vol. 10, pp. 41–55.

HAUG, M. (1973) 'Social Class Measurement and Women's Occupational Roles', *Social Forces*, vol. 52, pp. 86–98.

HOBSON, D. (1981) 'Young Women at Home and Leisure', in Tomlinson (1981).

HORTON, C. (1986) 'The Impact of the Family Life Cycle on Male and Female Trade Union Participation' (Paper presented to the British Sociological Association Annual Conference, Loughborough).

HUNT, P. (1980) *Gender and Class Consciousness* (London: Macmillan).

HWANG, C. P. (1978) 'Mother–Infant Interaction: Effects of Sex of Infant on Feeding Behaviour', *Early Human Development*, vol. 2, pp. 341–9.

JACKSON, R. H. and WILKINSON, A. W. (1976) 'Why Don't We Prevent Childhood Accidents?' *British Medical Journal*, vol. 1, pp. 1258–62.

JENKINS, R. (1983) *Lads, Citizens and Ordinary Kids: Working Class Youth Life-Styles in Belfast* (London: Routledge & Kegan Paul).

JERROME, D. (1983) 'Lonely Women in a Friendship Club', *British Journal of Guidance and Counselling*, vol. 11, pp. 10–20.

JOHNSON, C. L. (1975) 'Authority and Power in Japanese-American Marriage', in R. E. Cromwell and D. H. Olsen (eds), *Power in Families* (New York: Sage).

JOHNSON, F. L. and ARIES, E. J. (1983) 'The Talk of Women Friends', *Women's Studies International Forum*, vol. 6, pp. 353–61.

JOLLY, H. (1975) *Book of Child Care* (London: Allen & Unwin).

JOSHI, H. (1984) *Women's Participation in Paid Work: Further Analysis of the Women and Employment Survey*, Research Paper No. 45 (London: Department of Employment).

JOSHI, H. (1985) 'Gender Inequality in the Labour Market and the Domestic Division of Labour', Paper for the Cambridge Journal of Economics Conference *Towards New Foundations for Socialist Policies in Britain*.

KOMAROVSKY, M. (1971) *The Unemployed Man and His Family. The Effects of Unemployment on the Status of the Men in 59 Families* (New York: Octagon Books; first published 1940).

KORNER, A. F. (1974) 'Methodological Considerations in Studying Sex Differences in the Behavioural Functioning of Newborns', in R. C. Friedman, R. M. Richart and R. L. Vande Wiele (eds), *Sex Differences in Behaviour* (New York: John Wiley).

LACOURSIERE, R. B. (1972) 'Fatherhood and Mental Illness: A Review of Material', *Psychiatric Quarterly*, vol. 46, pp. 109–24.

LAND, H. (1980) 'The Family Wage', *Feminist Review*, no. 6, pp. 55–78.

LAND, H. (1981) *Parity Begins at Home* (Manchester: Equal Opportunities Commission).

LAND, H. (1983) 'Who Still Cares for the Family? Recent Developments in Income Maintenance, Taxation and Family Law', in J. Lewis (ed.), *Women's Welfare, Women's Rights* (London: Croom Helm).

LAND, H. (1986) *Women and Economic Dependency* (Manchester: Equal Opportunities Commission).

LAWSON, N. (1986) 'Budget Speech', *Hansard, 1376* (London: HMSO, 18 April).

LEES, S. (1986) *Losing Out: Sexuality and Adolescent Girls in London* (London: Hutchinson).

LEONARD, D. (1980) *Sex and Generation: A Study of Courtship and Weddings* (London: Tavistock).

LEVIN, E., SINCLAIR, I. and GORBACH, P. (1984) *The Supporters of Confused Elderly Persons at Home* (London: National Institute for Social Work Research).

MACFARLANE, A. (1979) 'Child Deaths from Place of Accident', *Population Trends*, no. 15, pp. 10–15.

MACFARLANE, A. (1980) 'Official Statistics and Women's Health and Illness', *Equal Opportunities Commission Research Bulletin* no. 4 (Manchester: Equal Opportunities Commission).

MACFARLANE, A. and FOX, J. (1978) 'Child Deaths from Accidents and Violence', *Population Trends*, no. 12, pp. 22–28.

MACFARLANE, A. and MUGFORD, M. (1984) *Birth Counts: Statistics of Pregnancy and Childbirth* (London: HMSO).

MACGILLIVRAY, I., DAVEY, D. and ISAACS, S. (1986) 'Placenta Praevia and Sex Ratio at Birth', *British Medical Journal*, vol. 292, pp. 371–2.

MAKINGS, L. and SAKS, M. L. (1983) 'Women Manual Workers and Images of Inequality' (unpublished paper, Leicester University).

MANPOWER SERVICES COMMISSION (1981) *No Barriers Here? A Guide to Career Development Issues in the Employment of Women* (London: Manpower Services Commission/Training Services Division).

MANPOWER SERVICES COMMISSION (1983) *Working in Hairdressing*, Working Series 57 (Sheffield: Careers and Occupational Information Centre).

MARTIN, B. (1984) ' "Mother Wouldn't Like It!": Housework as Magic', *Theory, Culture and Society*, vol. 2, pp. 19–36.

MARTIN, J. and MONK, J. (1982) *Infant Feeding 1980*, Office of Population Censuses and Surveys, Social Survey Division (London, HMSO).

MARTIN, J. and ROBERTS, C. (1984) *Women and Employment: A Lifetime Perspective* (London: HMSO).

MASON, J. (1986) 'Gender Inequality in Long Term Marriage' (Paper presented to the British Sociological Association Annual Conference, Loughborough; revised version this volume).

MATERNITY ALLIANCE (1983) *One Birth in Nine – Trends in Caesarean Section* (London: Maternity Alliance).

McCABE, T. (1981) 'Girls and Leisure', in Tomlinson (1981).

McCABE, T. (1982) 'Girls and Leisure', in Hargreaves (1982).

McRAE, S. (1986) *Cross-Class Families: A Study of Wives' Occupational Superiority* (Oxford: Clarendon Press).

McINTOSH, S. (1981) 'Leisure Studies and Women', in Tomlinson (1981).

McKEE, L. and BELL, C. (1984) 'His Unemployment, Her Problem: The Domestic Consequences of Male Unemployment' (Paper presented to the British Sociological Association Annual Conference, Bradford).

McKEE, L. and C. BELL (1985) 'Marital and Family Relations in Times of Male Unemployment', in Roberts, Finnegan and Gallie (1985).

McROBBIE, A. (1978a) *'Jackie, an Ideology of Adolescent Femininity'* (stencilled paper, Birmingham University: Centre for Contemporary Cultural Studies).

McROBBIE, A. (1978b) 'Working Class Girls and the Culture of Femininity', in Women's Studies Group (eds), *Women Take Issue* (London: Hutchinson).

McROBBIE, A. (1980) 'Settling Accounts with Subcultures: A Feminist Critique', *Screen Education*, no. 34.

McROBBIE, A. (1984) 'Dance and Social Fantasy', in A. McRobbie and M. Nava (eds), *Gender and Generation* (London: Methuen).

McROBBIE, A. and GARBER, J. (1975) 'Girls and Subcultures – an Exploration', in Hall and Jefferson (1975).

McROBBIE, A. and McCABE, T. (eds) (1981) *Feminism for Girls* (London: Routledge & Kegan Paul).

McROBBIE, A. and NAVA, M. (eds) (1984) *Gender and Generation* (London: Macmillan).

MEISSNER, M., HUMPHREYS, E. W., MEIS, S. M. and SCHER, W. J. (1975) 'No Exit for Wives: Sexual Division of Labour and the Cumulation of Household Demands', *Canadian Review of Sociology*, vol. 12, pp. 424–39.

MIRZA, H. (1985) 'Distortions of Social Reality: A Case for Reappraising Social Class Schema Definitions' (Paper presented to the Postgraduate Women's Seminar, University of London, Goldsmith's College).

MORGAN, D. H. J. (1975) *Social Theory and the Family* (London: Routledge & Kegan Paul).

MORGAN, D. H. J. (1985) *The Family, Politics and Social Theory* (London: Routledge & Kegan Paul).

MORONEY, R. M. (1976) *The Family and the State* (London: Longman).

MORRIS, L. D. (1985) 'Renegotiation of the Domestic Division of Labour in the Context of Male Redundancy', in Roberts, Finnegan and Gallie (1985).

MOSS, P. (1986) *Child Care in the Early Months: How Child Care Arrangements Are Made for Babies*, Working and Occasional Paper No. 3 (London: Thomas Coram Research Unit).

MUSGROVE, F. (1964) *Youth and the Social Order* (London: Routledge & Kegan Paul).

MUSSEN, P. H. and JONES, M. C. (1958) 'Self-Conceptions, Motivations and Interpersonal Attitudes of Late and Early-Maturing Boys', *Child Development*, vol. 29, pp. 61–7.

NISSELL, M. and BONNERJEA, L. (1984) *Family Care of the Handicapped Elderly: Who Pays?* (London: Policy Studies Institute).

OAKLEY, A. (1974) *The Sociology of Housework* (London: Martin Robertson).

OAKLEY, A. (1976) *Housewife* (Harmondsworth: Penguin).

OAKLEY, A. (1981) 'Normal Motherhood: An Exercise in Self-Control?', in B. Hutter and G. Williams (eds), *Controlling Women* (London: Croom Helm).

OAKLEY, A. and OAKLEY, R. T. (1979) 'Sexism in Official Statistics', in J. Irvine, I. Miles and J. Evans (eds), *Demystifying Social Statistics* (London: Pluto Press).

OFFICE OF POPULATION CENSUSES AND SURVEYS (1978) *Birth Statistics 1976*, Series F.M.I. no. 3 (London: HMSO).

218   *Bibliography*

OFFICE OF POPULATION CENSUSES AND SURVEYS (1985) *Social Trends*, 15 (London: HMSO).

OFFICE OF POPULATION CENSUSES AND SURVEYS MONITOR (1986) *General Household Survey 86/1*, Office of Population Censuses and Surveys, 3.

OPEN UNIVERSITY (1985) *Birth to Old Age*, Health and Disease Course U205.

PAHL, J. (1983) 'The Allocation of Money and the Structuring of Inequality Within Marriage' *Sociological Review*, vol. 31, pp. 237–62.

PAHL, R. E. (1984) *Divisions of Labour* (Oxford: Blackwell).

PARKER, G. (1985) *With Due Care and Attention* (London: Family Policy Studies Centre).

PARKER, R. (1982) 'Tending and Social Policy', in E. M. Goldberg and S. Hatch (eds), *A New Look at the Personal Social Services*, Discussion Paper No. 4 (London: Policy Studies Institute).

PARKER, S. (1971) *The Future of Work and Leisure* (London: Longman).

PAYNE, G., FORD, C. and ULAS, M. (1981) 'Occupational Change and Social Mobility in Scotland since the First World War', in M. Gaskin (ed.), *The Political Economy of Tolerable Survival* (London: Croom Helm).

PHILLIPSON, C. (1983) *Capitalism and the Construction of Old Age* (Oxford: Blackwell & Robertson).

PLATH, S. (1963) *The Bell Jar* (London: Faber & Faber).

POCOCK, S. J. and TURNER, T. L. (1982) 'Neonatal Hyperbilirubinaemia, Oxytoxin and Sex of Infant', *Lancet*, vol. 2, pp. 43–4.

POLLERT, A. (1981) *Girls, Wives, Factory Lives* (London: Macmillan).

POOLE, M. E. (1983) *Youth: Expectations and Transitions* (London: Routledge & Kegan Paul).

PORTER, M. (1978) 'Worlds Apart: The Class Consciousness of Working Women', *Women's Studies International Quarterly*, vol. 1, pp. 175–88.

POULANTZAS, N. (1973) *Political Power and Social Classes* (London: New Left Books).

POVALL, M. and HASTINGS, J. (1983) *Managing or Removing the Career Break* (Sheffield: Manpower Services Commission/Women and Training).

PRENDERGAST, S. and PROUT, A. (1980) ' "What will I do?" Teenage Girls and the Construction of Motherhood', *Sociological Review*, vol. 28, pp. 517–35.

PRESDEE, M. (1986) 'Agony or Ecstasy: Broken Transitions and the New Social State of Working Class Youth in Australia' (Paper presented to the British Sociological Association Annual Conference, Loughborough).

RAPOPORT, R. and RAPOPORT, R. (1975) *Leisure and the Family Life-Cycle* (London: Routledge & Kegan Paul).

REICHER, S. and EMLER, N. (1985) 'Delinquent Behaviour and Attitudes to Formal Authority', *British Journal of Social Psychology*, vol. 24, pp. 161–8.

RICH, A. (1980) *Compulsory Heterosexuality and Lesbian Existence* (London: Only-Women Press pamphlet).

RICHARD, M. P. M. and DYSON, M. (1982) *Separation, Divorce and the*

Development of Children: A Review (Cambridge: Childcare and Development Group).

RICHMAN, J. (1982) 'Men's Experiences of Pregnancy and Childbirth', in L. McKee and M. O'Brien (eds), *The Father Figure* (London: Tavistock).

RICHMAN, N. (1976) 'Depression in Mothers with Young Children', *Journal of Child Psychology and Psychiatry*, vol. 17, pp. 75–8.

RIMMER, L., POPAY, J. and ROSSITER, C. (1983) 'One Parent Families', Family Policy Studies Centre, Occasional Paper 12 (London: Study Commission on the Family).

ROBERTS, B., FINNEGAN, R. and GALLIE, D. (eds) (1985) *New Approaches to Economic Life* (Manchester: Manchester University Press).

ROBERTS, K. (1984) *School-Leavers and their Prospects* (Milton Keynes: Open University Press).

ROBERTS, W. L. and ROBERTS, A. E. (1980) 'Significant Elements in the Relationships of Long-Married Couples', *The International Journal of Ageing and Human Development*, vol. 10, pp. 265–72.

RODHOLM, M. and LARSSON, K. (eds) (1979) 'Father–Infant Interaction at the First Contact After Delivery', *Early Human Development*, vol. 3, pp. 21–7.

ROMNEY, M. L. (1980) 'Predelivery Shaving: An Unjustified Assault?', *Journal of Obstetrics and Gynaecology*, vol. 1, pp. 33–5.

ROSSITER, C. and WICKS, M. (1983) *Crisis or Challenge: Family Care, Elderly People and Social Policy* (London: Study Commission on the Family).

SARSBY, J. (1983) *Romantic Love and Society* (Harmondsworth: Penguin).

SCHOFIELD, M. (1965) *The Sexual Behaviour of Young People* (London: Longman Green).

SCRATON, S. (1986) 'Images of Femininity and the Teaching of Girls' Physical Education', in J. Evans (ed.), *Physical Education: Sport and Schooling* (Barcombe, Sussex: Falmer Press).

SCRATON, S. (1987) 'Boys Muscle in Where Angels Fear to Tread: The Relationship Between Physical Education and Young Women's Subcultures', in J. Horne, D. Jary and A. Tomlinson (eds), *The Sociology of Leisure* (University of Keele Sociological Review Monograph).

SEITER, E. (1986) 'Feminism and Ideology: The Terms of Women's Stereotypes', *Feminist Review*, no. 22, pp. 58–81.

SHARPE, S. (1976) *Just Like a Girl: How Girls Learn to be Women* (Harmondsworth: Penguin).

SILVERMAN, D. (1970) *The Theory of Organisations* (London: Heinemann).

SIMMONS, C. and WADE, W. (1984) *'I like to say what I think'* (London: Kogan Page).

SINFIELD, A. (1981) *What Unemployment Means* (Oxford: Martin Robertson).

SOLANTAUS, T., RIMPELA, M. and TAIPALE, V. (1984) 'The Threat of War in the Minds of 12–18 Year Olds in Finland', *Lancet*, vol. 1, pp. 784–5.

SPENDER, D. (1980) 'Education or Indoctrination?', in D. Spender and E.

Sarah (eds), *Learning to Lose* (London: The Women's Press).

SPENDER, D. (1982) *Invisible Women: The Schooling Scandal* (London: Writers and Readers Publishing Co-operative).

STACEY, M. (1981) 'The Division of Labour Revisited or Overcoming Two Adams', in P. Abrams, R. Deem, J. Finch and P. Rock (eds), *Practice and Progress: British Sociology, 1950–1980* (London: Allen & Unwin).

STAGEMAN, J. (1980) *Women in Trade Unions*, Occasional Paper No. 6, Industrial Studies Unit, University of Hull (Hull: University of Hull Industrial Studies Unit).

STANWORTH, M. (1984) 'Women and Class Analysis: A reply to Goldthorpe', *Sociology*, vol. 18, pp. 159–70.

STOKES, G. (1984) 'Out of School – Out of Work: The Psychological Impact', *Youth and Policy*, no. 2, pp. 27–9.

STREET, J. (1985) 'Playing with Money: Political Economy of Popular Music', *Youth and Policy*, no. 14, pp. 1–5.

TALBOT, M. (1981) 'Women and Sport', *Journal of Biosocial Science*, vol. 13, pp. 33–47.

TAYLOR, B. (1983) *Eve and the New Jerusalem* (London: Virago).

THOMAN, E. B., LEIDERMAN, P. H. and OLSON, J. P. (1972) 'Neonate-Mother Interaction During Breastfeeding', *Development Psychology*, vol. 6, pp. 110–28.

THOMAS, G. and ZMROCZEK, C. (1985) 'Household Technology: The "Liberation" of Women from the Home?', in Close and Collins (1985).

THOMAS, R. (1984) 'Research and Development on the Statistical Treatment of Women's Occupations' (Paper presented to the Offices of Population, Censuses and Surveys).

THOMAS, R. (1986) 'Classification of Women's Occupations', *Survey Methodology Bulletin*, no. 18, pp. 5–16.

TILLY, L. A. and SCOTT, J. W. (1978) *Women, Work and Family* (New York: Holt, Rinehart & Winston).

TOMLINSON, A. (ed.) (1981) *Leisure and Social Control* (Brighton: Brighton Polytechnic, Chelsea School).

TOWNSEND, P. (1963) *The Family Life of Old People* (Harmondsworth: Penguin).

TOWNSEND, P. (1979) *Poverty in the United Kingdom* (Harmondsworth: Allen Lane).

TOWNSEND, P. (1981) 'The Structured Dependency of the Elderly', *Ageing and Society*, vol. 1, pp. 5–27.

TROWN, A. and NEEDHAM, G. (1980) *Reduction in Part-Time Teaching: Implications for Schools and Women Teachers* (Manchester and London: Equal Opportunities Commission/Assistant Masters and Mistresses Association).

ULLAH, P. (1984) *A Qualitative Study of Unemployed Black Youth in Sheffield*, Social and Applied Psychology Unit, Sheffield University.

UNGERSON, C. (1983a) 'Why Do Women Care?', in Finch and Groves (1983).

UNGERSON, C. (1983b) 'Women and Caring: Skills, Tasks and Taboos', in E. Gamarnikow, D. Morgan, J. Purvis and D. Taylorson (eds), *The Public and the Private* (London: Heinemann).

VAN GENNEP, A. (1960) *The Rites of Passage* (London: Routledge & Kegan Paul).

VENESS, T. (1962) *School Leavers* (London: Methuen).

WALKER, A. (ed.) (1982) *Community Care* (Oxford: Blackwell & Robertson).

WALKER, J. (1986) 'Romanticising Resistance, Romanticising Culture: Problems on Willis's Theory of Cultural Production', *British Journal of the Sociology of Education*, vol. 7, pp. 59–80.

WALLACE, C. (1985) 'Masculinity, Femininity and Unemployment' (Paper presented to the International Sociology of Education conference, Westhill College, Birmingham).

WALLACE, C. (1986) 'From Girls and Boys to Women and Men: The Social Reproduction of Gender Roles in the Transition from School of (Un)employment', in S. Walker and L. Barton (eds), *Youth, Unemployment and Schooling* (Milton Keynes: Open University Press).

WARD, J. (1976) *Social Reality for the Adolescent Girl* (Swansea: University College of Swansea, Faculty of Education).

WARR, P. (1983) 'Work, Jobs and Unemployment', *Bulletin of the British Psychological Society*, vol. 36, pp. 305–11.

WENGER, C. (1984) *The Supportive Network* (London: Allen & Unwin).

WESTWOOD, S. (1984) *All Day Every Day: Factory and Family in the Making of Women's Lives* (London: Pluto).

WHITE, D. and WOOLLETT, A. (1981) 'Fathers at Birth' (Paper presented at the British Psychological Society Conference, City University, London).

WHITEHEAD, A. (1976) 'Sexual Antagonisms in Herefordshire', in Barker and Allen (1976a).

WHITEHEAD, A. (1984) 'I'm Hungry Mum!', in Young (1984).

WILLIAMS, R. (1973) *Base and Superstructure in Marxist Cultural Theory* (London: New Left Books).

WILLIS, P. (1977) *Learning to Labour: How Working Class Kids Get Working Class Jobs* (London: Saxon House).

WILLIS, P. (1984) 'Youth Unemployment: Thinking the Unthinkable', *Youth and Policy*, no. 4, pp. 17–36.

WILLMOTT, P. and YOUNG, M. (1960) *Family and Class in a London Suburb* (London: Routledge & Kegan Paul).

WILSON, R. (1966) *Feminine Forever* (New York: Evans).

WIMBUSH, E. (1986a) *Women, Leisure and Well-Being*, Report to the Health Promotion Research Trust (Edinburgh: Centre for Leisure Research).

WIMBUSH, E. (1986b) 'Transitions in Work, Leisure and Health Experiences in Early Motherhood' (Paper presented at the British Sociological Association Annual Conference, Loughborough).

WOMEN'S STUDIES GROUP, CENTRE FOR CONTEMPORARY CULTURAL STUDIES (eds) (1978) *Women Take Issue: Aspects of Women's Subordination* (London: Hutchinson).

WORLD HEALTH ORGANISATION (1978) *Primary Health Care* (Geneva: World Health Organisation).

YEANDLE, S. (1984) *Women's Working Lives: Patterns and Strategies* (London: Tavistock).

YEANDLE, S. and LEAVER, G. (1986) 'Women's Social Contacts in Later Working Life' (unpublished paper, Department of Sociology and Anthropology, University College, Cardiff).

YOUNG, K. (ed.) (1984) *Of Marriage and the Market: Women's Subordination Internationally and Its Lessons* (London: CSE Books).

YOUNG, M. and WILLMOTT, P. (1957) *Family and Kinship in East London* (London: Routledge & Kegan Paul).

Author Index

Subject Index